GERALDINE
THORSTEN

ILLUSTRATED BY ANNETTE REIMER

Portions of this book were previously published in *God Herself.*

A FIRESIDE BOOK
Published by Simon & Schuster Inc.
NEW YORK   LONDON   TORONTO   SYDNEY   TOKYO

THE GODDESS IN YOUR STARS

FIRESIDE

Simon & Schuster Building
Rockefeller Center
1230 Avenue of the Americas
New York, New York 10020

Portions of this book were previously published in
God Herself.

FIRESIDE and colophon are registered trademarks
of Simon & Schuster Inc.

Designed by Marysarah Quinn
Manufactured in the United States of America

10 9 8 7 6 5 4 3 2 1

Library of Congress Cataloging in Publication Data

Thorsten, Geraldine.
The goddess in your stars / Geraldine Thorsten;
illustrated by
Annette Reimer.
p.   cm.
"A Fireside book."
ISBN 0-671-67780-2
1. Zodiac. 2. Astrology. 3. Women—Miscellanea. 4. Goddesses—
Miscellanea. I. Title.
BF1729.W64T49 1989
133.5'2'082—dc20

89-34660
CIP

ACKNOWLEDGMENTS

Each of you who is a part of my life is a part of this book. I take full responsibility for the views expressed in these pages, but to you belongs the credit for enabling me to write them. Thank you all for your love and advice, your help and encouragement. Some debts are so great, however, that I wish to acknowledge them specifically.

I give special thanks to my parents, Tressie and Robert Williams; my brother Ken Thorsten and his wife, my dear friend Ann Thorsten; my brother Robert Williams; my sister Lili Williams-Otto and her husband, my dear friend Joseph Otto; and my darling niece Kathryn Tressie. You enrich my life beyond measure. Thank you for *being*.

I am profoundly grateful to my children Julia YangNim Mamun and her husband Abdullah, and Betty YangNae Thorsten and James MyungSun Thorsten, who generously took on every task they could to free me for writing, who read the manuscript with unflagging interest and encouraged me ever onward, and who have filled my life with joy and pride.

I thank my treasured friend Rosalee Abrams for the priceless gift of her friendship. I do not know what I would have done without her and her husband Robert Abrams, and their children Michael and

Katy, to lighten the burdens and multiply the joys throughout the years.

I also thank my beloved friend Pamela Williams for all she has so generously added to our lives and, specifically, for her editorial advice and for typing the first half of the manuscript.

I am grateful, too, to Margot Colbert for all I have learned from her and enjoyed with her in the almost forty years of our friendship.

I owe very special thanks to Marge Mendel, who taught me about visualizations; shared her ideas, images, and books with me; and inspired me by her own example. I am grateful that she and her husband Steve Mendel and their children, David and Lisa, are my friends.

I also thank Teri and Philip Meskin and their daughter Kira who have sustained me with their love and encouragement.

In addition to the pleasures of the friendship enjoyed with Judith and Bill Werner and their children, Elizabeth and Joseph, I wish to thank Judith for her astrological advice, particularly on Moon Sign interpretation, and Bill, for the use of his computer.

Thanks for specific help with this book are due to Mario Pardillo for his astrological guidance; Diane Korte for urging me to follow up the work started in *God Herself*; Betty Estelle for her encouragement; Thomas Disch and Charles Naylor for an assortment of good times and great advice on writing; Jayne Black, Barney Collier, Rick Alexander, Fran Baron, Dave Cwirka, and our fellow seminarians who helped me past a terrible jam in the writing and buoyed me by their support; and to Maureen Messina, who finished typing the manuscript.

Last but not least, my thanks are due to my editor Barbara Gess for her understanding and faith in me, to Cynthia Lao for her ever-gracious help, and as always to my great friend and agent, Elaine Markson and her wonderful cohorts Geri Thoma, Lisa, Lily, and C.J., who have worked so hard on my behalf.

CONTENTS

This book is dedicated to my mother,
        Tressie Williams,
                whom I love with all my heart
                                and thank for all her gifts to me,
                the first of which was life itself.

INTRODUCTION

When I started to work on this book, I just wanted to explore a few questions. I had no idea how fascinating and exciting the answers would prove to be, and I'm eager to share what I've learned with you. In one sense, I feel as if I were returning from a wildly successful expedition with all sorts of treasures: beautiful feminine things that have been hidden away for many centuries. The delightful part is that these are not just lovely museum pieces for us to admire. They are vital, dynamic concepts and facts, and they work! In fact, they not only work for us right now, they are better than any we've had before and they can make a very positive difference in how we see ourselves and what we do with our lives.

I assume that you and I are interested in astrology for pretty much the same reason: We want to understand ourselves and other people better, and astrology is one of the very best ways to do this. We begin with the zodiac, the path that the sun and moon and planets seem to follow in the sky during the course of a year. This great wheel of the heavens, which exerts a direct influence on us here on earth, is divided into twelve signs. Each sign occupies thirty degrees of space, and relates to specific concerns, activities, and qualities. When you have a natal horoscope drawn up and interpreted for you by an accredited astrologer, you are getting a picture of the sky at your time and place of birth—and it is a very specific picture, pinpointing the location of the sun and the moon and of the eight planets and four asteroids in the circle of the zodiac. An astrologer can tell you astonishing things about yourself from the distribution of these heavenly bodies among the signs, and from their relationship to each other. It may be a bit expensive, but it is certainly very well worth it to have your horoscope drawn up.

But even without professional guidance, we can use astrology to help ourselves. There are three major points in our horoscope: our Sun sign, our Moon sign, and our Rising sign or Ascendant. Of these, the Sun sign is the easiest for an amateur to locate. It takes the sun about a month to travel through a sign; therefore, all you need to know is your date of birth and you're in business. The only possible difficulty comes from the fact that the sun enters a sign at different times of day from year to year, so that it may be leaving Leo on August 23 and entering Virgo on August 23. If you were born on August 23, then you are "on the cusp" and should read both Leo and Virgo. Most of us think of ourselves in terms of our Sun sign, identifying ourselves as Taureans, for example, if the sun was in Taurus when we were born. Our Sun sign is an excellent guide because it does determine our basic characteristics, the key features of our individuality. From it, we learn a great deal about the qualities, skills, and traits we have to work with in shaping our lives.

The problem with concentrating on our Sun sign—apart from the fact that it simply isn't the whole picture—is that it encourages us to think of ourselves as static beings. We are most emphatically not. Each and every one of us on this planet is constantly involved in a process of change, of *becoming*—a process governed by the moon. And like the moon, we each have a monthly cycle, an annual cycle, and larger cycles of development that take seven to nine years. It is important for us to pay attention to the moon's effects upon us so that we can work with our energy instead of against it. We respond to the moon's transits of the signs in the course of the month. These transits shape our patterns of rest and activity, the ebb and flow of our moods and energies, making us more sociable one day, more private the next, and so on. One of the special features of this book is that it presents a revitalized, more complete portrait of your Sun sign qualities and shows how the basic you responds and changes during the month in accord with the moon's cycle.

It's pretty clear that whether we are working with a total horoscope or just key points of our horoscope, our concept of the signs is crucial. I have always felt that astrologers tend to underrate the feminine signs and that this is wasteful and silly. It's perfectly possible for us to learn to see and appreciate the valuable aspects of the feminine as easily as we discern them in the masculine. All we need is a little guidance and a little practice.

I sought guidelines in a couple of different ways. One resource was people I knew who were raised differently than we, who came from matrilineal (mother-line) communities and received their family names from their mothers instead of their fathers as most of us do. According to these friends, a girl's first menstrual period was reckoned as one of the most important events there was, and it was celebrated by the entire community with a grand party. Obviously, there were lessons to be learned from people who had such refreshing attitudes. Those whom I couldn't meet personally, I might learn a little about from anthropology.

Another source was cultures that were patriarchal and promasculine like ours, but still had valuable views to contribute. One such instance occurs in regard to the feminine element, water. Our culture regards water as shifty, unreliable, and dangerous. It signifies great emotional depth, but threatens us with loss of control. In contrast, China sees water as the model of personal integrity and discretion, and the perfect example of how to behave in difficult or dangerous circumstances. To someone like myself who has her sun plus three planets in watery Scorpio, this definitely seemed a viewpoint worth exploring.

There was also the possibility that our own history might be a source of profeminine views. We had started out with a lunar calendar, tracing the feminine moon through Her annual cycle of thirteen moons or months. It seemed reasonable to expect that during that period we would have considered the moon extremely important and, if so, we might have extended our appreciation of Her to other things in the feminine realm.

Well, history is where we strike gold! It turns out that from our simplest beginnings well into the time we developed written languages, sophisticated arts and sciences, and complex cities, we considered the universe essentially feminine, born of the Great Mother. The Great Goddess was a complex deity, prayed to by more than ten thousand names, which still did not name all of Her powers. Her spirit was the life's breath of all and She could appear in any form, but we cherished Her most as the moon. She was our guide to time, the focus not only of the lunar calendar, but later of the zodiac and the solar/lunar calendar. Originally, the zodiac represented and honored the gifts given to us by the Goddess, and astrology guided us to appreciate and use the special qualities, traits, skills, and other gifts we received from the Great Mother, according to which of the twelve signs the sun was in at our birth.

The idea that the zodiac celebrates the gifts bestowed by the Great Goddess is somewhat different from the concept we're familiar with. The view we've been raised with is only five thousand years old—a mere drop of time in the historical bucket—and it was developed during the period when male gods, especially solar gods, were substituted for the Great Mother. This religious shift accompanied and rationalized a change in social organization in which communities substituted father-right and patriarchy for mother-right. Since these transitions weren't particularly easy, swift, or peaceful, a lot of anti-feminine propaganda was generated and we got stuck with it. It's time we got rid of it.

I think you're going to enjoy discovering the original version of the signs very much. Never fear, it's not going to turn astrology absolutely topsy-turvy, but it does extend and complete it. We receive more information and, consequently, we learn more about ourselves. Another valuable aspect is that the original signs were developed at a time when there was no political ax to grind, at least not one concerned with gender, and both feminine and masculine elements were valued. And I must say, it probably gives us the most positive interpretation of the feminine that we've ever encountered.

Each chapter starts with the fascinating story of how your sign originated and what it means. We also learn the story of the women who "were made in the image of the Goddess," our great-aunts and great-grandmothers so many thousands of years removed from us, who did so much to create civilization. I think it helps us now to open the album of the human family and find that we are descended from women who were mothers *and* architects, governors, designers, artists, warriors, surgeons, teachers, musicians, pharmacists, psychologists, priestesses, and farmers.

Next, the focus shifts to you, giving you a portrait of your basic "self," drawn from the original meaning of your sign and updated to accommodate the range of your concerns as a contemporary woman . . . or man. Let me say here that although I have addressed myself to women, this material is relevant to men and men are certainly welcome to read it. In any case, you'll notice a few changes in the signs. The very fact that the feminine signs are portrayed in strongly positive terms is enough to make them seem different. However, the changes are by no means confined to the feminine signs. The masculine signs have a new look, too. Consider Leo, for example. We're used to seeing Leo as a proud lion in our zodiac, but originally Leo was a proud lion walking at the heels of a beautiful, stately Goddess who carried a bow and arrows. The Goddess was not there as a decoration; She meant something. As a matter of fact, She was the focal point of the image and the sign. When we work again with the completed image, we add back a positive feminine dimension, which naturally affects the interpretation of Leo. I hope you'll find that the change is distinctly for the better.

Since you are not just a catalog of characteristics, but a dynamic, changing, growing person, each chapter includes information about your monthly and annual cycles, and even those seven- to nine-year cycles that may present some special aspect for you. Of course, you may not be able to arrange everything to suit yourself—who of us can?—nevertheless, it helps to know when your creative and physical peaks and lows occur on a yearly basis. It's an even greater help to know your monthly pattern and how you respond to the moon's transits of the signs. Just as an example, let's suppose you wanted to ask for a raise or a promotion. If you know that you can assert yourself more easily during a Sagittarius transit than at any other time of the month, you can time your request for that transit when your mood and energy work to your advantage. Although the information is necessarily general, I hope it serves you as a guide to learning about your own patterns and to thinking about yourself as an organic being intimately connected to life's rhythms, rather than as a machine. You'll find the transits set forth in the charts beginning on page 254. These charts give the time the moon enters each sign for every month from the year 1989 through 2000.

At the end of each chapter, you will find a section devoted to visualizations. Every section begins with a general introduction on the benefits and techniques of visualizing, and then offers you images of the Goddess appropriate to the sign, to help you tap into the Eternal Feminine within you and to cope with the problems and stress each of us meets up with in life.

May your own visions of the Goddess shine with the reflections of the women who have gone before us, who did so much to enrich our lives. May you see yourself in your own true strength and beauty, adding your own gifts to that great heritage. May the Goddess smile upon us all.

TAURUS
April 20–May 21

TAURUS: Three young women enact the Great Goddess's control over the earth's power and energy by performing acrobatics on the back of a powerful bull. Based on the "Toreador" fresco from the Palace at Knossos, Crete, 1550–1450 BC, preserved in Archaeological Museum, Heraklion, Crete.

Taureans, prepare to see yourselves in a new light—a warm, glowing light from the past spotlighting Taurus as the lead sign of the zodiac. When astrology first began, over three thousand years ago, our ancestors believed that God was feminine, that humans were made in Her image, that She created and nurtured all and welcomed us back into Her mysteries at death and prepared us for rebirth. We saw Her everywhere—as Sky, as Moon, as Water, as Earth, in countless forms and concepts—and our zodiac symbols and signs commemorated the many gifts we received from the Great Mother, She of Ten Thousand Names.

Your sign Taurus celebrated the awesome, creative powers of the Goddess as Earth. As the herald of spring, the start of the new year, Taurus was an intensely dynamic time, marked by joyous celebrations and prayers. People did not see Earth as a passive, inert, heavy mass and, consequently, did not interpret Taurean aspects of personality in the heavy, stodgy terms later astrologers have tended to use. Earth, to them, was boundlessly creative. From Her were born an infinite variety of forms—from tiny, delicate flowers to great, sheltering trees. In our ancestors' thankful prayers to the

Goddess as Earth, we glimpse the stunning achievements of those earliest human women who first figured out which plants nourished us, which healed us, which yielded sacred beverages. It was they, in their concern to have shelter for their children, who figured out how to transform vines, trees, and grasses into homes. And it was they who taught themselves to use the sacred body of Mother Earth to form pottery and utensils, and even bricks for houses. Above all, it was they who learned not only which plants to gather to sustain us but how to plant them and thus bring our food supply under human control.

Our first mothers not only invented agriculture but also tamed the animals that were attracted to their gardens, and they transformed these into guards, workers, and food. Cattle were among the first animals to be domesticated, a feat accomplished around 7500 B.C. Their contributions were so vital to our lives that the Goddess Herself was often represented as a cow or as wearing a cow's horns because She nurtured us, sending Her milk in the form of dew and rain to feed our crops, to make our lives possible. Like a human mother, the Earth nourished and sustained us; like a human mother, the Earth worked the miracle of bringing forth sons, beings *unlike* Herself.

But the Earth was no human mother; the Earth was Gaia, Mother of All. She was Hera, Ceres, Persephone, Dikte, Ea, Tiamat, Ishtar, Isis-Hathor. Her names were legion, and Her powers far exceeded our small human abilities. Far from being passive and yielding, She could unleash devastating powers in the form of earthquakes, avalanches, tidal waves. She could level a city with a shrug of Her mountains. She could stretch and yawn, and swallow up an entire community in a twinkling. She was the Goddess with absolute power of life and death over all: wonderful, terrible, awesome.

Your sign's emblem, the bull, was the favored symbol for the incredible diversity of life born of the Goddess, and for those powerful energies and forces which only She could control. The bull was Her son. He was Moloch, Apis, Mithra, and more. Everywhere people worshipped the Goddess, images of the bull decorated Her temples and religious shrines. Bulls' horns were set atop temple walls to keep out intruders. Carved into temple walls were stranger sights: minotaurs—half man, half bull. In reality, there were no such beings. Instead, there were men who were selected to participate in the religious and civic affairs of their community and who wore the regalia of the bull to indicate their promotion to semidivine status as representatives of maleness or "otherness." These were the men sanctioned to join the priestesses in those ritual prayers that honored the range of the Goddess's powers, and they prayed that the Goddess would subdue those powers, prevent them from destroying human life, and prevent us from destroying our communities through our passions, anger, greed, jealousy, and lust.

If you wish to read this information in terms of your Moon rather than your Sun, you'll need to shift your thinking from your identity, your will, your essential self—the way you manifest being you in the world—to focus instead on the inner you, the emotional you—your self at the deepest levels of your unconscious. Your Moon not only has to do with your feelings but also includes those things you take for granted in your self—those things you assume everyone else feels or is like, since they are so essential to your personality. Your Moon gifts might not be the most obvious features in your personality. They are ever present but elusive qualities you know intimately and yet can't quite put your finger on. The Moon also has to do with what went on in your family of origin, your home, your background. It concerns all those things that give you a sense of emotional security.

Specifically, Moon in Taurus endows you with very deep feelings. You will need to guard against your sensitivity insofar as it prompts you to see insults where none were intended. On the other hand, you are virtually guaranteed a rich emotional life and a powerful intuition you'd do well to respect and nurture carefully. Your family will almost certainly take top priority over all other relationships. Despite their idiosyncrasies, or the difficulties you may experience with individual members of your family, they call forth your deepest loyalty and sense of responsibility. However, guard against being manipulated through guilt, or subordinating your needs to other people's.

Moon in Taurus also blesses you with a vivid imagination, resourcefulness, appreciation of beauty, and a great capacity both for contentment and enjoyment of life's pleasures, great and small. The discipline of meditation comes easily to you and offers you the tremendous rewards of enhanced health and use of your personal gifts. Your Taurus Moon expresses itself through the feminine side of your nature in a profound sensuality. This is not confined solely to your sex life, although it will be abundantly present there, of course. It affects the *whole* of your life and your presentation of yourself. Delicious scents and tastes, luxurious textures, harmonious sounds, beautiful colors, and the pleasing arrangement of forms are highly important to you. It is for you that precious gems are mined and rare perfumes distilled. May I plead with you, however, to forgo the silken luxury of sable and other furs in deference to the nonhuman members of our planet, and content yourself instead with fine quality fakes.

In terms of human temperament, Taurus also represents great strength and resources combined with the need and ability to exert control over these energies. Your first gift from Sun in Taurus is a lavish supply of energy and stamina; inactivity depresses you. However, I'm not suggesting that you're a hamster in a wheel, unable to be still for a minute. But your strength and agility need to be used in order for you to feel really comfortable. Think back to when you were a child and how much you loved to play, how totally absorbed you could become in making something or in active games. In this respect, you're not very different now, nor will you ever be. Only the ways you express yourself physically will change. There are all sorts of activities you could take up: belly dancing, scuba diving, walking, tennis, gymnastics, what-you-will. There's no point to my continuing this list when you'd be better off consulting the brochures at your local Y or community center, and choosing what appeals to you. And do follow your own responses. "Playing" may, but does not necessarily, mean trying to achieve a better figure or even a degree of excellence in an activity. Goals like these can be pleasant stimuli as long as they're not allowed to turn what should be pleasure into work or cause anxiety; ultimately, they're irrelevant. Another obstacle to satisfying this basic need of yours may be the feeling that "play" is undignified or inappropriate for you "at your age." Be guided, instead, by your own physical capabilities. If you can enjoy an activity without undue strain, then go ahead and enjoy it. You may, for instance, cherish fond memories of roller-skating as a kid and long to skate again; if that's what you want to do, get yourself an inexpensive pair of skates and skate to your heart's content. For all you know, you may inspire other people to risk enjoying their own special dreams. But, be that as it may, the point for you is that a certain amount of action is necessary. Nothing more quickly signals Taurean "blues" than prolonged inactivity. And it works rather like the chicken or the egg. Are you depressed because you're inactive, or inactive because you're depressed? Either way, movement will help you: in the first case, it dispels depression; in the second, it's a relief. One Taurean friend scrubs and polishes her apartment until it glitters whenever she's stymied by a problem; that takes a lot of muscle, but it gives her a sense of control over some portions of her life and it distracts her enough so that her subconscious is free to work on the difficulty and send some sort of solution to the surface.

Of course, there's no gift without drawbacks and responsibilities. The first, rather minor drawback is that you do expose yourself to the risk of injury and illness. A friend of mine who has a Taurus Moon and a Taurus son is now an expert with an Ace bandage; she pointed out that because her boy is outside playing hard in all kinds of weather, he gets a cold or an injury because he is taking more risks than an armchair sports lover. It's possible, however, to quickly learn what the risks are in the athletic activities you prefer and how to protect yourself against them to keep injuries to a minimum. When you become ill, you tend to regard it as a personal insult or a punishment, and you fret yourself trying to find the reasons why you're being chastised this way. It's very difficult for you to feel curtailed and helpless, and while I'm not belittling the unpleasantness of this frustration, it seems a shame to aggravate it further by blaming yourself. If you can, try to distract yourself from slipping into a sense of failure. Treat yourself as much as possible like invalid royalty, and keep busy within the limits of your strength. The last stages of a cold or the flu might be the very time to bring your photograph album up to date or to read articles you've been saving.

The real difficulty attached to your abundant energy and stamina is that you're tempted to squander it, to behave as if there were no limit to your strength. This is a rather tricky business. For one thing, Taurus gives you very strongly felt attachments to other people, and you tend to feel like an emotional cheapskate if you don't put all of your resources at the disposal of those nearest and dearest to you. Add to this the fact that we're raised with a definition of feminine that presents self-sacrifice as a cardinal virtue, and you can see what sort of trouble can arise. Who wants to be unwomanly? Who wants to stint the people you care about most? Self-control in this area can get downright uncomfortable, since you may feel as if you're going against your own grain. I can't offer any pearls of wisdom that will point a clear path through these dilemmas. But I urge you to consider the less virtuous, less publicized aspects of self-sacrifice: that it builds up debts of resentment for all concerned, it saps your energy, and it encourages that useless inner bookkeeping of totting up who has done what and how much for which ingrate. All too often it results in some pretty ugly scenes. On the other hand, if you take good care of your own needs, you are free to enjoy the satisfaction of helping other people. As for what is "womanly," nobody on earth is better qualified to define that for you than you yourself. There are as many ways of being a woman as there are women, and efforts to herd us in one direction seem rather pointless. In fact, I suspect that all such statements are manipulative, and that the interests they serve are not yours or mine. That's not to say that there's no room for compromises in human relationships. If your partner or your friends remark that your snoring or blowing your nose at the table is not the highlight of their life, you might want to change your behavior to accommodate them. When you hurt someone's feelings or anger people, as we all inevitably do, you have to deal with that. However, dealing with it may mean standing your ground when the alternative requires too great a denial of yourself.

But let's return to the positive aspects of your energy. Aside from sports and activities of that nature, one popular avenue of expression is through your sex life. Abstinence is definitely not your long suit. You discover sexual pleasures early in life, and you enjoy them for the rest of your days. For you, lovemaking is a delicious, juicy, warm experience to be savored leisurely. You do not stint your partner, and you do not appreciate being rushed or treated to a series of routine caresses. Your own responses range from affectionate to passionate; partners who behave impersonally, or who go in for a lot of cerebral fantasizing and analysis, will baffle and then bore you, and you give them pretty short shrift. You're generally pretty candid about your own feelings and preferences, and responsive to those of your partners, but you'd much rather be enjoying the action than talking or reading about it.

Taurus inclines you toward fidelity and a preference for long-term intimacies. By and large, dating is a tedious business for you. There may be brief flashes of seeing it as a glamorous and exciting chance for variety, but this usually wears thin quickly. You're not comfortable knowing people superficially, and prolonged periods without a close partner can make you feel rather desperate. When circumstances force you to be alone, there is little you can do about it except to begin again when you're ready. The temptation for you, however, may be to continue with an unsatisfactory relationship rather than do without companionship entirely. Well, who can advise you on this, really? There's little to say that would make an extended solitary state any more palatable for you, and the fact is that each of us proceeds in these matters at our own very individual pace. So what's left is simply the reminder that you not only can survive such periods but survive them very well indeed. Among the very solid compensations that time alone has to offer you are increased self-knowledge and respect for your courage and abilities to cope.

You possess considerable sexual and personal magnetism, and tend to be pleasantly although subtly aware of your powers, which means that you have the grace to enjoy yourself without finding it necessary to elbow the rest of us out of the way. You are generally aware of and appreciative of other people's attractiveness as well. Unless you're feeling threatened within a relationship, you tend not to begrudge other women their charms. And as to men, even when you do not act on your responses, you've noted who has a lovely, sensual mouth or any of the other characteristics that appeal to you. It never ceases to amaze me how, without seeming to notice a thing, a Taurean will come away from a social gathering with a full report on just what sexual undercurrents, maneuvers, and ploys were going on. Taureans seem to absorb this information as naturally as breathing, and I must say it makes for a very interesting rehash of experience.

This sexual awareness is responsible, in part, for your attractive appearance, which you manage to achieve with a minimum of fuss. You have to be very depressed indeed before you let yourself be sloppy or indifferent to how you look. This relates also to your preference that things, in general, are attractive and sensually appealing, but let's wait on this until we take up what it means to be an earth sign.

In general, your energy pattern starts as a swift rush, evens out at a fairly high level, and then gradually tapers off. You need to be alert to signals that indicate that it's time for you to slow down, to limit your responsibilities and activities during these resting intervals. On an annual basis, spring and autumn are peak periods for you, although there may be a brief period at the beginning of autumn when it's hard to make the transition from summer's slower pace to your busy fall schedule. You may feel as if you'll never catch your breath; you will—in fact, within a week or so, it may be hard for you to remember what summer was even like—so try not to harass yourself during that transition. The move from winter to spring is a lot easier. For one thing, your energy does not drop as low as it does in summer; for another, you tend to maintain a more active schedule even when you're not feeling quite up to it, which, I suppose, is rather like staying in fighting trim. Nonetheless, it wouldn't hurt to ease up on yourself a little, to vary your activities so that you get a change of scene or pace, however brief, from your usual routine.

Your monthly cycle follows the same general pattern, starting with a "revving up" when the Moon transits Taurus. This is a very positive transit for you in the sense that it's a marshaling of energies, but you may chafe at the feeling that you're at a standstill. However, the last part of the Taurus transit, plus the Gemini and Cancer transits that follow, are a great relief. You're active and tend to feel in harmony with yourself. Leo and Virgo transits generally represent a fairly high plateau of energy and good spirits, which dip, however, in Libra. The washed-out, listless feeling of this transit is succeeded by Scorpio's stronger sense of purpose and determination. You're just as determined in a Sagittarius transit, but you're also more likely to see the droll side of life and not be quite so demanding on yourself. Capricorn and Aquarius transits are excellent times to solidify plans, fill in the details on a project, and bring things to completion. Pisces is a more abstract transit usually; it's a time of sorting through, perhaps unconsciously, what you've gleaned from the recent past and getting ready for the next cycle. It's a time of less physical energy, but in general, you're quite content to be less active. The Aries transit, however, can be tricky: you tend to feel "unlike" yourself—restless and yet confused as to what it is you'd like to do. I suggest that you treat this like a Void-of-Course Moon period and let it be as much of a holiday as possible.

The last point to be made in connection with the Bull emblem concerns your self-control. There's no question that your emotions, your likes and dislikes, your values, and the views you form on issues are powerful and very deeply felt. Your outward demeanor often belies this. One thing Taurus gives you is a conviction that all living things are equally entitled to life, and one way this is expressed is in a tolerance and appreciation of other people's needs and views. You live by the values you cherish and you are certainly capable of arguing your viewpoints, but you don't see discussions as a fight to the death where the other person and her or his opinion must be squashed in utter defeat. You are able to control your own feelings to allow other people room for theirs. People generally find you an amiable, responsive, sensitive companion, which is a tribute to the self-control that makes this possible. And while it always seems effortless—a natural gift of grace—it means that you've been inwardly busy selecting what's worth making an issue about and what you'll simply let pass. The one flaw in this generosity of spirit is that you tend not to extend it to yourself, especially during your first three decades. It's hard to say whether this is the influence of Taurus or of our culture. It seems that it takes most of us a good thirty to forty years to shake off the conviction that we are somehow unworthy and to develop confidence and respect for ourselves. Try then, as we all must, to be as gentle toward yourself and as appreciative of your own gifts as you are toward those of others. Try, also, not to let your self-control work against you and prevent you from asserting yourself or expressing your angry feelings. We are each of us a unique expression of life, and you owe yourself the same kindness and respect you are willing to give to other people.

One sharp difference between patriarchal and matriarchal attitudes is in relation to the earth. We're familiar with the patriarchal view through astrological descriptions that equate earth with passivity and ponderous qualities. Our matriarchal ancestors, on the other hand, had a very different sense of the earth. Not only did they view it as a gift to be shared and cherished, but they believed it was a very active quantity. To them, the earth was teeming with life, both within itself and on its surface. More than that, it mysteriously transformed materials into phenomena and into food to support the life systems of those phenomena. That great oaks from little acorns grow was considered no paltry accomplishment. Our image of Mother Earth stems from that earlier time when the earth was worshipped as a primary manifestation of the nurturing Great Mother. Women were also likened to the earth; like her, they nurtured, they were capable of miraculous biological transformations, and they figured out how to take the materials of the earth and transform them into useful, beautiful objects that did much to enhance life.

Praise and respect for these talents changed to denial when the economic base shifted from communal to private property. Women as well as the earth were classified as passive, and women were accused of being materialistic creatures who were incapable of abstract thought or spirituality. For quite a long time it was claimed that we had no souls. Presumably, we're too grounded in concrete reality: we can't see beyond our noses, our children, our mates, and our homes; and those things we can see, feel, touch, smell, and taste. Shame of shames, we take our clues and ideas from our environment rather than create ideas solely from the free play of thought. My, my, my! Doesn't that just make you want to crawl off and hide somewhere?

Well, perhaps I'm not the one to do justice to these charges.

Apart from severe doubts about their general accuracy, I'm hard put to see a base in reality as a limitation. I think of those women who preceded us, and frankly I'm impressed that they had the mother wit to figure out how to grow plants and create food and medicine from them, how to weave cloth and build homes, how to control fire and make pottery. It seems a little picky to complain that they modeled their pots on the shape of their breasts or that they learned a few weaving tricks from spiders and birds. And as to the claim that abstract thought or spiritual concerns are alien to us, who can take it seriously when women of the past formulated a religious philosophy unrivaled in its egalitarianism and wisdom, and transformed us into social beings by the light of its precepts?

And here you are, very much a part of today's world and yet connected through Taurus to this great heritage. I believe that one of your earth-sign gifts is a flair for recognizing which concerns deserve top priority, and for stripping problems down to their basics and solving them imaginatively. You are based in reality insofar as you prefer to see that there's food on the table before you'll indulge in "pie in the sky." Food, shelter, and clothing are not the only items on your list of basics, however. The instinct for self-preservation and, indeed, for the preservation of all life is very strong within you, and you are also very much concerned with the quality of that life. This is often interpreted as a desire for wealth and material things, and I disagree strongly with that view. It has not been my observation that Taureans are especially interested in sheer accumulation of possessions or in the status attached to them. You view things more in terms of the pleasure they can provide and the uses they can serve. Your closets may very well be stuffed to bulging, but that's because you hate to discard anything potentially useful; it's hard to part with things when you have a sneaking suspicion that they'll come in handy at some future date. An Aries transit, by the way, is a good time to clear things out if you're pressed for space. You're likely to be indifferent to the marvelous possibilities of an article and it will be less difficult to throw it away.

Your relationship with your possessions is apt to be very personal: you take excellent care of them because you appreciate the beauty or convenience they contribute to your life. Your skis get waxed and stored away carefully so they'll be ready for your next trip to the slopes; your tools are oiled against rust; sweaters made soft and comfortable by time are guarded against moths and mended until they can be patched no more, because you find them a pleasure to wear. You choose and buy things carefully in the expectation that they will be with you for a long time. To you, it seems unintelligent and wasteful to spend money replacing things instead of buying excellent quality in the first place.

Your "carefulness" most definitely extends to people, too. Your concern for the quality of life reaches beyond physical well-being into the emotional and spiritual areas. Among your Taurean values is a conviction of basic equality: that each person is entitled to develop her or his potential to the fullest extent and that each is obliged to learn consideration and respect for others. Hierarchies and elitism of any kind tend to be distasteful to you because they stroke some egos at the expense of too many others. You live very much as you believe in this respect.

The fact that you are realistic or "human centered" influences your intellectual life. Ideas, no matter how awesome or how fashionable, are checked out against your values to test whether they benefit most of us rather than just a favored few. Theories have a limited attraction for you if they cannot, in fact, be implemented. You may find them interesting to read or think about, but you classify them as entertainment and will not invest serious time in and attention to them. It is also very much in line with your character to give your own personal imprint to your thoughts. The information and ideas you absorb are not parroted forth, but are blended with your own experience and transformed so they are distinctly your own.

Generally speaking, Taurus leads you to concentrate on the private sector of your life in your first three decades and then increasingly on the public sector from your mid-thirties onward. You are more likely to have and raise your children in your twenties and, when they are fairly well launched, to turn your attention more seriously to your own career and to society at large. As to choice of career, you have a great deal of latitude in that both arts and sciences are favorable for you. And it often happens that if you choose to enter a science, you will concentrate on an art avocationally, or vice versa. Rather than make a list of career choices suitable for you, I prefer to list those qualities you possess that you might do well to consider in making your decision.

The first is that yours is a sociable nature. Work that requires you to be alone much of the time will ultimately wilt your spirits. And you need to have some sense that whatever it is you're engaged in will result in some benefit to other people. It's far easier for you to tolerate and cope with the frustrations that inevitably attend group endeavors than to pursue your goals in solitary splendor. It's not impossible for you to work alone, but your gifts are more fully and comfortably realized when you are in a social context.

The second relates to the basic premise of this book: that we are dynamic beings who undergo several cycles of development, transition, and change in the course of our lives. Although the person you were in your late teens and the person you are now have a great deal in common, there have been some changes. Therefore, the image you formed of yourself as an adolescent is not the most complete basis from which to project your future plans. It's quite possible that you were shy then and had difficulty in expressing yourself, and are now a very convincing, persuasive speaker who enjoys sharing her views. Assuming that enough time has elapsed, you also have evidence that you possess the stamina to pursue a goal despite setbacks; indeed, you can persist even if it should take years to achieve. Add this information to some of the qualities mentioned already: your ability to reduce problems to their essentials; your capacity to deal with problems imaginatively and effectively; your concern for the welfare of others and your tolerance for other people without losing your own identity; and your ability to work with the resources at hand. You also possess an excellent memory and a quick, lovely sense of humor that can point out the funny side of a situation without making the joke at someone else's expense. You're able to deal with people diplomatically yet help them stay directed toward the important goals, and you can create a very personal, humane work situation that will call forth people's best efforts. These qualities strike me as a terrific combination for someone in a position of authority, and I recommend that you consider such a possibility for yourself and look at career choices in terms of the leadership opportunities they offer. One caution is that you avoid work that is overly routine or that does not allow you to make any personal imprint upon it.

In conclusion, the energy and stamina you possess, which allow you to work and play hard over sustained periods, may be felt as a handicap during transitional intervals. The reluctance to make changes, which we all experience to greater and lesser degrees, and the disorientation we feel as we shift from one cycle to the next can seem interminable to you. If you can, resist the impulse to berate yourself, to compound misery with recriminations like, "Why can't I be like so-and-so?" and "I should be this or do that" or "Why am I such a. . . ?" There are no goddesses and gods here on this earth, no perfect creatures who manage everything splendidly. All of us bristle with penetrating insights and surefire remedies when the difficulties belong to somebody else, and we all thrash about in bewilderment when we're in the throes of our own crises. So it is during these intervals when you can put your patience to best use, deal kindly with yourself, and exercise your faith that you will emerge from your trials with hard-won self-knowledge and deepened strength and compassion.

Taurus has endowed you with many rich gifts and the ability to use them well to shape a satisfying life for yourself. You can create and achieve much, and you may be justly proud of this. Not the least of these accomplishments is the fact that your presence here on earth will have enriched the lives of many others.

TAURUS VISUALIZATIONS

You possess an extraordinary resource within you: your imagination. Through the power of your inward eye, you can tap into your innermost self, and into the energies of the universe. The thoughts you think, the messages you give yourself, the images you create in your imagination have tremendous power. You can literally transform your reality to fit the positive images you create mentally simply by creating those images often enough, and as specifically and clearly as you possibly can. Through such focused, purposeful "daydreaming," you can achieve an astonishing range of goals: practical goals such as weight loss, physical fitness, or money management; spiritual goals such as enhanced self-esteem, inner peace, and a deeper sense of connection with other living beings. For further information on this process, I recommend two books I've found useful. Shakti Gawain's *Creative Visualization*, and Shad Helmstetter's *The Self-Talk Solution*.

My primary concern here is empowering you to get in touch with the Goddess within you, the Eternal Feminine whose creative, nurturing, renewing energies live within us all. The Great Goddess is always ready to comfort, to heal, to strengthen, and to guide us whenever we are in need. Her images come to us from all parts of our world and from across great stretches of time. By visualizing Her in our mind's eye, by meditating on Her image, you and I not only receive help with specific problems and enhanced self-esteem but also reap the additional benefit of greater esteem for all women, past and present, and for the wonderful contributions women have made in creating and advancing civilization.

The images I sketch for you came to me through my research and through my own meditations. They may work differently for you than I've envisioned. And, of course, they're not the only images available to you. I suggest you read Merlin Stone's *Ancient Mirrors of Womanhood* and Barbara G. Walker's *The Woman's Encyclopedia of Myths and Secrets* to see what stories, prayers, and images resonate for you, and use them. I think you'll also find it illuminating simply to gaze within your own mind and see how the Goddess manifests Herself to you. I would be delighted to read your visualization experiences, so if you would like to share them, please write to me c/o the publisher.

How to go about visualization is very much a matter of personal choice: you may sit, stand, or lie down—whichever position you feel you can most comfortably maintain for ten to twenty minutes. You're probably best advised to be in a quiet, darkened room and to keep your eyes closed. Begin by relaxing your entire body. One technique is to imagine a comfortably warm, golden light surrounding you and taking away all tension in the area you're thinking of. Start with your feet and work up to the crown of your head. Once this is done, begin to construct your visualization in your mind.

Certain images work to give us power, strength to weather difficult periods, or freedom to set forth on new paths. I offer you the following images as particularly useful for the Taurean aspects of your self, and for certain difficulties you may encounter as a Taurean.

It may happen that you will long for change, for some movement in your life, and yet feel yourself clinging even more fiercely to that which you possess, to things as they are. Instead of recriminations, which do nothing to enhance your self-esteem, try this. Visualize yourself standing on the earth, perhaps near a forest. Feel your bare feet squarely against the earth. Become aware of the incredible power and activity of the earth under you. Visualize the roots of trees reaching far beneath the earth's surface. Wiggle your toes and imagine that you are a tree, anchored deep within the earth by a vast, complex root system, bathed and nourished by an underground stream of cool, sweet, pure water. Stretch your arms skyward as if they were branches. Feel the power of Gaia, Great Mother Earth, coursing through you: through the soles of your feet, through the veins of your legs, through the trunk of your body, up through your neck and head, up through your arms, pulsing out through your fingers. Allow yourself to experience the power, the stability, the richness of Gaia. Let this fill your being. Now allow the power to gently subside down through your arms, your head and neck, the trunk of your body, your legs, your feet, back into the earth. Become aware that the power and strength of Gaia are always available to you. Become aware that She is both stability and change, that you are welcome to stay or to move, whichever is appropriate for you at this time. Repeat this visualization often to strengthen your sense of your own center. Allow the messages from your innermost self to come forth to guide you. When you are in touch with the power of the Earth Mother, you are operating from a position of strength. You will know that you are free to be rooted in what is, or to move on to what may be—and you will know which is best for you now.

An alternate visualization that might be useful when you have been launched into the sea of change, or are about to set forth but are reluctant to do so, is this one based upon a spring ritual from ancient Crete. The Cretan ritual took place in a stadium, into which were led great bulls reputed to be larger and heavier than their modern counterparts. To the sound of cymbals and flutes, young male and female acrobats marched into the arena to confront these bulls and perform daring feats symbolizing the Great Goddess's control over the potentially dangerous force She gave birth to. The young athletes wore simple loincloths and arm bands of gleaming gold; their bodies and curly hair also gleamed with fragrant oils.

In the Cretan murals surviving, we can see these girls and boys grasp the horns of a bull and vault onto his back in graceful somersaults. Imagine yourself as one of those consecrated acrobats. (It doesn't matter what age you are or what physical condition you're in; you can be whatever you want to be in your mind.) Imagine that you stand now, after long, hard training, in the soft powdery dust of the arena feeling the power of the bull of change vibrate through the earth and through the soles of your bare feet as he comes pounding toward you. Allow yourself to feel your fear coursing through you. Be with your fear completely: look at its color, its shape; smell it, feel its texture, embrace it as yours. Offer your fear to the Great Mother, and feel it transform itself into its sister, excitement. The bull is almost upon you now. You hear his great gasps, smell his sweat and anger. With one smooth, fluid motion you grasp his horns and lift yourself off the earth, forming a perfect arc. Now you complete the somersault onto his back. An exultant cheer bursts from the crowd. You flip yourself forward once again into a forward position and stretch out your strong, supple arms toward your teammate, who even now is vaulting onto the bull's back to you. Together you stand, riding the bull once more around the arena, feeling his powerful muscles move beneath your feet, seeing the earth move swiftly beneath you. When the circuit is complete, you draw power once more up through your legs and leap into the air, back-somersaulting onto the ground. Your partner joins you. Together you bow to the cheering crowd and walk proudly to the arena exit. Feel confidence surge through you, having met the worst that change can offer and, through the grace of the Great Mother, having triumphed.

All of us experience times when we feel lost or helpless, or overwhelmed by responsibilities, and we'd dearly love for someone else to take charge and relieve us of our burdens and comfort us. It is possible to receive the comfort you need, to be as a little child again and draw strength from one greater than you, without loss of dignity or without reneging on your responsibilities. Simply visualize yourself within a cave inside a great mountain. There before you sits the Great Mother on a throne. Her skirts swirl around Her ankles and become the waters of the earth. Sheaves of grain growing from the earth flank Her throne. Flowers are twined in Her hair and grow in profusion around Her. The air is rich with Her fragrance, the sweetness of blossoms, the delicious scent of foods. The air is alive with soft murmurs, the drowsy hum of bees, the trills and songs of birds. She sits in the midst of plenty, full bodied and majestic yet graceful. She smiles at you in welcome; Her eyes are like sunlight warming your soul. She lifts you gently onto Her lap, one arm around your shoulders, and cuddles you to Her. Allow yourself to relax into Her loving embrace, to feel Her stroke your hair, to hear Her tell you that all is well and that you are doing fine, that you are a daughter She is proud of. You are free to smile or to cry, to stay as long as you need to, to leave when you want, and to return whenever you will.

At certain points in your life you may feel invaded by jealousy or by bitterness at what you don't have that others have, or at the hardships you endure, or at disappointments over things you have been denied even though you've struggled to achieve them. Jealousy and bitterness are invasive; they spread their poison into all aspects of our lives and kill off our ability to perceive and appreciate, and thereby enjoy life. My sister-in-law, Ann Thorsten, shared a wonderful image with me which I now offer you. I don't know if she used it as I'm suggesting here, but it struck me as a wonderful balm to counter poisonous feelings.

Imagine you are on a wide, comfortable ledge near the top of a great mountain that rises solitary from the surrounding landscape. You are standing next to a natural pillar carved out of the mountain's side by time. It gleams golden brown in the sunlight. Visualize yourself embracing that pillar. Feel its warmth, its solidity, its world-old strength. Feel the strength and power of the mountain beneath your feet. Realize that you are holding on to a form of the Great Goddess Dikte, to whom mountains were beloved. Allow the presence of Dikte, She who is greater than the pillar, greater than the mountain, greater than all, to fill your own being. Then look where She directs you.

Before you lies the whole shining earth: seas, forests, deserts, cities, jungles—all the splendors of earth. In the utter safety of Her presence, allow yourself to look up at the sky and then out to the furthest reaches of the horizon. Look with love and wonder on the variety and richness and abundance before you. Become aware that there is enough for everyone, there is enough for you. Take out your jealousy, your bitterness as if they were merely chiffon scarves of an unappealing poisonous green. See how small and insignificant they are in the context of the panorama before you. Release them into the air and watch as they shred like clouds and dissolve into nothingness. Feel the warmth of the pillar suffuse your spirit, now buoyant through your awareness that there is plenty for you, more than enough for you, and that life holds more riches than you had ever dreamed of.

GEMINI
May 21–June 21

GEMINI: The "Heavenly Couple," who signified that the Great Goddess brought forth all opposites, such as female and male, to form the oneness of life. Based on a bas-relief from Khanjurāho, India, eleventh century AD, preserved in Archaeological Museum of Khanjurāho, India.

Interpretations of Gemini often present you as the butterfly of the zodiac: a charming but frivolous soul. You are depicted as witty and congenial, but incapable of persistence and, therefore, a waster of your considerable mental gifts. Those interpretations specifically directed to women see you as the epitome of feminine inconsistency, incapable of anything approaching a serious, long-term relationship. Although I feel that a great deal is otherwise accurate regarding Gemini, I part company with traditional interpretation on the matter of inconstancy and inconsistency. Gemini, in my opinion, is the sign of intimacy and sharing, and Gemini will help you to have relationships characterized by an extraordinary degree of closeness.

The fickle, scatterbrained image of you results from a common misreading of your emblem, the twins. These are interpreted as two warring personalities competing for dominance within you so that, as a result, you're always changing your mind or darting off first after one thing, then after another. This is really ironic since the major idea originally celebrated in Gemini was the union of opposites to create the wholeness of life. At that time, most people believed in the Great Goddess whom they worshipped as the origin of all that existed. They believed that She was life and death, night and day, female and male—all those opposites which are essential to form the Great Round of Life.

This idea was conveyed in a variety of ways. Sometimes you'll see the Goddess pictured as a great sea serpent encircling the globe, holding Her tail in Her mouth to form a completed circle—without end, without beginning. Another image emphasizing the cyclical nature of life is the Goddess as the Great Cosmic Egg, which contained the universe and from which all life was born. The Celts of Europe combined the sea serpent and egg motifs in one ritual that may be familiar to some of us. Each year, at the spring equinox, their priestesses and priests gathered at the seashore to conduct a symbolic hunt for the blood-red egg that the Great Goddess Oestris had laid originally in Her sea-serpent form.

Gemini, however, is not a single but a double image. The constellation itself consists of two stars equal in beauty and brilliance. We call these stars the Twins—Castor and Pollux—who were ancient heroes, or so the story goes. What is usually left out of that story is that Castor and Pollux were twins sacred to the Great Goddess, She Who First Bore Twins. Young men competed in athletic contests for the honor of "being" Castor and Pollux for a calendar year in various religious rituals. The winners wore little rounded caps with jagged edges, designed to resemble the halves of the cosmic eggshell. One twin symbolized spring and summer; the other, fall and winter. Together they meant that every period of increase is balanced by a period of decrease, and these seeming opposites make up the unity of life.

The Twins are a relatively late development, however. In the original zodiac, Gemini is portrayed as a woman and a man. The Egyptians drew Gemini as the Heavenly Couple: the lion-hearted Goddess Tefnut followed by Shu, the God of Air. The Chinese believed that the Goddess Nu-kua established cosmic equilibrium by inventing marriage, the partnership of *yin*, the dark, feminine powers, with *yang*, the light, masculine powers, when She took Fu-hsi as Her husband. Chinese and Hindu zodiacs still depict Gemini as a human couple—female and male—signifying (1) that society is based on the united efforts and characteristics of both sexes, beginning with their physical union which produces children, or the population necessary for a society; and (2) that each one of us is a union of feminine and masculine characteristics that blend to make up the wholeness of our individual psyches. It certainly seems simple enough, doesn't it? Yet think how threatened or outraged we tend to feel if someone questions our gender or suggests that we are behaving as if we were a member of the opposite sex. Many a man would rather drop dead than shed a tear or admit to feeling vulnerable. And it wasn't until football star Rosie Grier took up needlepoint that other men felt safe enough to indulge in that hobby. As for ourselves, think of all those subjects like math and science that we were encouraged to ignore because they were too difficult for little girls. We've sat by as spectators for years because it wasn't the thing for girls to play rough. And how about the jobs and pay raises that we let pass us by without making a peep because it would have seemed "unladylike" and "too aggressive" to complain about such injustices.

By the way, if you wish to read this information in terms of your Moon rather than your Sun, you'll need to shift your thinking. Instead of concentrating on your identity, your will, your essential self—the way you manifest being you in the world—you need to focus on the inner you, the emotional you, your self at the deepest levels of your unconscious. Your Moon affects not only your feelings but also those things you take for granted in your self—those things you assume everyone else feels or is like since they are so essential to your personality. Your Moon gifts might not be the most obvious features in your personality. They are ever present but elusive qualities you know intimately and yet can't quite put your finger on. The Moon also has to do with what went on in your family of origin, your home, your background. It concerns all those things that give you a sense of emotional security.

A Moon in Gemini sharpens your powers of observation, a gift that works to speed up your learning processes. You master intellectual and physical skills quickly because you are able to note exactly how they are done. This may also express itself in a gift for mimicry and humor, and will most certainly work to your advantage in your relationships with people as well as in your artistic self-expression. A Gemini Moon, by the way, makes self-expression a strongly felt need and since it also bestows versatility, it provides you with a variety of avenues through which to satisfy this. You may appear to be emotionally "cool" but you are disposed to be friendly and yours is a loving heart. In particular, you are likely to be deeply attached to your parents, regarding them with rapt fascination and love from your infancy onwards, and delighting in their company all your life. As they age, you will be as concerned with their emotional well-being and their intellectual stimulation as you are with their physical welfare. Naturally, these concerns will be manifest in all your deepest relationships but they are particularly marked in that with your parents. A Gemini Moon expresses itself in the feminine side of your nature through gracefulness of movement, and graciousness in social contacts, and of course, almost limitless charm. No matter what else is going on in your horoscope, the Gemini influence will be felt in your talents for sociability and for communication, and your shrewdness in assessing people and situations. For you, opportunity need only knock once.

Generally speaking, a strong Gemini influence, whether Moon, Sun, or Rising Sign placement, enables you to perceive and realize your "essence," your essential self rather than be locked into the rather limited definitions society presents us with. For most of us, our sense of personal identity is very much bound up with the behavior and responses our culture defines as appropriate to our sex. Yet those definitions are really very arbitrary; Gemini makes us innately aware of this. If we were Tuaregs in North Africa, our men would wear veils and jewelry and flirt coquettishly to keep us interested, and we'd spend most of our time in the marketplace tending to business. In our culture, it's been pretty much the reverse. Men have been expected to concentrate their energies outside the home and women to stay in the home or, if they venture forth, to enter service professions in which, presumably, they duplicate home functions. As we know, these categorizations are crumbling under the pressures and realities of life in a technological society of the late twentieth century. Even those among us who'd love to stay at home often find that we can't, either because two salaries are needed to maintain our families or because there's only the one salary—ours, as widows or as divorced or single mothers—to keep the home fires burning.

Our society and each of us is, to some extent, struggling with a reevaluation that is far more profound than the issue of who does what job where. Along with our division of labor went a division of traits and qualities, many of which have little to do with one's sexuality, but nevertheless we see them as a function of gender. For example, men are expected to be cool, competitive, logical, aggressive, and unemotional . . . except for anger or wild outbursts of enthusiasm at sports gatherings. Women, on the other hand, are supposed to be warm, cooperative, intuitive, passive, and emotional. Since, in actuality, we are all aggressive and passive, logical or intuitive, cool or warm by turns, it's been a bit uncomfortable having to learn that half of our responses are inappropriate on no sounder basis than our genitalia. The situation has been made more unpleasant in that one half—those defined as masculine—have been assigned superior value to the other, feminine constellation. In the largest social sense, this has often meant that we've thought it better to take an aggressive, competitive stance and that we've feared that cooperation and concern for the welfare of all would transform us into so much mush. In our individual lives, it has meant that men are reluctant to reveal their "feminine" side and that they suffer the consequences of such self-denial; that women are reared with an underlying sense of inferiority and, in trying to release ourselves from these toils, have had to fight to prove the "masculine" aspects of our selves to win the social rights and opportunities that should be available to all. As a result, it sometimes seems as if the "feminine" is getting blasted from all directions.

It is in regard to this issue that you get a great deal of help from Gemini and, ultimately, could yourself be a great help to the rest of us. For one thing, it is not your nature to see anyone in terms of absolutes. The idea that someone is all strong or all weak, or is only aggressive or only passive, strikes you as a rather bizarre joke because it is so evidently an impossibility. From earliest childhood, you've been quietly aware that the images people have of themselves are not necessarily accurate. And perhaps the loveliest part of this clarity you possess is that you love people quite as much for their imperfections as for their sterling qualities. You see through pretensions with an amused eye and past foibles with a fond glance. Even when you criticize and quarrel, there is an undercurrent of good humor and love that makes it easier for others to accept your remarks for consideration.

It's not likely that you share your culture's evaluation of masculine and feminine, or see this hierarchical view as anything other than an unfortunate quirk. In a certain sense, you are able to be the most level-headed of us all on this issue precisely because you regard these clusters of traits as equally valuable. No matter how rugged or invulnerable they strive to appear, you see the men in your life perhaps more completely, and certainly more tolerantly, than they see themselves. There's nothing odd to you in a man's crying or washing the dishes or wanting to be included in the gossip or rushing around getting the home ready for company or the groceries in. To you, these things are the commonplaces of life. Consequently, you treat such behavior matter-of-factly and do not make men feel foolish to have been caught in such actions or treat their behavior as landmarks of our liberation or of their evolution. In fact, it has often struck me that if only we all expected such behavior from men as you do, half of our battles would be over.

If anything, you favor humanity's feminine side, are not drawn to violence or violent people, and are very leery of aggression. While it is an exercise of good judgment to avoid, as much as possible, people of either sex who use aggression as their primary response to life, it is equally wise not to confuse aggression with assertion, a mistake we often make. For one thing, a great deal of attention has been focused on aggression. We try to explain it, we evaluate other people in terms of their aggressive responses, and apparently we extol it. Our good guys never win over the bad guys through sweet reason, or emotional ties, or even law and order; they beat them into the ground. For another thing, we've been raised to think of things as simple polarities: issues are black or white, decisions are either good or bad, people are either aggressive or passive, and that's that. But that is by no means that. Issues and responses are rarely so simple. There is the great middle range, which is far from gray, it is full of color and life and, thankfully, options that make it possible for us not to be helpless and yet not have to drive anyone else into the dirt. It is possible to say, "No, I'd rather not do this," or "I don't have the time for that," or "Yes, I am going to try for that position," without having to behave or feel like a psychological killer. Aggression is a most useful part of our human responses; our difficulty lies in learning that it doesn't cover as much territory as we've been led to believe. I stress this because I feel that even with Gemini helping you, you are susceptible to our cultural training and may be shy about fending off the bullies. The sense of helplessness that occurs when we'd rather not be aggressive and we don't yet know how to be self-assertive will result in bad dreams, and bad feelings about yourself. It is during these periods that you may be attracted to partners who are defiant and who, in effect, will act out aggression or self-assertion for you. Attachments of this type will not be long-lived because you do not find defiance intrinsically attractive and because, with any luck at all, you begin to assert yourself so that you do not need a vicarious version of the experience.

In a backhanded way, this returns us to the first point I made about Gemini: that it leads you to share experiences. The Twins symbol figures as a partnership far more than a rivalry, from everything I've witnessed about Gemini-influenced character. There is no aspect, no detail of life that you would withhold from someone with whom you felt truly compatible. Like the Balinese, who feel that if there is a floor to be swept it's much better done and more fun if twenty people rather than one set out to accomplish the task, so you, too, feel that any experience benefits a thousandfold if it is shared with friends or a lover or relatives. Even your most difficult trials are handled best in the company of people close to you; it may be that they are in the next room, but it will be important to you that they are there. The difficulties that may beset your relationships are not from lack of candor, for you do not keep your feelings, thoughts, or preferences secret. Some difficult moments do arise when your partner, friend, or relative needs to concentrate on a project or for some reason is not able or willing to share with you as you would like. The tendency is to see this as a personal rejection when it is more likely that the other person has needs different from yours, at least for that time period. It is during such intervals that you have hard work to remember you are a distinct person and to turn your attention to the fact that you do, indeed, have interests of your own. The rub in this, of course, is that it always feels like second best when it has not been of your own choosing . . . but it nonetheless helps and it's a lot more pleasant to be writing your paper or doing whatever it is that you must do or want to do than sitting around feeling unloved because the light of your life is focused elsewhere for the time being. It is also not so terrible to learn that if you can survive this, so can your nearest and dearest if you should need to concentrate totally on a project.

One possible disadvantage of a Gemini influence is that it does make it hard for you to be alone. As the most sociable, most sharing sign in the zodiac, you can't see any particular value in being by yourself and you generally arrange to have company most of the time. It helps us to be able to enjoy our own company. Each of us, by whatever path is appropriate, needs to learn and accept ourselves in all our aspects, from the grand to the petty, the good and the evil, the childish and the mature. When we don't, we project portions of ourselves onto others and live through them. But as Gail Sheehy pointed out in *Passages*, once we've integrated these aspects and claimed them as our own, "we make tremendous power available to ourselves."

Gemini contributes an extremely affectionate, sensual quality to your nature, which, as you might expect, surfaces in your sex life. You are hampered by few inhibitions and, in a close relationship, even these few disappear. You're generally curious about how things work and this, too, carries over into the sexual realm. When you're young, you can't wait until you can be fully sexually active because you're eager to see what it will be like, and you're pretty sure that you're going to enjoy yourself. And indeed you do. You're willing to try all sorts of positions and techniques, as long as they're neither violent nor painful. And you have what we've come to regard as a masculine attitude toward sex: you find many people attractive and, if you're unattached, you see no reason why you shouldn't enjoy their company in bed without necessarily thinking of them as possibilities for long-term or even brief relationships. It seems foolish to you to neglect one of your most basic needs during those periods when you're without someone whom you care for especially. When you're in a partnership, you do not cease to find other people attractive and, in fact, are often beset by impulses to make love with others. For you, fidelity is an active choice and a matter of self-discipline, a decision you make on the basis of doing as you would be done by.

Within partnerships, you are lavish of your affection and attention. You tend to find all aspects of your partners fascinating, and your partners will undoubtedly learn a great deal about themselves simply from the attention you bestow. You are susceptible to jealousy—and remarkably candid about it—because, for one thing, you suspect that your partner is as likely to be attracted to other people as you are and, for another, you resent any interference with the intimacy between you.

There's a strong possibility that you will marry early in life, since you enjoy the closeness of family life and prefer to live within that context. If you had your way, you'd pile all your closest relatives into your new home with you and, barring that, would prefer that they all live nearby. In a way, you'd have been more at home in the old matriarchal clan setup where your husband or lover would have moved into your home with all of your people. But even in a contemporary setting, you will do whatever you can to make yours an extended rather than a nuclear family.

As far as activities within the home are concerned, you enjoy cooking and making things and decorating, but you find housework a colossal bore and do only what you absolutely must as swiftly as you can. Raising children, however, strikes you as one of the great treats in life. You are very patient with them, and their activity, energy, and diversity give you a lot of pleasure. You love the sense of a busy, bustling house, full of life; the only drawback to this is that it will be a bit more difficult for you when your children are grown and out on their own. The transition from the period of motherhood, which absorbs most of your energies, to the next stage, when your responsibilities and involvement are lessened, may be the most difficult you undergo in your life. Naturally, we can hardly plan for these things in advance, but it might be better to plunge into a whirl of activities, perhaps get a job even if you don't need one, rather than sit at home brooding or falling prey to self-destructive impulses like drinking.

It seems to be the pattern of your transitions that they are extreme reversals of previous behavior. Although there is a great deal of turmoil churning about inside you, other people are often unaware of this and are puzzled by the strenuous pace you maintain and the changes wrought in your personality. During these periods you experiment with many different activities and ways of being, and it does seem as if you are burning your bridges to your past. However, your experiments can be very valuable in that they allow you to learn what you really want to discard and which new direction you wish your life to take. The assumption generally is that you crave the new and that these "outbursts" are merely the long-withheld expression of your desire to try the untried. However, these intervals are not always the gay, mad whirls they appear to be, and you experience a great deal of unexpressed sorrow at relinquishing your past self and style. It is this bewildered anguish that prompts you to prefer action rather than reflection during a transition. You will, however, sort yourself out and be able to think about the past you've left with fewer pangs once you have found your new ways to live a satisfying life. One Gemini gift of yours that can be of great assistance to you in these difficulties is that you tend to gravitate toward satisfying your own needs and paying attention to your own responses to life. And the further off you move from images of what you "should" be, the better off you are.

At whatever point in life you decide to concentrate on a career, you might review the following advantages that you possess through Gemini. First, of course, is your love of a lively, social context, which means it would be folly for you to think of entering any work that would be routine or isolated in nature. Second, you are exceptionally alert and imaginative, eager to learn what makes people and things tick, and equally eager to share your information. You're likely to be a gifted storyteller, a talent I've had the pleasure to experience through my sister Lili, who has a Gemini Moon. Many a family evening has been enlivened by her marvelous stories. These talents make it advisable for you to consider the whole field of communications—writing, film, radio, television, journalism—and you might see if you could combine these with traveling, which you enjoy tremendously. You tend to be on the lookout for the positive aspects in people and places, and you approach the new and unfamiliar with a remarkably unbiased attitude. This attitude would work very well for journalism or writing travel pieces.

More than most of us, your talents are extraordinarily varied, ranging from physical agility and grace, and an aptitude for gymnastics and dance, to a love for beauty and the manual dexterity to create in your own right, either in crafts or in the arts. The ability to express yourself well and your lack of self-consciousness combine very well for teaching, lecturing, and dramatic arts as well as writing. Your talents are almost equally suited for business or the sciences; in terms of running your own business, you have the ability to be a shrewd bargainer, but you're apt to let your sympathetic nature get the better of you. Here, you'd be well advised to work with a partner whose heart was a bit more immune to your customers' plights or charms.

You may not take your desire for leadership seriously, in part because it is subtly expressed and in part because the image of a boss, particularly a woman boss, seems to require that we annihilate our femininity . . . or so we've come to believe. However, it is possible to treat other people humanely and manage a business or hold an executive position. Nothing but custom dictates that it is easier to accept directions from a man than from a woman, so if this is something you want for yourself, by all means pursue it. This desire will undoubtedly become easier for you to realize and deal with as you get older. You are extremely idealistic, especially in your youth, hence the disadvantage that others may exploit you. Selfish behavior is both a surprise and a disappointment to you. You expect others to be as willing to share their time and resources as you are, and it comes as a shock to meet with people whose primary aim is to use others to their own advantage. It takes time for you to accept this as a reality and a bit more time before you are able to discern it quickly and protect yourself from it. However, when you do recognize this trait, you manage to enjoy such friends' company without becoming their prey, which speaks for a great generosity of spirit.

In terms of energy, yours is characterized by short increases followed by brief declines. Mind you, I'm not talking about fifteen-minute intervals, but rather two and three hours at a stretch. You have a natural tendency to balance yourself out and not prolong an activity to the point of exhaustion. Your energy and sense of well-being are restored by changes in activity rather than inactivity. It's hard for you to do absolutely nothing. Even when you are resting, you may thumb through magazines, make lists and notes to yourself, or work at some handicraft. It would help if you could get interested in meditation or yoga, since these are excellent ways to renew your strength. You tend not to have as much stamina as your energy would lead you to believe, and therefore you need to be cautious about not overextending yourself and leaving yourself vulnerable to colds and illness. Restlessness and fidgeting tend to crop up when you are faced with tasks you fear or which bore you. You often put these off in the hope that they will disappear or that someone else will do them. And, as you know, you're much better off if you just jump in and get them over with . . . a little reminder that's always easier said than done.

On a monthly basis, you generally feel lighthearted, optimistic, energetic, and full of plans and ideas when the Moon transits Gemini, Libra, and Aquarius. Fire transits are also usually positive for you. The Moon's passage through Leo and Sagittarius brings steadiness of purpose, clarity, and a lot of satisfaction in accomplishing what you set out to do. Aries transits are usually exceptionally positive and your activities are characterized by a sense that everything is going well. The transits through Virgo, Capricorn, and Taurus strengthen your organizational abilities, and they also make you more inner directed than usual. They are the times when it may seem on the surface as if nothing much is happening and yet a great deal of private reflection is going on. The Moon's transits through the water signs are a bit more complex. During Cancer transits you may feel much closer to people; this works to intensify your intimate relationships and yet can leave you vulnerable toward people not so close to you and who may take advantage of your warm feelings. Scorpio and Pisces generally make for closeness also, but you're more controlled during Scorpio days and more nostalgic during Pisces.

Your annual cycle is characterized by two high periods in spring and fall, a low occurring in summer, and fairly even energy throughout winter. Your creative energy peaks in spring, in the sense that this is the period in which you tend to have most of your ideas. Don't be discouraged by your summer slump. It probably enables you to have that peak period in the fall, during which you set out to translate your ideas into reality. In general, too much variety or too many demands bring on fatigue characterized by nervousness, anger, or weeping. Pay attention to these signals and check out how you can ease up on yourself immediately. Even if it means that you drop everything and go out for a drive or to a movie, do that rather than push yourself into a cold or some other ailment born of physical and emotional exhaustion.

Gemini sharpens your wit and you have a flair for satire, which enables you to puncture the pompous without injuring other people's self-esteem. You are good-humored and witty, and a pleasure to be with. In your close relationships, you are extremely sympathetic and quick to encourage those dear to you. You are kind and also very appreciative of kindness from others. Simply make it your business to be as tenderhearted toward yourself as you are to others, and avoid the temptation to place your energies too much at other people's disposal lest you exhaust yourself. Gemini has bestowed a wealth of lovely qualities and abilities upon you and has given you the special gift to create and enjoy truly intimate relationships. You bring a great deal of pleasure into the lives of those associated with you. I leave you with the wish that your many talents and your ability to love bring you deep satisfactions and delight in your own life.

GEMINI VISUALIZATIONS

You possess an extraordinary resource within you: your imagination. Through the power of your inward eye, you can tap into your innermost self, and into the energies of the universe. The thoughts you think, the messages you give yourself, the images you create in your imagination have tremendous power. You can literally transform your reality to fit the positive images you create mentally simply by creating those images often enough, and as specifically and clearly as you possibly can. Through such focused, purposeful "daydreaming," you can achieve an astonishing range of goals: practical goals such as weight loss, physical fitness, or money management; spiritual goals such as enhanced self-esteem, inner peace, and a deeper sense of connection with other living beings. For further information on this process, I recommend two books I've found useful, Shakti Gawain's *Creative Visualization*, and Shad Helmstetter's *The Self-Talk Solution*.

My primary concern here is empowering you to get in touch with the Goddess within you, the Eternal Feminine whose creative, nurturing, renewing energies live within us all. The Great Goddess is always ready to comfort, to heal, to strengthen, and to guide us whenever we are in need. Her images come to us from all parts of our world and from across great stretches of time. By visualizing Her in our mind's eye, by meditating on Her image, you and I not only receive help with specific problems and enhanced self-esteem but also reap the additional benefit of greater esteem for all women, past and present, and for the wonderful contributions women have made in creating and advancing civilization.

The images I sketch for you came to me through my research and through my own meditations. They may work differently for you than I've envisioned. And, of course, they're not the only images available to you. I suggest you read Merlin Stone's *Ancient Mirrors of Womanhood* and Barbara G. Walker's *The Woman's Encyclopedia of Myths and Secrets* to see what stories, prayers, and images resonate for you, and use them. I think you'll also find it illuminating simply to gaze within your own mind and see how the Goddess manifests Herself to you. I would be delighted to read your visualization experiences so if you would like to share them, please write to me, c/o the publisher.

How to go about visualization is very much a matter of personal choice: you may sit, stand, or lie down—whichever position you feel you can most comfortably maintain for ten to twenty minutes. You're probably best advised to be in a quiet, darkened room and to keep your eyes closed. Begin by relaxing your entire body. One technique is to imagine a comfortably warm, golden light surrounding you and taking away all tension in the area you're thinking of. Start with your feet and work up to the crown of your head. Once this is done, begin to construct your visualization in your mind.

Let me share with you an image that came to me one night as I was thinking about your sign in terms of its element, air. Ancient Egyptian titles of the Great Goddess drifted through my mind: the Lady of Breath, She by whose grace we live, unknowable in Herself, essential to life; the Lady of the Great Voice, before whom all trembled yet who feared none. I heard the murmur of ancient prayers to the Lady of Heaven, Great Set, who formed the arch of the sky itself with Her own beautiful body. I thought of Merlin Stone's description in *Ancient Mirrors of Womanhood* of "Amunet, She who existed on the Isle of Flame that rose out of the primeval waters and helped all life come forth from the great Cosmic Egg," and of Amn, She who was as "invisible as the air that we breathe, yet as real as the breeze or the wind."

Suddenly, I saw our sky in my mind's eye, but more beautiful than I had ever seen it before. It was a deep, rich, bright cobalt blue, so intense it was breathtaking. Etched in silvery white against this vivid background were the flowing, transparent robes of the Great Goddess, Her flowing hair, Her graceful limbs, the profile of Her beautiful, powerful face—silver kohl outlining the midnight of Her eye; Her mouth upturned in a silver smile.

How fortunate you are! When you are lonely or sad, in need of comfort, you may turn inward to the Goddess and She will wrap you in the caresses of a warm, gentle breeze, soothing you, calming you.

She may appear to you as the Goddess Isis, Her great wings outstretched, signifying that She was life itself and that we all live by Her spirit within us. She may enfold you in those infinitely soft yet strong wings, allowing you to sense that you are Her child, that you are never alone.

When life seems narrow and confining to you, and restlessness seizes your spirit, you may turn to the Goddess and she will lift you up and carry you throughout the heaven as far away from or as close to the earth as you wish. You may gaze like an eagle upon mountains, or hover near the earth, watching your life, regaining your perspective.

During transitions and other potentially stressful periods, you may wish to visualize the Goddess as Mother Night, who brought forth the World Egg. You may gaze upon that wonderful blackness, embroidered here and there with stars and veillike nebulae. Rest in Her silence; be restored and refreshed in Her darkness.

At those times when you are trying to achieve harmony within yourself or within your life, contemplate the magnificent Celtic Arianrhod, She who Barbara Walker describes in *The Woman's Encyclopedia of Myths and Secrets* as the "keeper of the endlessly circling Silver Wheel of the Stars." Her twins, Dylan (Darkness) and Lleu (Light) were born from Her simultaneously. As you see Her in your mind's eye, think about how things join, become one; how darkness becomes light becomes darkness, in an endless wheel. Look at the elements in your self and your life, and see how that which seems so separate may be reconciled into a satisfying unity.

Each of us is bound to come up against situations in which someone is apt to get hurt no matter what decision we make. Sometimes we want someone or something fiercely, and yet hesitate to act because of the possible consequences for others. Few of us really want to live our lives in a childlike way, just grabbing what we want and shutting our eyes to the effects of our behavior. But neither do we wish to martyr ourselves, denying our own needs or turning our backs on opportunities out of a possibly mistaken perception that we will injure too many other people or hurt others too deeply if we go for what we want.

When you are faced with such a dilemma, you may offer your problem to Maat, an ancient Egyptian form of the Great Goddess. Slender, beautiful Maat wears an ostrich plume upon Her head. In one hand, She holds a sceptre and in Her other She holds the ankh, the Egyptian symbol of life. The Egyptians honored Her as "The Eye," for it was She who looks deep within the human heart and knows us for whom we are. It is She who at our death weighs our good deeds against Her ostrich feather to judge whether we are worthy of rebirth. You may meditate upon Maat in Her single form or see Her as She occasionally appeared—as twins. Maat as twin sisters—a duplication and intensification of Herself—is She who established and maintained the rhythm and order of the universe,

She who guards justice and truth, She who balances Truth with Kindness. Gaze upon Her eye. Let Her look deep within your heart and reveal you to yourself. Listen to the guidance that She brings you.

Gemini blesses you with creative, artistic talent, the ability to communicate with others in writing or through some other medium. You may deepen and enrich your talents by placing yourself in touch with the Great Goddess Sarasvati of India, Mother of the Written Word. The beautiful Sarasvati River was named after Her, and you might use for your image the swift movement of the water, the sun glinting golden on the surface as it moves along swift as thought. You might picture the river in the moonlight, the water reflecting the sky's velvet blackness, the moon's silver light. Imagine the Great Goddess Sarasvati Herself, golden skinned, Her gleaming night-black eyes smiling at you. She is draped in a silken sari of blue shot through with gold and silver threads. Her hair of deepest black ripples down Her back, to Her ankles, and becomes the river. Her voice is the music of the water and the winds. It is She, Sarasvati, who dispenses the gifts of language and of poetry, music, carving, and painting. Stand in Her presence and listen to what She shares with you. Allow your thoughts to be gently suffused with Her presence. Allow your mind to open to Her gifts. She is the source of your inspiration. She wants you to do well. Gaze upon Her. Listen to Sarasvati, She Who Created Language. Allow yourself to learn.

Or you may choose, when you need inspiration, information, or guidance in your communications, to think on Seshat/Sefchet, Egypt's title for the Great Goddess of Writing and the Ruler of Books. Go deep within your mind to the source of language, to the great vault of insight and information stored like treasures within. Be patient and receptive, and allow the Goddess to release ideas and insights like lotus petals into the current of your mind.

The winds of the Goddess sweep away confusion, clear away the old, and ready your mind for the new. Use the vision of the Goddess to help you focus on what is most valuable in your life, to clarify for you what your values really are. An idea you might find useful comes to us from the Dahomey people in Africa, who believe that the Great Goddess Mawu endows each of us with the breath of life. She bestows a piece of Herself within each one of us—what we would call soul and they call *sekpoli*. They teach that we should not fight one another because we are fighting and destroying another part of Mawu Herself when we treat another human being as an enemy. In meditating on your relationships with others, including yourself, recall this idea and see what effect it has upon you to regard all of us as sharing in the soul of the Great Goddess.

CANCER
June 21–July 23

CANCER: A vision of the Moon Goddess, based upon ancient myths and contemporary Native American writings. The Goddess wears Her emblem on Her pendant and Her moccasins as She walks through the night sky, guarding all She has created.

Y ou have an astrological heritage of which you may be very proud. Cancer, the sign ruled directly by the Moon, honors the many beautiful, life-enhancing lunar qualities of the Great Mother of All, whom people worshipped thousands of years ago, when astrology first began, and even earlier. The Great Mother could assume any form but it seems the one we humans loved best was Her nightly appearance as the Moon.

We certainly had reasons enough to be grateful. The Moon transformed the night sky from a jumble of stars into a map, and once we developed the concept of a moon, or month, we had a handle on time, a framework that allowed us to recall the past and anticipate the future. We were released from the eternal, haphazard present.

The Goddess of the Moon brought many gifts, the most precious being Her light in the midst of darkness, which was equated with wisdom and insight. Nocturnal animals such as cats and owls, whose eyes seemed to grow roundest at the time of a full moon, were regarded as Her special favorites and believed to share many of Her qualities. Our rather trivialized "wise old owl" was once a most noble bird, the emblem of Athena, Goddess of the Moon, thousands of years ago in pre-Hellenic Greece. To the Egyptians, the grace, poise, and wisdom of the Moon and the pleasures of love She provided were personified in the Goddess Bast, whom they adored. Bast was depicted as a slim, beautiful woman with the head of a cat, and their reverence for Her was so intense that all cats were considered royalty, treated with the utmost care and respect while they lived and buried with the highest funeral honors when they died.

The earliest concept of human wisdom was modeled not on the sun's dazzling light but on the moon's ability to penetrate darkness, and on its coolness as well. The most widespread image of intelligence and sagacity is feminine in nature. The very words *mind* and *mental* are derived from the word *moon,* as are so many other words for mental activity. Most people in ancient times held their council meetings the week of the new moon each month so that grievances were not allowed to get very "old." They patterned their idea of justice on their experience of motherhood, and since everyone was a child of our Universal Mother, the Moon, everyone had an equal right to present a complaint before Her representatives. These were usually the oldest, wisest women of the group, or the priestesses—and often this amounted to the same thing. Whether they were seated around a council fire under the stars or inside a splendid palace, everyone had a chance either to make a complaint or to give an explanation for antisocial behavior. Reparations were preferred to the strict eye-for-an-eye code. Among the social virtues, honesty was the most highly esteemed as the basis of social trust. In ancient Rome, the only place the common people felt their money was safe from fraud and lies was in the temple of the Great Goddess Ceres, Goddess of the Moon and of All Living Things.

Massive monuments to the Great Goddess of the Moon mark a path from Asia and the Middle East through Africa and Europe up to North Jutland, Sweden, and Zeeland. Their counterparts in Central and South America, especially in Peru, echo the same beliefs. We marvel at how our ancestors ever managed to set up megaliths such as Stonehenge, which would tax our engineering abilities even today. These monuments stand as testimonials to human ingenuity. They are also an index of the depth of religious feeling that people had for the Great Mother. She was the intelligence that animated the universe. All forms of life were born from Her, received Her maternal care, and were subject to the laws She gave as life's framework. She could be black or white; a maiden, a mother, a wise old woman. She was the essence of "being" and "becoming." We learned that although Her faces changed, She remained the same, just as the seasons change and return to their beginning. We also follow Her pattern. We undergo cycles of growth, but our essential selves remain stable as we shift into new patterns.

If you wish to read this information in terms of your Moon rather than your Sun, you'll need to shift your thinking from your identity, your will, your essential self—the way you manifest being you in the world—to focus instead on the inner you, the emotional you, your self at the deepest levels of your unconscious. Your Moon not only has to do with your feelings but also includes those things you take for granted in your self—those things you assume everyone else feels or is like, since they are so essential to your personality. Your Moon gifts might not be the most obvious features in your personality. They are ever present but elusive qualities you know intimately and yet can't quite put your finger on. The Moon also has to do with what went on in your family of origin, your home, your background. It concerns all those things that give you a sense of emotional security.

Specifically, your Moon in Cancer blesses you with a highly active, highly developed imagination, a gift that can enhance your life immeasurably. Nourish it, and avoid as much as possible the violent images we are so routinely exposed to. A Cancer Moon creates a need for balance between sociability and privacy. You prefer to be with other people much of the time, to entertain, to share ideas. This, coupled with Cancerian idealism, prompts you to be part of great enterprises aimed at making the world a better place. Contribute your energies and talents to issues and projects you consider worthy, but honor your need for individual expression and your periodic need to work alone. Do not lock yourself into any overly restrictive arrangement. Moon in Cancer contributes an appreciation for the past, your own personal history as well as history in general. You are able to value what others have contributed to your life, to learn the lessons of the past, and to view life in cyclical terms. A Moon in Cancer expresses itself through the feminine side of your nature, through your ability to sympathize with others and to cherish the people, places, and things you care most about. Your femininity might be characterized as "maternal" provided you include in "maternal" the ability to see life and issues in very broad terms far beyond the immediate present, the desire for excellence, and the ability to assume great responsibility and exercise leadership.

If you have Sun in Cancer, the chances are extremely good that you possess great personal ambition and the abilities to achieve the recognition and financial success you desire. You are, after all, influenced by the sign of the Great Goddess Herself. It's certainly not "unfeminine" of you that you wish to share your gifts with an audience larger than your immediate family circle. It seems a mistake to insist that you are happiest when devoting your energies to your home, when it's just as likely that you will be happiest devoting yourself to a very interesting, multifaceted career, and indeed, may choose not to have children, or a home as that is traditionally understood.

Cancer gives you great personal flair and a distinct style. You are able to assess your strengths and weaknesses objectively and to proceed to make the most of your assets. On the most superficial level, your appearance reflects your instinct for what suits you best, so that you present yourself to excellent advantage. This is no mean skill to have, especially if you are going to put yourself forth to the public. People do remember you. They recall either your exquisite taste or your highly original, interesting style, but whatever it is that captures their attention, you definitely do not fade into a blur in people's memories.

More interesting, at least to me, is the fact that this originality is also expressed in the life you create for yourself. It often entails a large portion of courage because you are as apt to go against the social grain as to abide by convention. Happily your decisions are grounded on what suits you, which is a much firmer basis for proceeding than choosing to be merely fashionable or trying to tailor yourself to other people's expectations of you. I'm not saying that this doesn't cost you, because of course it does. The great stress on the craving Cancerians have for security is connected to this, although somewhat mistaken in my opinion. Often the parallel is drawn between you and the crab: that you are hard on the outside and soft on the inside. I've never gotten that impression, as this image too frequently implies, that you are a frightened little soul hiding behind a tough exterior. You take great risks and, by refusing to stay within tidy stereotypes, you expose yourself to a great many unpleasant reactions. In addition, many of your efforts are very private, independently initiated and executed. Given this, who wouldn't want a little reassurance and security? None of us is impervious to qualms and doubts. It's a great help to have friends you've been close to for years, whose acceptance you can count on and who will cheer you on in your ventures. I fail to see this as an inordinate craving.

You are capable of putting an enormous amount of effort into your undertakings and are conscientious and thorough in the work you do. Your organizational skills are excellent, and you are quick to see ways in which you can save yourself time or can delegate responsibilities to save your energy for major tasks. Learning new skills and the best ways to proceed on a project generally give you pleasure and satisfaction through an increased sense of competence, of being effective in the world.

Cancer's influence increases the possibility that your work will be varied and that you will change positions or alter career directions quite a few times. It may be that one career will branch into another, or that you will explore several related facets of a particular interest. In considering careers, it might be well to keep in mind certain Cancerian traits you've been granted.

To begin with, you have a keen sense for ideas you intuitively know are workable, have great appeal to the public, and are needed at a particular time. You can capitalize on your inner timing in such fields as publishing, writing, teaching, movies, television, radio, and drama. You also have a talent for publicity, an ability to sense where and how to get the best public exposure for yourself or your clients, and you are willing to follow these efforts through to see that the ideas you cherish get maximum exposure.

Another point to consider is that you are an independent spirit, and are capable of working alone, although you will then need to balance this by social contact during your leisure so that you don't become too isolated. In working with others, you're better off in jobs that allow you a great deal of independent action, permitting you to initiate projects and pursue them on your own, or in which you are in a managerial or executive position relative to other people. The ability to do things in a style distinctly your own does have a drawback, in that it makes you impatient and irritable with other people's ways of doing things. You may find your nerves rubbed raw by what you feel is inefficiency, slow-wittedness, or lack of dedication to a project. This last is especially difficult for you because you devote yourself so utterly to a project or a cause; it's hard for you to accept that your colleagues might not be as committed as yourself or might not express their commitment in the same way or to the same extent as you do.

Despite the fact that you can work on your own, you'd be well advised to review your ideas periodically with friends whose opinions you respect. It never hurts to have someone act as a sounding board; not only is another opinion a valuable assistance in giving balance to your work but it allows you to step back from it briefly and look at it objectively once more.

You have a strong sense of adventure, and your commitments to people and ideas will certainly provide you with much of it in your life. You are quite capable of picking up and moving to another city or country to start a new life—*if* it suits you and only as long as it suits you. This is by no means flightiness, because however strong your urge, you are careful to research and plan in advance of your move. But you won't hesitate to make radical changes in your life in order to be near someone you care for or to pursue a goal if it's best done in a setting other than your usual environment. You approach adventures confidently, expecting the best to happen, and even if they don't live up to your hopes, you are able to draw much that is valuable from the experiences. You enjoy travel and learn very quickly that the best way to adapt to the new is to bring along a few easily carried, cherished items from your familiar world to create some sense of home in a strange place.

There's a great deal of stress on the Cancerian love of home, and it is certainly true that you use your resources imaginatively to create a home that is comfortable for you and that gives you pleasure. This seems effort well spent, in my opinion, because the demands that both you and circumstances place upon your energy make it absolutely vital for you to have a place in which to restore and refresh yourself. Your home acts as a buffer between you and the outside world, and it's important that it be serene. You enjoy entertaining, and even during periods when money is not super-abundant, you manage to carry this off with elegance and originality. However, entertaining is an occasional pleasure. You're not eager to have your home continually swarming with guests; this is just as well, since you need the respite your home affords too much to let it become Grand Central Station.

Since we're close to the topic, we might as well proceed to your energy pattern right now. My other strong objection to traditional interpretations of Cancer is the insistence on your "moodiness." We are all moody, regardless of sign or sex, so this doesn't give you much help. What distinguishes your pattern is that your moods tend to get you firmly in their grip; they are insistent and strongly felt, and you can't shake them off easily. Some signs need only to change from one activity to another; others need to remember that neither the bad mood nor the good is going to last forever. You need to know your mood pattern intimately to maximize your energies. On a monthly basis, a Sagittarius transit is very difficult for you—either wonderfully high but followed by a sharp drop into depression, or just plain depressed—so tread carefully on these days and try not to take anything terribly seriously. The fire transit, Leo, on the other hand, is generally very positive without a depressed aftermath, and it tends to sustain your strong sense of creative energy from your Cancer transit. Pisces and Aries days can also be funny combinations. You'll probably feel very inner directed in the Pisces transit and may experience Aries as a frustrating time when your energies are all dammed up. Taurus and Gemini transits, however, are a great relief and are very sociable periods, so you might try to schedule important business that involves social contact for those periods. The other air transits, Libra and Aquarius, are generally plain, pleasant times when life seems to go about its business with a minimum of friction. Virgo and Capricorn transits are also positive days in which you'll feel as if your energies are fully released and things flow easily. They are excellent times for creative work. Water transits are usually days of profound inner reflection, even when they do not seem so on the surface. Your Cancer and Scorpio transits are powerful periods of introspection, while Pisces, as mentioned, can be difficult in that this may be negatively toned.

Your annual energy is usually high during the summer, particularly if you have the opportunity to vacation or travel, and remains strong through fall and spring. Winter is a low point for you, and you might try to balance your schedule in favor of social activities. In general, your energy and stamina seem to be of equal weight. You, like Scorpio people, have to learn to balance your strong need for quiet and for time to reflect with an almost equally strong need to be with other people. Difficulties arise for you when you have been either too private or too sociable. You can help yourself by paying attention to your restlessness, which can signal for you when you've been alone too long or when you've been socializing to the point where you feel it's merely "gadding about."

I've spoken at length about your ambitions because I feel they too often get lost in the shuffle of traditional astrological interpretations. But there's no denying the fact that you're interested in your more private relationships and bring to them a deep loyalty and commitment. Sexually, you tend toward one relationship at a time and give yourself to it utterly. Your late teens and early twenties is the time, generally speaking, when you enjoy having brief affairs that engage your affections superficially. You tend to give yourself over to having a good time and are not interested in serious attachments. However, do not allow yourself to be careless about your health. Wear protection yourself and insist that your partner wear fresh protection each time you have intercourse. Given the health risks you face these days, forego intercourse on a casual basis.

This is a good period, despite the likelihood that it's attended by self-doubts. Whether you realize it or not, you are developing your social strengths, getting to know yourself, and learning which people are really compatible with you. Many of the friendships you make in this period will last your lifetime, through all the changes wrought by time and circumstances.

But from your mid-twenties onward you enter the pattern more generally characteristic of you: long-term relationships to which you commit yourself fully. I do not suggest by this that you lose your sense of self, because that is certainly not the case. But you bring candor to your relationships and a well-defined personality, complete with strong likes and dislikes, as well as an awareness of your needs. You are also able to accept your partners on their own terms, even when you dislike certain traits or actions. Yours are definitely partnerships of equals.

You are delighted by romance and adventure: anyone who desires to capture your attention is advised to develop a flair for outrageously romantic gestures. No matter how long you've been with someone, you do not lose your taste for a grand and glorious surprise. A lovely, unexpected gift or an impromptu vacation will do more to refresh your ardor than any amount of new techniques from the manuals. You prefer partners with strong personalities of their own, and especially appreciate wit and generosity.

Occasionally, this penchant for the exotic can lead to disappointments. You may be very much attracted to someone who is delightfully witty and ingenious, but who proves rather a butterfly incapable of returning the strong love and loyalty you offer and require in turn. If you're not deeply involved or do manage to extricate yourself from these affairs without severe disillusionment and bitterness, you are able to remain friends and enjoy the magical qualities of your former lovers without hurting your heart or expecting more from them than they can give. In line with this is the likelihood that at some point or another you plunge into a passion for someone that absorbs you so totally that it feels like an obsession. Rarely is this a happy experience, and it often occurs out of love for an image or for the state of being in love rather than from a genuine relationship with the object of your desire. You may be compelled to encompass your lover totally and will be upset and agitated if your partner is not as absorbed as completely in you. There's no denying that this is painful to go through, or that when it happens it is certainly not perceived as being in love with love or anything as objective as that. There is, however, one compensation to be gained from this experience, should it come your way; you can emerge from the disappointment with firsthand knowledge that living for someone else, at the sacrifice of your most important needs, is not the way you wish to spend your life, nor is it something that you can really ask of anyone else, especially once you know what it feels like.

Such difficulties as these, however, are relatively minor compared to the loss of someone you've profoundly loved or to separation from someone to whom you've been attached for years. These times of grief are hard for us all, and although you may seem fairly cheerful on the surface, you are in reality shaken to your depths. You heal slowly, and you are well advised to follow your own inclinations in this regard. Often your friends, with the best intentions in the world, try to help you ease your sorrow by urging you back into the social whirl before you're really ready for it. But you do not form real attachments hastily and you do not disengage from them or acclimate to their loss very swiftly. You will recover— in your own time and in your own way—and there is no one who can presume to say how long this process should take. People sometimes say things like, "Well, it's time you were over that" because they do not know how to cope with your grief. In their discomfort and frustration at not knowing how to help you, they simply wish it were over with. That is their problem; you will do what you can and must from your own inner promptings. Fortunately, you will be carried through the hardest parts by your instinct for self-preservation, without falling victim to brooding depression. You have enormous reserves of strength and resilience and these, too, come to your aid.

In a more cheerful vein, there is the lovely fact that you are a person who can have deep, loving attachments that give you an enormous amount of pleasure. Although you are self-reliant and resourceful, you are aware of and responsive to the enriched dimension a relationship gives to your life. If and when you choose the traditional pleasures of family life, you bring the same energy and high standards to managing your home as you would to a career. In short, you take it seriously. Your organizational abilities stand you in good stead, and you're able to accomplish a great deal because you use your time well. Much as you enjoy your children, there may be some difficulty in delegating responsibility to them. Children are not likely to be very efficient or skilled at their assigned tasks; this may irritate you, because you like things to be done well. As regards this, it will take conscious effort on your part to restrain yourself from "doing for" or taking tasks over from them. If you can learn to abide with their initial clumsiness and slowness, you'll benefit your children and yourself. They'll have the chance to develop their sense of responsibility, plus enjoy the pleasures of becoming self-reliant and competent—pleasures that you can certainly empathize with. You, on the other hand, will not be overburdening yourself by taking on all the work, and you can avoid the pitfall of martyrdom, a state that has yet to improve anyone's disposition.

You enjoy extending your skills beyond the basic level into the realm of the inventive and unusual. For example, you no sooner learn the rudiments of cooking than you're off to conquer baking breads or becoming expert at the cuisines of other countries or specialties of that sort. You're dexterous and can become accomplished in several crafts, especially fine work such as needlepoint and creating jewelry. Again, your ingenuity asserts itself, and once you've acquired the basic stitches, for instance, you go on to create your own combinations and particularly your own designs. It's quite possible that the skills you develop in conjunction with homemaking will reach a very marketable degree of excellence. These hobbies could quite easily be adapted into a business of your own, if your interest in them is sufficiently high. This is certainly a possibility worth considering when your home responsibilities have lessened to the point where you'd have the time and energy. Fortunately, there are excellent books and articles available now for women who want to start their own business ventures and could use a little advice on how to get credit and how to cope with the mysteries of marketing.

Another area you might do well to involve yourself with is politics, at any level—local, state, national, or international. Cancer not only sharpens your interest in current affairs but it makes you very aware of the workings of power—and you yourself could handle power very well. You are not only concerned about good, efficient government but are acutely affected by injustice and the curtailment of people's rights. You tend to regard the social inequalities that hamper women as inane, unworthy survivals from the stupidities of the past and would like to see them ended as swiftly as possible. Your feminism is expressed in very practical terms: you direct your energies toward immediate improvements in hiring practices, health care, and laws that affect women's access to property, as well as toward eliminating all kinds of restrictions that limit our political, social, and educational opportunities.

In regard to this, your sense of humor, especially your ability to be sharply witty, adds freshness and power to the message you wish to get across. Your sensitivity extends from yourself to other people's feelings, and you are able to deal with people diplomatically without sacrificing your own values and opinions. Honesty and tact are a hard combination to come by, especially in politics, but they serve you well—and they can also benefit the rest of us.

In conclusion, I remind you that perhaps the greatest gift the Moon gives is wisdom. It is not based merely on logic or on experience; it combines these with the insights gained intuitively and the sensitivity to the human condition born of one's own pains and pleasures. It is a gift most definitely available to you. It comes gradually, of course, and requires not only that you show the courage to bear the disappointments that crop up in anyone's life but that you accept yourself without flinching from your limitations and without ignoring the many valuable assets you possess. The regard you show toward yourself is not confined to egotism; it extends to others, and in the course of your life, it deepens into genuine compassion for others and a strong concern that we should all strive to improve the workings of this world. The considerable effort you expend and the risks you take can culminate in your later years in the satisfaction of sharing your hard-won knowledge with the rest of us and helping to guide us toward those precepts of which the Goddess Herself would be proud.

CANCER VISUALIZATIONS

You possess an extraordinary resource within you: your imagination. Through the power of your inward eye, you can tap into your innermost self, and into the energies of the universe. The thoughts you think, the messages you give yourself, the images you create in your imagination have tremendous power. You can literally transform your reality to fit the positive images you create mentally simply by creating those images often enough, and as specifically and clearly as you possibly can. Through such focused, purposeful "daydreaming," you can achieve an astonishing range of goals: practical goals such as weight loss, physical fitness, or money management; spiritual goals such as enhanced self-esteem, inner peace, and a deeper sense of connection with other living beings. For further information on this process, I recommend two books I've found useful, Shakti Gawain's *Creative Visualization*, and Shad Helmstetter's *The Self-Talk Solution*.

My primary concern here is empowering you to get in touch with the Goddess within you, the Eternal Feminine whose creative, nurturing, renewing energies live within us all. The Great Goddess is always ready to comfort, to heal, to strengthen, and to guide us whenever we are in need. Her images come to us from all parts of our world and from across great stretches of time. By visualizing Her in our mind's eye, by meditating on Her image, you and I not only receive help with specific problems and enhanced self-esteem but also reap the additional benefit of greater esteem for all women, past and present, and for the wonderful contributions women have made in creating and advancing civilization.

The images I sketch for you came to me through my research and through my own meditations. They may work differently for you than I've envisioned. And, of course, they're not the only images available to you. I suggest you read Merlin Stone's *Ancient Mirrors of Womanhood* and Barbara G. Walker's *The Woman's Encyclopedia of Myths and Secrets* to see what stories, prayers, and images resonate for you, and use them. I think you'll also find it illuminating simply to gaze within your own mind and see how the Goddess manifests Herself in you. I would be delighted to read your visualization experiences so if you would like to share them, please write to me, c/o the publisher.

How to go about visualization is very much a matter of personal choice: you may sit, stand, or lie down—whichever position you feel you can most comfortably maintain for ten to twenty minutes. You're probably best advised to be in a quiet, darkened room and to keep your eyes closed. Begin by relaxing your entire body. One technique is to imagine a comfortably warm, golden light surrounding you and taking away all tension in the area you're thinking of. Start with your feet and work up to the crown of your head. Once this is done, begin to construct your visualization in your mind.

The images of the Great Goddess as the Shining One, the Moon, are so varied, so many, and so beautiful that it is difficult to choose among them. They come from every part of the world: Africa, Asia, Europe, the Pacific Islands, Australia, and the Americas. In fact, you could easily make a hobby of collecting stories and lore of the Goddess as the Moon.

From Asia comes an image that might solace you when you are downhearted and in need of comfort. Look within your mind at the gentle Chiang-o, Great Goddess of China. Her hair is piled softly on Her head and bound by a wide ribbon; She wears a flowing, richly patterned robe over a silvery white gown. Her expression is tender. In Her arms, She cradles a rabbit, an animal beloved of Her for its fertility. You, too, are beloved of the Goddess; Her cool, gentle hand smoothes the worry from your brow. She cradles you in Her arms as if you were a little rabbit, and as She smiles at you, feel your strength return to you and your heart feel light within you.

There may be times when you feel constricted by your life. Perhaps you feel burdened by responsibilities, especially if you feel that you haven't chosen them but instead have had them thrust upon you. The way to release yourself from this sense of helplessness and victimization is to choose whatever you have. Empower yourself by choosing exactly what you have. Further empower yourself by stepping out, in your imagination, for a walk through the universe with the Iroquois Goddess, the Eternal One, whose Moon emblem decorates Her dress and moccasins and the pendant She wears around Her neck.

Walk with Her through the night sky as She guards all She has created. Hold Her cool, firm hand so that you may walk confidently and gaze around you, above you, below you. Enjoy the beauty around you, the blazing stars, the swift flash of meteors, the Milky

Way flung like a gossamer stole into the heavens. Look below at our beautiful earth, all blue and white, shining with hope. Let the sense of wonder and of love fill you, and push out the boundaries of your life so that you return from your meditation with a broadened perspective.

The image of the Mayan Goddess, Ix Chel, can serve you well for several needs. If you wish to become pregnant, Ix Chel is one name of the Goddess you can call upon to make you fertile. If you wish to become fertile in thought, pregnant with ideas, again call upon Ix Chel. If you are about to deliver a child, hold the beautiful image of Ix Chel, the Sacred One, smiling at you in your mind, easing the difficulties of childbirth. If you are ill, remember it was Ix Chel who taught the people of the Yucatan and Guatemala to heal themselves, and Her image they held in their prayers for health. Lastly, if you are ending an unsatisfactory relationship or debating whether or not to do so, gaze inwardly upon your image of Ix Chel, She who taught women that they must be free to come and go as they please, that they must not tolerate abusive treatment from anyone.

As a Cancerian, there are going to be many occasions in which you will need to call upon your inner resources to bring forth ideas and intuitions. You have exceptional insight into the possibilities of a situation, and can see opportunities where the rest of us wouldn't. However, because the chances are good that you will persevere to the end of any course of action you embark upon, you must be especially careful before you make a commitment. Like our ancestors, you may call upon the cool, subtle wisdom of the Moon Goddess, the Mother of Insight. Meditate upon the image of China's Shing-Moo, Perfect Intelligence. Or turn your inward gaze upon the Christian Virgin Mary, Moon of the Church, who was prayed to as Perfect Wisdom.

If your task is less to judge and evaluate, and more to create and innovate, then visualize the wonderful Goddess, Spider Woman, to whom the Pueblo people prayed as Thinking Woman or as Thought Woman. As Merlin Stone wrote in her wonderful book, *Ancient Mirrors of Womanhood:*

Once the lights of heaven were in place, Spider Woman
. . . made people. Upon them She placed a covering of
creative wisdom, that which She spun from Her own Spider
being. To each She attached a thread of Her web . . . each
person has a delicate thread of web connected to Spider
Woman . . . [and] we may draw upon this link to the creative
wisdom of Spider Woman.

The Pueblo believe that we keep our link by chanting, and that
if we close the door in our minds, we become cruel and small in
spirit. So it is a good idea to keep our connection to the creative
wisdom of Spider Woman/Thought Woman.

It is also a good idea to remember the Moon, the Great
Goddess of Mercy, at those times when you are feeling sharply
critical of yourself or others. In this visualization, think of the night
sky as velvet-black, picked out just here and there with a small spark
of starlight. This is the deliberate creation of the Goddess of Mercy,
who hides Herself from view to give respite to all the poor little
hunted things. It is Her sacred reenactment of the original darkness
of the womb in which all were carried and nurtured safely, calmly,
lovingly. Allow yourself to feel the calm and the gentleness of this
nightscape. Imagine brushing your hand lightly across the grass,
touching the light, refreshing dew the Moon sends to nourish us.
Allow the patience and love suffusing this nightscape to enter your
own feelings and to soothe you and inspire you with mercy and
patience toward yourself and others.

When I think of you in terms of your water element, I see an
ancient seashore. There are great boulders on the sides of this vision,
and the ocean waves rise up like magnificent wild horses to leap over
these rocks. The central portion of the vision is calm. There is no
one there except a priestess of the Moon, standing where the water
laps the land, the hem of her robe seems to become water, to swirl
around her ankles. She gazes upward at the Moon, She who rules
the waters of all living beings, including ourselves, whose moods
and energy levels are linked to Her. Like the priestess, you can feel

the Great Goddess as Moon pull the waters of earth first forward, then back.

The priestess holds a silver vessel in her hand. She fills the vessel with water from the ocean. She turns and smiles at you and tells you that this is the ocean of life. She tells you to fill your vessel to the brim, that there will be enough for you no matter what size vessel you brought, that there is enough for all of us. You stand by this ocean, enchanted by its beauty, and you are filled with a buoyant sense of confidence and delight, knowing that there is an abundance of wonderful things for you. Now, next to you on the shore, are all the people you know, all the people you have ever loved, have ever seen or heard of or thought of. Each has a vessel, and each can fill her or his vessel and still there is enough—still the ocean ebbs and flows in its ancient rhythms, its ancient fullness— and the Great Goddess smiles down on us all.

Another image I would like to share with you is one that seems to pop into my mind whenever I'm feeling glum, misunderstood, lonesome, and blue—in short, sorry for myself and a bit short on a sense of humor. What happens then is that, in my mind's eye, I see myself as a sea otter. Do likewise: see yourself floating on your back, your paws clasped on your stomach in perfect contentment and good humor. You are buoyed up by the vast ocean of life that is the Great Mother from whom we all came. Feel yourself rocked gently, first forward, then back, by the Great Mother, the Moon. Look within your mind at your jolly otter's face, and see yourself playing in the water, diving, somersaulting, having fun. If you have children or you work with children, you might see yourself as a mother otter, clasping your happy babies to you as you are rocked in the loving cradle of the sea. Feel your sense of humor return to you. Rest confidently in the sense of love connecting and supporting us all.

LEO
July 23–August 23

LEO: The Great Goddess, Cybele, in Her chariot drawn by lions, which signified that She had dominion over all animals, however fierce. Based on a bronze statue, Rome, second century AD, preserved in the Metropolitan Museum of Art, New York.

Traditionally, the sign Leo represents the sun at its maximum brilliance. Dazzling, forceful, it is the ultimate in solar power and it seems only fitting that the lion, that most magnificent of animals, should be its symbol. There is nothing wrong with this image—except that it's incomplete. And because we've been working with an incomplete image, our interpretations of Leo have tended to depict it as the sign of unrestrained vanity and egotism.

In ancient astrology, at the time when people throughout the world worshipped the Great Goddess as the supreme divine force animating the universe, the sun was regarded as the child of the Great Goddess. He was Her brilliant, powerful son who both enhanced and menaced life. The summer solstice was his time of greatest splendor and potential danger, so that, as in Taurus, people prayed that the Goddess would restrain Her child and control his power for their benefit. The image of the lion was assigned to the constellation that signaled the solstice, perhaps because the sun seemed the great golden lion of the sky.

However, he did not stalk the heavens alone but followed at the heels of the Great Goddess. The brilliant star cluster we know as the

Sickle of Leo were the Bow Stars to the Egyptians, and they signified
the Goddess as Satis, who strides through the sky, armed with bow
and arrows, followed by Her lion.

The Goddess is shown in command of lions and other wild
animals throughout the world. Elsewhere in Africa, an Amazonian
Gorgon Goddess is shown strangling a brace of lions in Her bare
hands. In Sparta, the Great Goddess calmly stands on a lion, while
in Crete She is shown either playing with them or standing on a
mountaintop while they flank Her adoringly. In Italy, the winged
Goddess Artemis carries bow and arrow and is shown holding two
lions by their paws. In Phoenicia and Mycenaea, the Goddess was
frequently presented in abstract as the Moon Stone (Cancer) or the
Moon Tree (Libra) with lions standing guard on either side of Her.
The Assyrian-Babylonian Goddess Ishtar and the Goddess Atargatis,
Queen of Heaven from Asia Minor, are depicted astride their lions,
while the Goddess Cybele, who had a wide following from Asia
Minor to as far west as Italy, was pictured as either riding lions
bareback or seated in a chariot pulled by a team of lions.

The Great Goddess was not only Mother of the Sun but
Mother of All—of beasts and birds, fish, insects, and people, of
everything in the universe. Her dominion over the ferocious as well
as the gentler creatures was also a tribute to human women, who not
only tamed wild animals into domestic companions but also
transformed our species from fierce hunters who killed and ate one
another into civilized beings capable of social harmony. It was our
mothers, so very long ago, who decided what "human" was ideally
supposed to mean and taught us how to live up to those ideals.

The sign Leo did not represent the untrammeled power of the
sun but the control of that power, the ability to direct it into
constructive rather than destructive channels. As I mentioned,
people had the wit to realize that the sun worked for and against
them; it could nourish their crops or shrivel them to dust. This
balanced view extended to astrology, a combination of psychological
and religious thinking. They did not celebrate the unbridled egotism
and vanity that wither human relationships but instead the generosity
of spirit that strength and the wise use of it permit.

If you wish to read this information in terms of your Moon

rather than your Sun, you'll need to shift your thinking from your identity, your will, your essential self—the way you manifest being you in the world—to focus instead on the inner you, the emotional you—your self at the deepest levels of your unconscious. Your Moon not only has to do with your feelings but also includes those things you take for granted in your self—those things you assume everyone else feels or is like, since they are so essential to your personality. Your Moon gifts might not be the most obvious features in your personality. They are ever present but elusive qualities you know intimately and yet can't quite put your finger on. The Moon also has to do with what went on in your family of origin, your home, your background. It concerns all those things that give you a sense of emotional security.

Moon in Leo imparts a special warmth to your personality. It is expressed through the feminine side of your nature in a kind of radiance, a magnetism that draws people to you. Physically, there is a glowing quality to your looks, which you will no doubt play up, and rightfully so. Psychically, you emanate confidence in yourself and warmth toward others and, consequently, people enjoy being with you. A Leo Moon also blesses you with a fertile imagination and the courage to gamble on new ideas. It allows you to take pleasure in your accomplishments and in the achievements of those dear to you. Emotionally, it imparts a basic optimism to your nature, a tendency to look for the best in yourself and others, and for the most favorable interpretation of events. Yours is more than just a sunny disposition, however; there is real passion in your love life and a passionate quality to all your deepest attachments, whether these be family, friends, ideas, or projects. You have your Moon in Leo to thank for your generosity of spirit and for your essential dignity and your respect for the dignity of others. In addition, it gives you a flair for leadership that you are able to exercise without being oppressive. Cultivate this.

The first gift you receive from Sun in Leo is energy in abundance and the stamina to maintain a pace that would floor most of us inside of a week. You get up early and stay up late. Into an eighteen-hour day you manage to pack the responsibilities of a demanding job—often more than one job, in fact—plus a full social life. Surprisingly, you rarely seem frantic or rushed, and you give each job or person your full attention so that it seems as if you had all the time in the world. But your demanding schedule is kept up for months and months at a stretch, and during these periods you're quite likely to put in a six-and-a-half or seven-day work week. Even your days off are probably spotted with interludes devoted to your job, and frequently you rest by doing different kinds of work rather than none at all. For example, your weekend may include a strenuous bout of gardening or working on a private project.

Living within a family context helps you keep a balance between your work and your private time. When you are on your own, you're quite likely to cut down drastically on the time you give to strictly personal pleasures, especially if your work involves a considerable amount of social contact, since that, seemingly, satisfies your need to be with other people. One close Leo friend who owns a nightclub takes a vacation about once every four or five years and rarely remembers to schedule a night off for herself to go out and relax with her friends. I'm not citing her as a model to emulate, mind you, but as an example of the extremes to which a Leo person can push her stamina.

Even though you may have the physical wherewithal to endure such a rigorous schedule, it's not a particularly grand idea to let your private life atrophy. We all need the refreshment gained through purely personal time. One hopes that we will live long enough to reach that stage when our work ceases to figure so largely in our concerns, at which point it's rather nice to have personal interests to turn to. In this regard, you do need to exercise self-control so that you don't fall into that "all work, no play" trap. This may be difficult because, along with lavish energy and endurance, your generosity and your demand for personal excellence inclines you to be prodigal with your physical resources. Other people frequently turn to you for help. They realize that you're responsible and that if you set out to do something, you will see to it that it is done extraordinarily well. It's hard for you to refuse a plea for help and even harder to treat something casually once you've committed yourself to it. Before you know it, you can find yourself with little time for yourself beyond the bare necessities of eating, getting dressed, and sleeping.

Just as "money attracts money," the fact that you're a responsible person draws responsibilities to you like a magnet. It takes time
and conscious control for you to learn to steel yourself against
people's requests and not to place yourself so freely at their disposal.
But that control is most definitely within the realm of possibility,
and it becomes easier the more you exercise it. As a matter of fact,
you're likely to become most aware of the need to control your
generous impulses when you enter the transitional periods in your
thirties and again in your forties. For one thing, you're a bit tired by
then of rescuing other people's projects from disaster, especially
when you inwardly recognize that often the largest part of their
trouble is their willingness to let you do their work for them. For
another thing, these transitions are the times when your personal
ambitions clarify and begin to take definite shape.

Transitions are always difficult to some degree; I guess it's their
nature to be so, as the needs we've yet to satisfy shift to the fore and
others merge into the background. The experiences we've undergone
have given us information we didn't have before and have developed
certain aspects of ourselves, often without our even realizing it. Our
transitional intervals are rather like bridges we cross; we carefully
pick our way because we don't quite know who we'll be and what
waits for us on the other side, and we are a little bewildered about
what of our past we should leave behind.

It seems most likely that the transition you make in your early
thirties is first marked by an increase in the help you extend to
others. You may swamp yourself with outside responsibilities, a kind
of double or triple dose of the familiar, which begins as a response
to nervousness and fear, a way of keeping change at bay. But it ends
by hastening that change, because there's nothing quite like an
overdose to convince you that this is definitely not the way you wish
your life to continue. At that point, you start to cut back. You may
take a vacation and do a lot of traveling. You may enroll in courses
that will help you toward the skills or degree you need to alter or
expand your career. You may get very serious about having children
if you've postponed having a family prior to this. You may change
from a volunteer to a salaried professional. But whatever direction
you choose to move in, your life is broader in terms of your personal

goals and, of course, more limited in the amount of time you can devote to other people's projects. And that's just fine. It may feel to you as if you're terribly selfish, but you needn't worry—you're not. You're taking care of your own vital needs and interests, and that's something that no one else can do for you. It is, after all, only by caring for ourselves that we are enabled to really care for others; if anything, your generosity will actually expand the more you respect your own needs.

As I mentioned, your transition into your forties is similar in many ways, and it is very much related to your work. The chances are very good that in this period you may start your own business or go freelance. All sorts of skills, experience, and contacts from your past come crowding into your awareness, and it is during this time that you begin to realize it is indeed very possible for you to launch out independently, an idea that may never have occurred to you before or that you might not have taken seriously. In this situation, natural generosity combines with inexperience to create a period in which you tend to overextend yourself, to take on more work or more clients than you really feel comfortable with. But this is short-lived, often lasting only a year, and here your cutbacks are designed to leave you enough time so that you can achieve the degree of excellence you want your efforts to exhibit.

Characteristically, the difficulties you experience during your transitions are not visible on the surface. Unless you speak about your discomforts, people are unlikely to be aware of them. The only indication may be that you may give voice to complaints or, rather, your suspicion that certain responsibilities could be handled just as easily by others—which shows that they no longer interest you particularly. And you may do a bit more "daydreaming" aloud. Generally, the people closest to you are delighted to hear that you're thinking of things that will benefit you personally for a change.

The one transition that may give you the most difficulty is the bridge between work and retirement, or its equivalent. Like Virgo people, who also possess great stamina and energy, it is very hard for you to come to terms with the fact that your strength is not as abundant as it used to be. It isn't the passage of youth, per se, that troubles you, because you make your peace with that quite early on.

But you may become irritable and frustrated because you physically can't support the same rigorous demands you're used to placing upon yourself. You may also cling to old roles and demand from them a satisfaction that they can no longer provide.

In view of these difficulties, it may help to remember that there is no rule that says that if you can't do everything you used to, you have to sit in a corner and do nothing. Neither is there a rule that says you must remain in a worn-out role and feel trivial, when you can put your sharp intelligence and considerable talents to other uses that would be interesting and pleasurable for you. Fortunately, few schools place age limits on entering students, and it's open to you to study those things you've always had a hankering to learn. This is also an excellent time to give your generosity free rein and get involved in volunteer or philanthropic work for the causes that have always been dear to your heart, in the arts or politics or teaching younger people how to start and manage their own business, for example. It is also the time to let yourself relax and do those things you enjoy for no other reason than that they are fun for you. As I said, it helps considerably if you've let yourself have time for a few hobbies and pastimes earlier on.

In terms of your annual energy cycle, generally your pattern is to be very strong in spring, early summer, and fall with a slump in midwinter, around January and February. Go easy on yourself for those few months in order to avoid illness. It is usually your way to force yourself to work despite a cold or what you consider a minor ailment. But who needs it? And while I'm not suggesting that all illness is born of fatigue or a need to change one's pace or have some private time, an awful lot of it is. So, since you detest being sick, you might take the lesser of two evils and slow down a little to avoid what can be avoided. The end of July and most of August is an interesting period for you; it is a power-building time when you can most easily do absolutely nothing—swim, lay about in the sun—in short, just relax. It may be your time to store up strength for the next long stretch, and I hope you do everything possible to guarantee yourself this opportunity to unwind. Even if it's only for two weeks, it can make a considerable difference to you in your next year.

On a monthly basis, you have a great deal of positive energy during the Moon's transits of Leo, Sagittarius, and Aries, and these days are very productive of new ideas, new approaches, and putting yourself forward to best advantage. Gemini also tends to bring ease in speaking up for yourself. But the other air transits, Libra and Aquarius, are rather so-so days for you in which life is fairly routine. You also react well to earth transits, and when the Moon is in Virgo, Capricorn, and Taurus, you're liable to feel as if things are going smoothly and you're able to accomplish a lot. The water transits are not so splendid, although you may feel a surge of power during Scorpio days, but a Cancer transit is often exasperating and depressing, and may be a good time for you to temporarily let your responsibilities go with the wind.

Naturally, your energy is not simply there; it is expressed in your actions and through the personal qualities you possess. As we've touched on before, Leo gives you great generosity of spirit and this is manifested in all of your relationships. You are a very warm, very personal person and you do not stand on ceremony. Formalities strike you as rather ridiculous, and even if you are forced to be in a situation in which everyone is behaving very formally toward each other, you cut through this fairly quickly so that people begin to ease up and relax into friendliness. People are never simply names attached to the services they perform—you are always aware of them as people. You search out the places that offer excellent goods or services, and it is characteristic of you that you build up friendly relationships with these people over the years. You make yourself at home in the world and do not permit it to be an alien, lonely place. It's probably not your way to simply dart into a supermarket and rush through your shopping; you talk with your butcher and with your greengrocer, and even your simple chores are warmed by sociability. People respond in kind to your friendliness. They enjoy doing things for you, they'll go out of their way to save the best for you, and they like to share their specialized information with you. Linked to this is your pleasure in seeking out exotic, interesting places to visit or to eat or shop in. You are, generally speaking, always game for a new experience if there's the slightest chance it will be interesting, and you are clever and resourceful at providing entertainment for the people you love as well as for yourself.

You tend to be optimistic, to see people in the best possible light, and to place the most cheerful interpretation upon events. This is neither naïve nor a way of avoiding reality. There's no doubt that you're aware of the less-than-savory aspects of life and that you see room for improvement in many areas and in many people. However, you generally choose not to focus on the negative, especially on things you personally can't affect, because it drains you of energy. You prefer to act, and can cope with obstacles best by concentrating instead on the possibilities a situation has to offer. Your ability to see the bright side enables you to deal with difficult people and, certainly, to find your way through situations that might otherwise be overwhelming. One Leo woman I know was left widowed with two young sons to raise. If she had sat around brooding about her fate, things would have become very dreary indeed for that family. Instead, she turned her homemaking skills to excellent advantage, she started working as a cook in a school cafeteria and went on to open her own catering business and gave cooking lessons besides. My own mother has a Moon in Leo, and she has rescued our family from disaster more times than I can count. She took in work at home and, when we were old enough, she went out to work, but she made sure we had what we needed and she has managed to see her obstacles as challenges and to live her life in a spirit of fun. It is hoped that circumstances will not present you with such drastic tests of your ingenuity, but it's nice to know that, should things get difficult, you can count on your ability to survive in excellent style.

Obviously, from the qualities I've dealt with so far, yours is a sociable nature and you flourish when you are around other people. There are certain kinds of work for which you require absolute privacy and find noise or the presence of others too distracting, but these situations are comparatively rare. Most of the time you'd rather be with other people and you are excellent in dealing with the public, which is well to keep in mind when you are thinking about the kind of career you wish to take up.

While we're on the topic of careers, there are a few other abilities and traits that you might also think about when making your choice. Your ability to see the best in people makes you alert to perceive talent and potential in others. The fact that your own self-respect is solidly developed and that you're magnanimous by nature leads you to encourage others without begrudging them their particular gifts. Fields such as teaching or being an agent are, therefore, good possibilities for you.

Even in the employ of other people, you are not the sort of person who sits back and lets all the ideas come from others. You are capable of initiating and implementing new ideas; in fact, you enjoy doing so. When you begin a project, you will devote enormous amounts of energy to it, especially if you like the work. You have a strong distaste for shoddy work, and any job you undertake will be done to the very best of your ability. You prefer working for people who are competent, well organized, and strong-minded. As a boss in your own right, your friendliness and appreciation of others again serves you well. Your employees are motivated to do their best for you; you encourage people to develop their skills and resources to the fullest, so that in a sense their employment with you can be a form of apprenticeship from which they will have gained valuable skills should they wish to branch out independently.

Your organizational abilities stand you in good stead in all aspects of your life and naturally they're an immense help to you as either an employee or an employer. You're not terribly fond of tending to the details, so it's a good idea to delegate those responsibilities to others whenever you can. You're excellent, however, in mapping out an overall plan, sensing what deserves top priority, deciding what equipment or contacts will be needed, and scheduling your time to accommodate the various phases of the project. You also react well under the pressures of a deadline and it is a matter of pride to you to accomplish a task within the time limit assigned. In these situations, you do not hesitate to tax your stamina and energy to the fullest, and it might be a good idea to reward yourself with a short recuperative period after any of these all-out efforts. You are essentially a practical person and will not spend much of your time yearning for the unattainable and the impossible. Your daydreams may run to grand, romantic schemes, but your efforts are directed to solid, tangible accomplishments.

Chances are that the arts will figure largely in your life. While you do appreciate the beauties of nature, you're even more responsive to human creativity. You most likely have artistic talent in your own right and should develop this as your hobby, if not as your profession. Your sense of basic equality with all other people, and your warmth and friendliness, free you from inhibitions and stage fright. It's easy for you to act, to entertain people at parties, to address large groups, or to perform on stage. And you have a lot of fun performing. Drama appeals to you—to such an extent, in fact, that if life grows too tame, you'll cast about for some way to liven things up. I very strongly recommend that you give your flair for drama and performing wide latitude, since it is not simply a talent but usually a very strong, genuine need. If you'd rather not be an actress, be a critic or get involved in community theater or teach, or at least play charades at parties. But use this ability and let it be a source of pleasure for you all of your life.

You may also be gifted at painting, sculpture, or ceramics, and your visual sense is highly developed. You enjoy seeing the work done by other people as well as being creative yourself, so don't stint yourself on the pleasure that comes from visiting museums, galleries, and art shows. You have a strong sense of color and form, and it is important to you that things be visually appealing. This trait shows up in a variety of ways, such as your personal appearance, your presentation of food, and the way you arrange and decorate your home and garden. You might consider opening your own art gallery or being an agent for other artists and artisans as well as yourself, since you have good judgment in selecting pieces, you can present them to excellent advantage, and you're at ease in dealing with the general public.

In your personal relationships, Leo certainly adds color and warmth to your sex life. You enjoy being attractive—and being attracted—and you savor all the drama of falling in love and staying there. This is one situation where details do not bore you. You enjoy making love, and all the grand and little things that lead up to it as well as the warmth and intimacy afterward. You genuinely wish to give pleasure to your partner—a lovely quality as long as you do not neglect your own satisfaction in the process, which is unlikely. When you're involved with someone, you have a keen appreciation of that person's best qualities and talents, and you give freely of praise and encouragement. You, too, need appreciation and praise and you flourish best with a partner whose generosity matches your own. People who tend to be critical, or who withhold themselves or are absorbed with themselves to the exclusion of others, are extremely poor choices for you.

Watch out for those who begrudge their affection for fear that they might commit themselves; as far as you're concerned, they're a dead loss. Your ardor and interest will be rewarded with frustration and, eventually, bitterness. Pay careful attention to whether or not someone is truly generous before you commit yourself deeply, although I know it's hard for you to rein in your affection. You are very likely to stay with your commitment once it's made, so it's important for you to be a little cautious at the outset. If a partnership proves disappointing, even disastrous for you, you will hang in there with it although your instinct for self-preservation may move you to have affairs. You do not begrudge your partners their interests and ambitions and are very supportive of their efforts to develop their capabilities to the fullest—but you do resent these if they occur at your expense or deny you your interests and needs and ambitions. And it would be a shame to waste your lively, generous spirit and your active intelligence on people who are incapable of thinking about anyone but themselves.

Your home is important to you and is never an empty showcase designed to impress others. You enjoy being with children and usually choose to have your own. If this is denied to you, you form loving, encouraging relationships with other people's children, either as a teacher or within your circle of friends and relatives. You don't mind the noise and disorder that invariably attend children; you concentrate on the pleasures afforded by their company instead. You see your children in terms of their best qualities and are careful to provide them with the maximum opportunities to learn. In this respect, you are generous with your time and resources; you try to get them everything you think they might need or like and take them every place they might possibly enjoy and benefit from. The only disadvantage to this, of course, is that you might err in the direction of too much generosity, so that they may be overwhelmed and feel unworthy to receive so much or their perceptions of their possessions may become blurred because there are simply too many of them. Difficult as it may be, you might try to hold yourself back a little from giving them everything in the world. Your attention and love, your ability to perceive them as individuals rather than as extensions of yourself, are the best gifts of all those you give, and there's no toy or piano lesson or trip that can compete with these real treasures.

The qualities and talents you receive through Leo help you achieve a great deal in which you can take genuine pride, and your self-confidence and self-esteem are an encouragement to others. Rarely do we perceive how our abilities and our lives affect those around us, but you may be sure that your resourcefulness, your optimism, and your ability to appreciate yourself as well as other people open up options for other women that they may not have seen before. It is part of your nature to enhance and enrich life, and it is your gift that you can do this without depriving yourself. Make the most of your gifts, take pride in a life well lived, and help us all to realize that self-confidence and self-expression are not crimes against humanity but are blessings instead.

LEO VISUALIZATIONS

You possess an extraordinary resource within you: your imagination. Through the power of your inward eye, you can tap into your innermost self, and into the energies of the universe. The thoughts you think, the messages you give yourself, the images you create in your imagination have tremendous power. You can literally transform your reality to fit the positive images you create mentally simply by creating those images often enough, and as specifically and clearly as you possibly can. Through such focused, purposeful "daydreaming," you can achieve an astonishing range of goals: practical goals such as weight loss, physical fitness, or money management; spiritual goals such as enhanced self-esteem, inner peace, and a deeper sense of connection with other living beings. For further information on this process, I recommend two books I've found useful, Shakti Gawain's *Creative Visualization*, and Shad Helmstetter's *The Self-Talk Solution*.

My primary concern here is empowering you to get in touch with the Goddess within you, the Eternal Feminine whose creative, nurturing, renewing energies live within us all. The Great Goddess is always ready to comfort, to heal, to strengthen, and to guide us whenever we are in need. Her images come to us from all parts of our world and from across great stretches of time. By visualizing Her in our mind's eye, by meditating on Her image, you and I not only receive help with specific problems and enhanced self-esteem but also reap the additional benefit of greater esteem for all women, past and present, and for the wonderful contributions women have made in creating and advancing civilization.

The images I sketch for you came to me through my research and through my own meditations. They may work differently for you than I've envisioned. And, of course, they're not the only images available to you. I suggest you read Merlin Stone's *Ancient Mirrors of Womanhood* and Barbara G. Walker's *The Woman's Encyclopedia of Myths and Secrets* to see what stories, prayers, and images resonate for you, and use them. I think you'll also find it illuminating simply to gaze within your own mind and see how the Goddess manifests Herself in you. I would be delighted to read your visualization experiences, so if you would like to share them, please write to me, c/o the publisher.

How to go about visualization is very much a matter of personal choice: you may sit, stand, or lie down—whichever position you feel you can most comfortably maintain for ten to twenty minutes. You're probably best advised to be in a quiet, darkened room and to keep your eyes closed. Begin by relaxing your entire body. One technique is to imagine a comfortably warm, golden light surrounding you and taking away all tension in the area you're thinking of. Start with your feet and work up to the crown of your head. Once this is done, begin to construct your visualization in your mind.

The sign-associated images that come to mind for Leo are powerful, beautiful, and dramatic. Here is one that may be useful for you when you are in need of comfort. In my vision, I see you youthful, no matter what your chronological age is. You are walking through the heavens with the Great Goddess Satis, Her quiver of silver arrows slung across Her back. You are near slim, reed-straight

Satis. Perhaps She holds you by your hand. Perhaps She rests Her hand reassuringly on your shoulder. Choose whatever appeals to you.

Beside you is the great lion. You rest your hand on its neck, enjoying the smoothness and softness of its fur, and the sense of its strength and power. The three of you proceed in dignity through the sky. The clouds are warm beneath your bare feet. You are filled with an inexpressible delight at being with Great Satis and Her lion, and you drink in the beauty of the world below you. Your spirit absorbs the calmness and love of Satis. You are warmed to the core of your being, filled with a calm joy as you are restored to a sense of worth, as you feel with each step how much you are valued by Satis, how pleased the Great Goddess is with your essential self.

When you've been overwhelmed with work and your life is out of balance, you might try to visualize yourself standing near the Great Goddess Tara of India, who is standing on the back of Her cosmic lion. She is a dainty Goddess. Her gleaming black hair streams down Her back to Her ankles; Her intricately worked dress, Her fine coat and headdress gleam with rich colors and glisten with gold and silver threads. Her beautiful eyes shine with mischief. She reaches one exquisite hand to you, grasps your hand, and enables you to spring lightly to Her side. You see that She holds the sun in Her other hand, balancing it on Her palm as if it were a lovely golden ball. You stand on the cosmic lion and feel the lion's powerful muscles beneath its marvelous soft fur. Practice keeping your balance. You are perfectly safe. The Goddess will not let any harm come to you, so you are free to enjoy your ride as much as you please. Allow your sense of fun, your sense of adventure to reawaken. The lion is your totem animal, and as long as you respect him, you are free to enjoy his companionship. You may ride him as you would a horse or lie down and stretch out on his back, or continue to stand on him. The Goddess will take you wherever you wish: past, present, or future, and anywhere in the universe you care to visit. Enjoy your trip!

If someone has insulted or belittled you, pay a visit in your imagination to the Great Goddess Cybele as She was known in the ancient Mediterranean area. The Goddess Cybele is enthroned in a chariot pulled by two huge, fierce lions. Climb into the chariot. Perhaps Cybele holds you on Her lap and allows you to hold the reins with Her as the lions race through the sky. The warmth of Her love and mercy is a balm to your sore spirit. The rush of sweet wind cools the anger and hurt on your cheeks. Pain slips away and in its place is interest in the world around you, and pride in your ability to control yourself. Use the sense of distance in this visualization to establish a sense of perspective for yourself so that you may return from this mental exploration able to evaluate your situation more objectively.

If someone in your life is physically, emotionally, or verbally abusing you, use this next visualization often to empower you to change the situation. First, I see you trudging along the Egyptian desert. The sand is dull gold; the sun beats down on you. You are dusty, weary; your spirit is heavy within you. You near the imposing statue of the Sphinx, who wears a beautiful woman's head on a lion's crouching body. You sense the Sphinx turn Her sightless stone eyes upon you, holding you motionless in that blind gaze, and ask you why you have given up your power. Her question vibrates within you. You continue sadly onward.

Now you are face to face with Sekhmet, She who rules the sun, She who rules fire. Her body is that of a lovely woman; Her head is a lion's head, with a lion's tawny fur and golden eyes. Look deep into the eyes of Sekhmet, into Her eyes of power. Allow yourself to be filled with Her strength, Her sense of outrage that Her laws on the sanctity of women should be so disrespected. Be filled with Her resolve that this situation shall not continue as it is, but as it should be.

Look deep and see in Sekhmet's golden eyes, as in a mirror, the image of the Great Goddess Artemis, armed as a hunter. She picks up two lions by their paws and holds them as if they were rabbits, for you to observe, for you to see the power and strength of the Goddess and to draw it into yourself. Take back your power. Visualize yourself standing between Satis of Egypt and Artemis of Greece as their human counterpart. Like them, you are armed with strength and resolve. Like them, you radiate beauty and energy and power.

Step forth into your life as befits a daughter of Satis, a priestess of Artemis: proud, courageous, daring.

You are capable of initiating and successfully carrying through great undertakings. Whenever you need inspiration or clarification of your ideas and plans, turn to your element—fire—for guiding images.

In your mind's eye, you may come face to face with the Great Goddess, Diana Lucifera, Light Bearer, She who brought fire to Italy. In form, She is strong, athletic; Her gaze is level, practical, unflinching. She wears the short, graceful tunic of the athlete. In Her hand, She carries a torch. Look into Her eyes. Look into the flames She has kept alive since the beginning, so many thousands of centuries ago. Allow the flames of that torch of truth to burn away indecision, fear, and confusion and leave you with a clear mind and firm resolve.

You may also approach the altar of the Great Goddess Vesta, as She was known in Rome. Her priestesses spoke only truth, and so it was they who were called upon to judge and it was they who kept the eternal flame of Vesta burning, sanctifying the city. In your mind, approach the altar upon which burns the clean, pure flame of Vesta. Look within yourself by the light of this flame, and gaze upon your own personal truth at the core of your being. Live by it.

You may also turn to Hestia, oldest of the Goddesses of Greece, She who taught our most ancient grandmothers how to capture fire, keep it alive, recreate it when we needed it. It was Hestia who created the hearths of our homes, the council fires of judgment, the eternal flame that dignified our communities as cities. Draw Hestia's clear-eyed courage into yourself, allow Her warmth to suffuse you, allow Her sense of purpose to penetrate you and become your own. Bring Her clarity, Her warmth, Her purpose into your own home, your own life, and be enriched.

People have mistakenly believed that the sun is universally a male image. Instead we have images from our most distant past as well as from relatively recently in which people have envisioned the sun as a Goddess. The Japanese worshiped the Sun Goddess Amaterasu, She who is Heaven Shining. The Toba people of

Argentina prayed to the Sun Goddess Akewa, who nurtured all with Her beautiful warmth. And the Eskimo, or Inuit, of North America worshipped Sun Sister. Perhaps the oldest culture we know of is in Anatolia, which is now modern Turkey, in the most ancient cities of Catal Huyuk and Hacilar of 7000 BC. There the people prayed to the Sun Goddess of Arinna. She was Mother of All, Source of All Warmth, Source of All Justice and Righteousness. Perhaps, from time to time, you will stand before this ancient Goddess and be renewed in Her beauty and strength as She gazes upon you with pleasure, acknowledging you as Her worthy child, as Her youngest daughter, living life now in justice and strength and beauty.

VIRGO
August 23–September 23

VIRGO: The Great Goddess of
Egypt, Isis-Hathor, "She Who
Gave Birth to the Universe"
and "She Who Nurtures All."
Based on an Egyptian bronze,
eighth–sixth century BC,
preserved in the Louvre.

Virgo has always had a very special place
in my heart, so it's been a particular joy to discover Virgo's meaning
both in astrology and in the history of our civilization. We can
discard the dismal interpretations of Virgo that traditional astrology
so frequently offers. A strong Virgo influence at work in your
horoscope does not mean that you are destined to be a carping nag
or sexually unresponsive or the drudge of the zodiac. The qualities
and strengths that Virgo contributes are qualities you can be proud
of and grateful for.

Buried under the dingy picture of Virgo that we're familiar with
is the awesome portrait of the Mother of the Universe, worshipped
as the Supreme Being in every portion of our planet from 30,000 BC
onward. Her names changed and multiplied; Her figure varied from
Rubenesque to reed thin; She was sometimes portrayed as mother
naked, and sometimes resplendent in gold and brilliant gems, but
certain facets of Her nature remained constant whatever the time or
place.

People believed that the Great Mother was the universe, and
from Herself brought forth all forms of life and all harmony and
order. Everyone, everything existed as manifestations of Her spirit,

and lived according to Her rhythms and Her laws. The Goddess was frequently worshipped as a Holy Trinity of Daughter, Mother, and Grandmother, or Crone; and three or multiples of three were sacred numbers the world over. The Great Mother was the source of life's three essential liquids: blood, milk, and water. She was the moon, the earth, and water. She ruled life, death, and rebirth; She was the three forms of matter. Sometimes She was portrayed with a serpent and a bird to signify Her dominion over the innermost regions of the earth, the earth's surface, and the farthest reaches of the sky. Often She was shown holding Her infant son in Her lap, signifying that just as human women miraculously brought forth beings unlike themselves, so the Goddess, on an inconceivably grander scale, brought forth the great diversity of life.

The gifts of the Goddess celebrated in Virgo were the blessings of agriculture and the intelligence, foresight, organization, and discipline it was based on. During Virgo—their lunar month *Pharmouthi*—the Egyptians planted flowers, identified with the Goddess as Daughter, and they harvested their corn, identified with the Mother aspect of the Goddess. The signal for harvest to begin was the appearance at moonrise of the star Spica, or "ear of corn." The Great Goddess Isis was sometimes pictured with ears of corn sprouting like wings from her back. The ancient Romans named the star Spica, "She Who Brings Forth the Grape Harvest." And we have heard of their Goddess Ceres, Mother of all cereal foods, and of Her Greek equivalent, Demeter.

The fact that people the world over identified their food as feminine is another aspect of the Great Mother. Peruvians prayed to their Corn and Cocoa and Potato Mothers; in Malaya, Java, Sumatra, and throughout Asia, they prayed to their Rice Mother; some North Americans prayed to Corn Mother and others to the Three Sisters, Maize, Bean, and Squash. In Europe, prayers were given to the Barley or Corn Mother while the Egyptians praised Isis for giving them grain, for teaching them how to make bread, and for thus delivering them from the sin of cannibalism. The list of feminine food deities is incredibly long, reaching even into Christianity with prayers to Mary, Madonna of the Sheaves.

In Virgo, we pay tribute to the triad form of the Great Goddess as Earth. She is Kore or Persephone, the Daughter Who grows and gathers flowers for their beauty, for food, medicine, or anesthetic, and as a lure for honeybees. The queen bee was revered as pure because she was vegetarian in her diet; and valued as a model of femininity because she was independent, the original meaning of our word *virgin*. The Goddess is also Demeter or Ceres, the Mother who grows grains, fruits, and vegetables; and She is Hecate, Grandmother, who supervises the harvest, the sacred offerings, and the equal distribution of food. These religious concepts parallel women's achievements in food production. Women first taught themselves to be skillful gatherers of nature's bounty, and then to grow, store, and cook foods and to make dyes, intoxicants, and medicines from them. In fact, the pharmacopoeia they developed was unrivaled until this century. Elder women did indeed supervise the harvests and ensure that every member of the community received a fair portion of food. Agriculture was considered women's magic, and the settled communal life farming made possible was the basis for the rise of cities, and all the complexities of civilization.

In ancient astrology, the main characteristics associated with Virgo were generosity, breadth of vision, creativity, and fair-mindedness. The service for which Virgo is justly renowned was understood in the largest sense, as the ability and imagination to cope with vital needs combined with the talent, concern, and spirit to shape and administer communal life.

If you wish to read this information in terms of your Moon rather than your Sun, you'll need to shift your thinking from your identity, your will, your essential self—the way you manifest being you in the world—to focus instead on the inner you, the emotional you—your self at the deepest levels of your unconscious. Your Moon not only has to do with your feelings but also includes those things you take for granted in your self—those things you assume everyone else feels or is like, since they are so essential to your personality. Your Moon gifts might not be the most obvious features in your personality. They are ever present but elusive, qualities you know intimately and yet can't quite put your finger on. The Moon also has to do with what went on in your family of origin, your home, your background. It concerns all those things that give you a sense of emotional security.

Specifically, a Moon in Virgo endows you with an intriguing combination of qualities that defies the narrow limits of what is usually understood as feminine. You may seem delicate and fine-boned yet possess great physical as well as emotional and intellectual strength and hardiness. Your ability to perceive and acknowledge weaknesses in yourself, in others, and in ideas may lead people to misread you as emotionally cool and detached. On the contrary, Moon in Virgo virtually guarantees that your emotions are deeply experienced, and that you are profoundly loyal and loving in your relationships. Moon in Virgo also lends an earthy quality to your personality, often expressed in a rich, full laugh, an appreciation of good food and drink and sensual pleasures, and a generosity of spirit. You love to share and to give pleasure to others, and consequently, the poverty and misery of others is experienced as a wound in your heart, and the chances are very good that you will work to mitigate these. Above all, your Moon in Virgo endows you with breadth of perspective and independence of mind and spirit, qualities to cherish and cultivate.

A virgin wasn't ignorant of sex and she certainly didn't abstain from it. So we can just toss the idea that Virgo is sexually indifferent right out the window. As a matter of fact, I've never met a Virgo woman yet who didn't count lovemaking as one of life's great pleasures and put it high on her list of priorities. Originally, a virgin was a person who was her own woman: free, independent, the property of no one, with full control over her own life and full responsibility for it. A Virgo Sun endows you with a strong independent spirit that acts as a powerful shield against social pressures. But you may be uncomfortable with this when you're young, the time when we are all most vulnerable to other people's criticism and most likely to feel that their views and expectations are more valid than our own. Fortunately, whether or not this makes you uncomfortable, it is well nigh impossible for you to be other than who you are. And, naturally, this honesty characterizes your romantic life also.

As in every other area of your life, you proceed at your own pace. You will not, for example, fake an orgasm to gratify anyone else's ego, but neither do you fix upon orgasm as if it were the only pleasure in lovemaking. Thanks to your broad perspective on life, you are aware earlier than most people that sexual responses are not monolithic, that they vary according to partner and mood or, rather, where both people are in terms of their physical and emotional cycles. This allows you to be patient with yourself and with your partner, and it enables you to weather the slumps that even the most passionate attachments are subject to. If difficulties persist, you will initiate an open discussion about them, and since you view them as part of everyone's experience, you're able to discuss them without resentment and with a genuine appreciation of your partner's feelings as well as your own.

A strong Virgo influence does give you fine powers of discrimination, and one result of this is that you are highly selective about your lovers. Now I don't mean to suggest that you sit around and analyze them coldly, because you certainly don't. But you do respond to people as total personalities rather than just in terms of good looks; it's rare indeed that you'll hop into bed with someone solely on the basis of physical attraction. You are drawn to people who can be friends as well as lovers, who share your ideals and interests, and even with whom you can collaborate in your work. It may be very fashionable to be casual about sex, but you need more than what a casual encounter can offer, and you're not especially interested in impressing anyone with your sexual prowess. You're not likely to succumb to social pressure in regard to marriage, either. Your parents may urge you to marry for fear that life will be too difficult for you as a woman alone. Your friends may feel that marriage is the mark of a successful woman, and think it strange that you do not share their eagerness to wed. But you marry when and if you want to, and yours is a marriage of equals. However, since differences in age, religion, race, or ethnic background matter very little to you, there's the possibility that your choice may cause some initial consternation among your friends and family.

During those periods when you are unattached, you won't languish at home or feel that the world is coming to an end because you lack a date for Saturday night. You're sociable and have a knack for making friends—and that includes men friends as well as women. Your social life definitely doesn't depend on your being a member of a couple, and you're quite comfortable going out with your friends for concerts, plays, parties, swimming, or any of the other sports you enjoy. On those days when you feel discouraged because there's no romance currently in your life, take heart from the knowledge that this certainly will not last forever. The very fact that you get out and do the things that interest you increases the likelihood that you'll meet a person compatible with you. You might also look at depressed days from another point of view: as possible energy troughs or periods when you actually need to be alone. Since Virgo involves you with other people much of the time, it may, in fact, be difficult for you to recognize your need for solitude. Of course, any prolonged depression or lethargy should be checked out medically, but in general, your "blue" days usually signal that you need some time to yourself to restore your energies.

In regard to marriage, your lack of haste to make this decision works to your distinct advantage, because you acquire the experience and self-knowledge that enable you to choose very wisely in terms of your own personality and needs. And if you decide to marry, the chances are extremely good that you will be married for a very, very long time. Virgo contributes several gifts that make your marriage a rich and satisfying relationship for both you and your partner. For one thing, jealousy plays a very small part in your temperament. You won't be hovering watchfully over your partner for fear that his or her affections will stray, and you certainly won't welcome your partner's keeping guard over you. Sexual fidelity, per se, is not crucial to you, although you can discipline yourself to be faithful if this matters a great deal to your partner. When the shoe is on the other foot, you tend to regard an occasional brief infidelity as a frivolous lapse on a par with drinking too much at a party. You'll complain about it mightily, but you're not likely to end your marriage because of it. However, you'll fight against anything that seems to be a genuine threat with everything in your power, including your shrewd sense of humor.

Traditional astrology to the contrary, you are tolerant of other people's foibles, and very little in human behavior surprises or shocks you. You don't object to being encouraged to develop abilities that you yourself feel the need for, but you're not likely to team up with someone who wants to remold you. Instead, you'll probably choose someone who, like you, is able to appreciate and nurture the other's abilities and ambitions, and who needs and thrives on real intimacy. Your partner may not be particularly shy about his or her body, but even if that was the case in the beginning, those inhibitions will be lost after living with you for a while.

Virgo bestows a remarkable physical ease and grace, and a lack of self-consciousness about the body. I sometimes wonder how nineteenth-century Virgoans ever put up with Victorian prudery. It must have been particularly stifling for them! You, at any rate, are very much at home in your own skin and have a sound respect for your physical well-being. You are concerned throughout your life with basic good health and regard it as a prerequisite for any achievement. In this respect, you follow the classic feminine pattern, which starts from the physical, material level and moves to the abstract, spiritual level.

Your instincts in regard to health are generally sound and often you back these up with research, since the subject is sufficiently important to you. You put good nutrition before gourmet cooking and won't waste your money on foods that are highly processed or that contain many chemical additives. Your justifiable wariness extends to cosmetics and drugs and a great many other "improvements" on our natural state. You usually demand to know just what these things are composed of and what their effects really are. The greatest favor you can do other women is to pass your information along. If you prefer to use a diaphragm rather than risk the side effects contraceptive pills may cause, don't hesitate to explain why to your friends, because they may not be aware that there's still no pill with a guarantee against blood clots or blindness or critical depression. It would be wonderful if one of the women's organizations campaigned for safe contraception and for a ban on vaginal deodorants. It seems a shame that so few of us know that our vaginas are about the cleanest part of the human body, that they cleanse themselves unobtrusively, and that all we need do is give them a wash on the outside when we shower or bathe. The companies that urge "feminine daintiness" are capitalizing on the shame we've been taught to feel about ourselves, and their concern for us is transparently green. Our natural scent is a lot more appealing than some artificial strawberry or lemon concoction that could damage us and, more important, if there is something wrong with our natural scent, it is usually a signal to us—in fact, it may be our only warning of an ailment as minor as an infection or as major as cancer.

Well, on to how Virgo affects you personally. Thanks to Virgo, you find real joy in physical movement. Not only do you value a limber, active body but you really like to stretch and jump and run and play, and you feel very uncomfortable when you've been inactive for too long. It's quite possible that your work will involve a good amount of physical activity; if it doesn't, you'll compensate for this in your leisure time. You favor total-body sports such as swimming, tennis, golf, walking, or biking, and these have the extra advantage that you can participate in them all your life. You also love to dance, both as a spectator and a participant, and this, too, is likely to be an important lifelong interest for you. Even exercise classes are fun for you, and I heartily recommend yoga as an especially wise choice, because it combines the physical release you crave with important meditational skills that can be of great assistance at difficult points in your cycles.

Your monthly cycle begins on a very positive note, with the Moon transiting Virgo. This transit is excellent for making plans and organizing yourself, so you'll be able to carry them out in the days ahead. It is a period of mental rather than physical energy, so try to avoid strenuous activity. Your perspective is especially keen at this point, so allow yourself its benefits; review the past month and make your plans for the forthcoming time. The Libra transit, which follows, is a happy combination of physical and mental energy. You're eager to get going on your plans and can make very fine beginnings on any complex project. Just be careful not to undertake too many things at once. Scorpio and Sagittarius transits affect you in similar ways because they both intensify your need to be sociable and the ease with which you relate to other people. Scorpio is the best, however, for serious contacts. It is an exceptionally good time for smoothing out personality clashes, for preventing crises, and for getting together about work. A Sagittarius transit, on the other hand, evokes a far more lighthearted feeling. It's a lovely time for just having fun and for handling lighter problems, but it can sour if you force yourself to stick with a rigid schedule. Avoid unnecessary frustration and treat yourself to the benefits of even a slight change of scene or routine.

The Moon's transit of Capricorn ushers in a quieter period. During Capricorn itself, your energy remains at a fairly steady level and you tend to be introverted. You feel fine, but you're simply not too responsive to outside stimuli. Aquarius is generally a difficult transit because it accentuates your awareness of inequalities and sharpens your desire to improve social conditions. The drawback to this transit is that it unleashes a flood of perceptions; you're aware of too many wrongs to right and feel overwhelmed by the immensity of the task. Even on a more intimate level, among your family and the people you work with, you're beset by your perceptions of other people's needs and feel an undue responsibility for making every-thing work smoothly. Needless to say, this is a transit in which you need to lavish yourself with every consideration. It is valuable in that it does eventually pinpoint those issues or problems you can and want to do something about. But it is exhausting because it makes you feel responsible for more than any one human being could possibly cope with. The next transit, Pisces, is a considerable relief in that it restores your perspective and releases you from the feeling that the world is on your shoulders. It, too, is an interval when you have less energy available; you'll feel better if you can keep your schedule as simple as possible. You'll be able to do a great deal more in the Aries transit which follows; it brings a strong upsurge in physical energy and an almost total lack of interest in anything intellectual—it's as if your mind has simply gone on vacation. All you crave is action and movement; if there are any strenuous jobs that need doing, this is the ideal time to undertake them.

Taurus transits bring a very lovely balance of energy. You feel mentally refreshed, especially warm and loving toward your family and friends, and you have plenty of physical energy at your disposal. It's an interval in which just about everything works well for you and you can do with it what you will. Gemini transits are not so ideal, however. They are very strong on creative energy and you'll certainly have no lack of ideas, but you may feel frustrated if you're not able to devote your time completely to your favorite projects. Cancer transits are a help in that you are better able to accept having to portion out your time to take care of various demands. They continue the supply of creative and intellectual energy, and are excellent for any mental work that requires concentration. In contrast, Leo transits are fine for routine work, for getting your files in order, settling up accounts, and taking care of details that exasperate you under ordinary circumstances. They seem to provide a peaceful lull that allows you to put everything in order, and they pave the way for the larger planning and organization you do in Virgo.

The high energy periods of your annual cycle occur in autumn and spring, with a really sharply felt low period in midwinter and a mild low in early summer. That midwinter slump is the most difficult for you, because chances are that circumstances provide you with more work to do, more demands to meet, than you feel you have strength for. During this period, you'd do well to take short rests as soon as your energy flags. Do some stretches, eye and neck exercises, take a walk, or just unfocus for a bit, but slow down so that you work with your body, not against it. You have excellent reserves of strength and good general health, but it's not wise to be prodigal with these resources. When you ignore your need for rest or change in routine, you're likely to compound the miseries of fatigue by feeling anxious and depressed about yourself. During these states you may succumb to overeating, which makes you feel even more uncomfortable physically and even less happy about yourself. Of course, I must add that Virgo's eating binges are not quite like other people's, as I've observed. One dear Virgo friend of mine used to toss willpower to the wind and abandon herself to the pleasures of eating seven or eight grapefruits at a sitting. To a cake-eater like myself, that seemed more an excess of virtue than the descent into the pit of vice that she regarded it as being. However, she learned to circumvent these citrus sprees by scheduling more frequent, short rests during her busiest times, with the happy result that she has the

energy and good spirits to do the nonstrenuous things that she enjoys
on her slack days. I recommend that you try it for yourself. If you
need a good excuse, consult a Void-of-Course Moon chart for those
intervals that make most of us wish "we'd stayed in bed"; they are
perfect times to forget about your regular routine and just doodle
around. Your summer slump is considerably easier for you to
handle, since you have no difficulty arranging a much lighter
schedule for yourself and may even be able to take a break from the
kind of activity you're usually involved in.

As far as your larger cycles go, the only transitions that may give
you trouble are the ones from your twenties into your thirties and
from your forties into your fifties. The crux of the difficulty in your
twenties-to-thirties transition is a conflict between your social ideals
and your leadership abilities and ambitions. To explain this more
fully, let me backtrack a little. Your adolescence involves sorting out
what your social ideals are as well as finding out who you are
emotionally and so forth. Not surprisingly, this period often brings
you into conflict with your parents and, also, with authorities in
your preferred field of interest. You exhibit a unique point of view
quite early in your life, and you usually emerge from this period
having decided to follow your own bent rather than convention.

Your twenties are very much taken up with living your life so
that it corresponds to your ideal. It is during this period that your
desire and ability to lead is usually suppressed because it feels like a
contradiction of your ethics. Let's suppose that you're a choreogra-
pher, for instance. During your twenties, you'd probably prefer to
experiment with improvisational techniques and encourage all your
dancers to work out their own ideas within a very loose structure.
You're likely also to invite nonprofessionals as well as trained
dancers to participate in your work. There's no doubt that this
approach would be interesting and a great deal of fun, and that you
would learn enormously from it. However, it does have its drawbacks, and among the stumbling blocks you'd encounter would be
that you do have very definite ideas of your own, which you'd like
to see executed at a high level of competence. So you are more or
less forced to face the fact that you wish to take charge, and that you
feel confident about your ability to do so; eventually you come to the

realization that you can take charge without acting superior or violating anyone else's rights. However, the transition that brings you to these realizations may seem both painful and interminable. Often you feel as if you're working extremely hard and getting nowhere, that your imagination is absolutely barren, and that you're going through life like an automaton. This is the period when you may seem to be obsessed with trivia and unable to get any sort of perspective on things. Be assured that despite the turmoil at the conscious level, your unconscious will come to your rescue. In the hidden workshop of your psyche, you are busily sorting out your experience, shifting your attention from the needs you have satisfied to those you've yet to fulfill, and regrouping your resources so that you can continue to learn and grow as a person. I recommend that you pay close attention to your dreams for clues to what is going on; this will probably relieve your anxiety to some extent.

The central difficulty in the later transition comes from your anticipating—and exaggerating—the physical limitations that will eventually be imposed by old age. Your tendency is to imagine that in no time at all you will be utterly decrepit. I don't mean to belittle your fears, but this is highly unlikely, for which you may thank your attention to diet and exercise. The chances are very good that you will be healthy and active, physically and mentally, until your last breath. However, there's no denying the fact that you will not leap as high or do as much at sixty and eighty as you did at twenty and thirty. Even the indomitable Martha Graham finally had to relinquish the stage. Of course, there is no one-sentence panacea that could smooth away your resentment and your struggle to come to terms with this fact of your life. It is very hard for you, but you do have the good fortune to possess a large measure of feminine creativity that urges you to transform life into something more, something better, whether it be changing a little patch of ground into a garden or getting funding for the arts so that younger artists may have a chance to learn and to show their work. You also possess the happy ability of being able to teach well, and can, like Margaret Mead, be an important influence and source of knowledge to other people when you are no longer willing or able to undertake the rigors of leading an expedition. There is no doubt that your later years will offer you many challenges and satisfactions, which you will enjoy profoundly once you arrive at and accept a realistic idea of your physical limits.

In terms of careers, there are several that are especially suitable for you: anthropology, archaeology (including the comparatively new field of underwater archaeology), education, sports, and above all, the arts, especially dance, choreography, acting, music, and writing. The arts are almost guaranteed to figure seriously in your life, either as your work or as a leisure-time pursuit, and possibly even both. You are very creative and, besides your ability to analyze, you are also gifted with the ability to synthesize several different arts into a new whole. You are not afraid to experiment and try out new approaches, and you are very responsive to and appreciative of other people's innovations.

There are, of course, a great many other fields open to you, but since I couldn't possibly list them all, I suggest that you keep these Virgoan traits in mind when you are thinking about a career. Your sociability is paramount to consider, because you will languish if you're working alone too much. And, by the way, I include the period when you may be concentrating on raising your children and running your home as part of the work category. It's true that this work involves you with people you love, but it certainly doesn't happen by magic, nor are you programmed and wound up each morning to whiz around like a robot. You have decisions to make, skills to use, schedules to arrange, lessons to teach, people to deal with. If that isn't work, I don't know what is. The difficulty of this period is that, much as you enjoy your children, you may feel too isolated from other adults. Socialize as much as you can afford to, and seek out ways—such as forming a parents' cooperative, or taking a part-time job, or taking courses—to supply you with the adult companionship you need.

The very qualities that make you an excellent marriage partner serve you well as a leader. You have a genuine respect for other people and their ideas, and are tolerant of their shortcomings. You enjoy cooperative effort, and once you recognize that it is all right to be the organizing force in a group, you are able to take the lead very gracefully. You are helped in this by your sense of humor, which might be best described as a sharp but not unkind eye for life's little ironies, and you are able to point up the absurd in a situation or deflate the pompous without injuring other people's feelings. You also have a talent for effecting compromises and untangling conflicts between people. These talents—plus your ability to analyze clearly, to separate the important from the trivial, and to see issues from a broad perspective—make you a natural for administrative work. Last, and far from least, you have a very deep concern for people, and it is extremely important to you that your work make some contribution toward improving social conditions or enlarging people's understanding.

In conclusion, Virgo has given you the gifts and the strength to meet life's challenges as well as the vision to create a rewarding life for yourself and a better life for us all. There is nothing second-rate about your desire to improve your lot, and there is nothing menial about the hard work you expend in achieving these goals. Enjoy your gifts and be proud of your contributions, for you, truly, leave the world a better place than when you found it.

VIRGO VISUALIZATIONS

You possess an extraordinary resource within you: your imagination. Through the power of your inward eye, you can tap into your innermost self, and into the energies of the universe. The thoughts you think, the messages you give yourself, the images you create in your imagination have tremendous power. You can literally transform your reality to fit the positive images you create mentally simply by creating those images often enough, and as specifically and clearly as you possibly can. Through such focused, purposeful "daydreaming," you can achieve an astonishing range of goals: practical goals such as weight loss, physical fitness, or money management; spiritual goals such as enhanced self-esteem, inner peace, and a deeper sense of connection with other living beings. For further information on this process, I recommend two books I've found useful, Shakti Gawain's *Creative Visualization*, and Shad Helmstetter's *The Self-Talk Solution*.

My primary concern here is empowering you to get in touch

with the Goddess within you, the Eternal Feminine whose creative, nurturing, renewing energies live within us all. The Great Goddess is always ready to comfort, to heal, to strengthen, and to guide us whenever we are in need. Her images come to us from all parts of our world and from across great stretches of time. By visualizing Her in our mind's eye, by meditating on Her image, you and I not only receive help with specific problems and enhanced self-esteem but also reap the additional benefit of greater esteem for all women, past and present, and for the wonderful contributions women have made in creating and advancing civilization.

The images I sketch for you came to me through my research and through my own meditations. They may work differently for you than I've envisioned. And, of course, they're not the only images available to you. I suggest you read Merlin Stone's *Ancient Mirrors of Womanhood* and Barbara G. Walker's *The Woman's Encyclopedia of Myths and Secrets* to see what stories, prayers, and images resonate for you, and use them. I think you'll also find it illuminating simply to gaze within your own mind and see how the Goddess manifests Herself to you. I would be delighted to read your visualization experiences so if you would like to share them, please write to me, c/o the publisher.

How to go about visualization is very much a matter of personal choice: you may sit, stand, or lie down—whichever position you feel you can most comfortably maintain for ten to twenty minutes. You're probably best advised to be in a quiet, darkened room and to keep your eyes closed. Begin by relaxing your entire body. One technique is to imagine a comfortably warm, golden light surrounding you and taking away all tension in the area you're thinking of. Start with your feet and work up to the crown of your head. Once this is done, begin to construct your visualization in your mind.

There is a basic modesty and humility in Virgo that may leave you perhaps more susceptible than any of us to psychic damage by our culture's subtle and not-so-subtle bias against women. It is your nature to analyze, to evaluate, to strive to be and to do the best you possibly can. And yet you are aware that results are always less than perfect, which is as it must be, since we are not goddesses. However, your honest attempts to appraise your efforts may be unduly skewed toward the negative, toward feelings of inferiority, because there is still so little real support of the feminine in our society. Therefore, in my opinion, you have an important, ongoing need to stay in touch with the patterns, the cosmic order of the Great Goddess. Frequent meditation on the basic femininity of life will sustain your spirit and shield you from thoughtless jokes, indifference, pressures to relinquish your independence, and other such drains on your energy. Fortunately, you have a great range of wonderful images to choose from, to satisfy every need, and suit every mood.

If you are feeling damaged or your life seems out of balance, look deep within your mind to the Chinese Great Mother, Nu-Kua, whose story dates back to at least 2500 BC. Mother Nu-Kua is mighty in strength, able to smother raging fires, able to subdue roiling floods and to restore Her creation—earth—to its proper order. Focus on Her so that you may see what is the source of disharmony in your life, and draw upon Her strength to help you repair it.

The path to your own pattern may lie in wandering the earth in the privacy of your mind. Perhaps you will start in Africa, where the human race was born, and where the Great Mother of All taught us to be honest, to be brave, and to care for each other. Walk through the beauty of Africa; enjoy the tawny veldt stretched out like a lion quietly sunning itself; enter the lush rain forest where the creativity and abundance of the Great Mother is evident everywhere, where the warmth and moisture create a visible womb rich with new life; walk alongside the lakes where the beautiful image of the Moon Mother floats in the waters; climb the mountains beloved of the Goddess, in which are hidden beautiful jewels. Stand on the mountaintop and look out over the orderly fields newly planted with seeds, green with young seedlings, crowded with ripe foods ready for gathering.

Wind your way up the Nile into Egypt and from there where shall you go? Perhaps you'll wander through Europe, past orchards of olives and grapes, and north toward apples and wheat, barley, and corn. Perhaps you'll visit the mist-shrouded fjords of Norway and marvel at the bounty of the earth that the Great Goddess Freyja has brought forth. Then, too, you may travel farther north into

Finland's beautiful blue-green forests where the Great Goddess Mielikki feeds little bear cubs sweet honeycomb.

You may visit the deserts of the Saharan sun, or ride across the wind-whipped steppes of Siberia and Tibet. Or maybe you'll climb the terraced hillsides of China or visit the rich, emerald-green rice fields of Korea. Wherever in your mind you go, you see the laws of the Great Goddess at work, the balance She creates between periods of increase and periods of decrease. Whether the time frame is a year or a day, rest alternates with activity, inner thought with outward expression. In your mind's eye, you see the Mother's shining silver face as She proceeds through Her lunar cycle, you see Her ever-changing body as Earth, as Gaia, as Hera holding sceptre in one hand and pomegranate in the other. You hear the Goddess singing the sprightly airs of spring, the mellow songs of summer, the melancholy farewells of autumn, the lullabies of winter. Allow yourself to merge with the rhythms, to join in the song, whatever is called forth from you. Be patient and allow your own connection to the cycles of earth to become apparent to you.

As I mentioned earlier in your chapter, there are transitions that are somewhat difficult for you. One image I feel may be especially fruitful for you is that of Changing Woman, the Great Goddess of the Navajo people. Visit the House of Changing Woman. What it looks like only you can know. Because Changing Woman was born amidst beautiful flowers under the sparkling arcs of rainbows, when I think of visiting Her I am in a meadow. The grass is cool and soft beneath my feet, and thickly carpeted with flowers of every color. The air in the middle of the meadow seems dense, seems to shimmer as if it is the portal to another realm. Softly glowing rainbows frame this shimmery air. I stand before it, I pass through.

Perhaps you stand before beautiful, always young Iduna, the Daughter, whose breath is as sweet as the spring breezes, whose eyes are as blue as the Norwegian sky, whose golden hair is wreathed in flowers red, blue, and violet. Lovely Iduna renews your energy, is your companion in the bubbling exciting time when ideas take shape and are born, when you have an urge to play, when things are new.

Perhaps you stand before Demeter—Ceres—the Mother who gathers you to Her in love, who spreads a feast before you of all earth's loveliest foods so that you may eat your fill and know that there is more than enough for you, there is more than enough for all, and that hunger should end in our world.

Perhaps you stand before the Grandmother, Great Wise Hecate, whose hair is silver, whose wrinkled cheeks are petal soft, whose old eyes have seen all the mysteries of life, of death, of rebirth. She smiles at you, and you realize how utterly and completely you are loved and accepted, how valuable your own experience is, how much you have to share with others. Stand with Her in the dark of the moon and look with the eyes of owls and of cats at life's secrets. Allow Hecate to teach you to nourish your mind, to nourish your spirit. Rejoice in the sense of abundance and richness and great magic that the Grandmother shares with you. Rejoice that you, too, may try to be like Her and share what you have learned with others.

In the House of Changing Woman you may see yourself as Daughter, Mother, Grandmother by turns and simultaneously. You may indeed be admitted in imagination into those ancient mysteries, the Eleusinian rites for Great Mother Demeter, wherein even the most barbaric nature was transformed into a civilized being and people's fear of death became a joyful, hopeful acceptance. No one can predict your experience in this meditation, but you can be sure that it will reward you with a deeper appreciation of yourself and of the Eternal Feminine.

There may be times when you need to set about working on some project, and yet you find yourself either confused as to how to get started or just too lazy to begin. It may help you to meditate on the bee, sacred to the Goddess for its vegetarian purity; its purposeful, well-organized activity; its production of honey, delicious in itself and as a sweetener and useful as a preservative. You may wish to present yourself to the shrine of the Great Goddess Aphrodite of Greece or of Asherah of Israel. There the High Priestess Melissa or Deborah will initiate you into the secrets of the bees, whose wings represented the veils of the Goddess, the hymen that shields the portal through which all humans enter life.

If you have chosen, for whatever reason, to live your life independent of men, know that your choice is acceptable to the Great Mother. At those times when your responsibilities feel too heavy to carry any more, know that you may present yourself to the Great Goddess and rest in Her. Her priestesses, who knew the pleasures of love yet were independent, smile at you and move quickly, smoothly, to assist and refresh you. They bathe your feet; they cool your brow with rose-scented water. Delicious cakes of honey and sesame—*mylloi,* made in the shape of our vulva—are set before you, and the nectar of wise blood and honey, which brings wisdom, magic, inspiration—are offered to you. You are welcome in and of yourself; you are accepted as complete, as valuable just as you are. Enjoy yourself.

LIBRA

September 23– October 23

LIBRA: The Great Goddess as the Tree of Life with Her son, Chonsu, who wears the lunar disk and crescent. A composite based on an Egyptian bronze Chonsu from the Twenty-fourth Dynasty, 672–525 BC; an Egyptian stella of the Eighteenth Dynasty, Kestner Museum, Hanover; and an Egyptian bronze vessel, 600 BC, Louvre.

Your sign Libra is represented in the zodiac as a pair of scales, and histories of astrology generally identify this as an appropriate enough symbol for the month in which the Egyptians weighed their harvest prior to selling or storing it. However, the scales actually represent the matriarchal justice and the all-seeing eye of the Great Goddess Libera, for whom your sign is named. Libera was one name of the Great Goddess worshipped in Libya, an area that in ancient times comprised most of Africa. In the city of Carthage, She was called Astroarche, Queen of the Stars. Variations of this basically Phoenician name were Astarte, Ashtoreth, and Asherah. We learn from *The Woman's Encyclopedia of Myths and Secrets* by Barbara G. Walker that "Her priestesses were famous astrologers whose prophecies were circulated throughout the Roman Empire." The Romans were among those who celebrated Her festival, the Liberalia, when wine flowed like water, slaves were freed for the day, and the emphasis was on love, pleasure, and high spirits—rather like our carnivals.

The Goddess Libera was very similar to the Egyptian Goddess Maat, She who weighed the human soul in the balance against Her ostrich feather to see if, in life, it had gained weight by the kind deeds the person had done and the truth she or he had spoken. Maat was revered as Truth, Justice, Mother. It was She who taught us righteousness, who gave us benevolent laws. This matriarchal law of the Goddess-worshippers was more humane, more benevolent than the later, vengeful law of the patriarchal gods. This can be seen in the "negative confession" an Egyptian was supposed to repeat to Maat to show she or he had lived in accordance with Her rules, from Barbara G. Walker's *Woman's Encyclopedia of Myths and Secrets,*

I have not been a man of anger, I have done no evil to mankind. I have not inflicted pain. I have made none weep. I have done violence to no man. I have not done harm unto animals. I have not robbed the poor. I have not fouled water. I have not trampled fields. I have not behaved with insolence. I have not judged hastily. I have not stirred up strife. I have not made any man to commit murder for me. I have not insisted that excessive work be done for me daily. I have not borne false witness. I have not stolen land. I have not cheated in measuring the bushel. I have allowed no man to suffer hunger. I have not increased my wealth except with such things as are my own possessions. I have not seized wrongfully the property of others. I have not taken milk from the mouths of babes.

Elsewhere in the ancient world, people worshipped the Lady of the Scales, She who gives us laws, as Ala in Nigeria, Inanna in Sumeria, Ishtar throughout the Semitic world and in Mesopotamia, Bachue in Colombia, and Themis in ancient Greece.

One important aspect of the Great Goddess that is especially pertinent to your sign was Her ability to transform spirit into matter, and vice versa. Libra celebrated the union of material and spiritual aspects of life, and the tree was a favorite symbol for these transformative powers. Most of the world's people thought of trees as feminine: their roots intertwined in Mother Earth, drawing strength from the realm of death and rebirth; their branches reached for the Moon Mother and the realm of the spirit; their bodies constituted a maternal bridge linking all the elements of nature to one another and to us.

The story of the labors of Hercules contains an interesting appearance of the Goddess as Tree, and it is an example of how stories were twisted to suit the politics of whoever ruled. In the story we know, Hercules is supposed to steal the golden apples of the Hesperides, which were guarded by the hundred-headed serpent Ladon. Since this garden and tree were sacred to the Great Goddess Hera, for whom Hercules was named, we can see that in the version we've inherited Hercules behaves as the betrayer and the enemy of the Great Mother by tricking the giant Atlas into stealing the apples for him. In the earlier version, Hercules is a ritual name given to the young man who serves as king for a year, empowered in a festival like the Liberalia by a marriage with the high priestess representing the Goddess. As a reward for his service, he receives the apples of immortality from the Great Mother as the Tree of Life, guarded by Her faithful serpent, in Her sacred garden in the land of the dead, which seems to have been located in Libya on the side of Mount Atlas. The Goddess as the Tree of Life is evident throughout the world, surviving today in our sacred poles and crosses, our once-lusty but now tame May Day celebrations, and of course as our Christmas tree. The original meaning of each of these symbols was the Great Mother's transformative, life-giving powers.

If you wish to read this information in terms of your Moon rather than your Sun, you'll need to shift your thinking from your identity, your will, your essential self—the way you manifest being you in the world—to focus instead on the inner you, the emotional you—your self at the deepest levels of your unconscious. Your Moon not only has to do with your feelings but also includes those things you take for granted in your self—those things you assume everyone else feels or is like, since they are so essential to your personality. Your Moon gifts might not be the most obvious features in your personality. They are ever present but elusive qualities you know intimately and yet can't quite put your finger on. The Moon also has to do with what went on in your family of origin, your home, your background. It concerns all those things that give you a sense of emotional security.

Specifically, Moon in Libra fine-tunes your emotions and gives you great sensitivity. It makes you particularly responsive to beauty, prompting you to take care of your own appearance and that of your surroundings. It is also very likely that the arts will be important to you. With Moon in Libra, the feminine side of your nature will be strongly marked by charm and an eagerness to please, which you need to be a little cautious with so that you neither make empty promises nor subordinate yourself to the needs and desires of others. By and large, a Libra Moon influences you toward peace and harmony except for sudden outbursts of anger, which occur rather like a brief, violent storm in the midst of a sunny day. It also endows you with a talent for cooperation, a generally friendly, tolerant disposition, and a delight in offering family and friends the hospitality of your home. On a deeper level, your Moon in Libra will make spiritual fulfillment a vital concern for you. Give this need your most careful attention.

The main trouble with traditional astrological interpretations of Libra is that they overemphasize Libran indecisiveness. I don't see Librans as folks who sit around endlessly picking through the pros and cons of an issue, unable to arrive at a decision. Perhaps if your horoscope were weighted almost entirely in Libra, you might find yourself unable to choose between coffee, tea, or milk and die of thirst in consequence, but barring this drastic circumstance, you have no more trouble than the rest of us in making up your mind.

The balance, harmony, and decision-making connected with Libra relate more to reconciling spiritual and material concerns, and to the whole issue of self-development, than they do to the questions that crop up in day-to-day living. And they are themes that work themselves out over the years instead of in days, weeks, or months. In fact, if we were to look solely at that daily surface, yours would appear to be an exceptionally delightful, untroubled life. In many respects, it is delightful, but it is not quite as carefree as others might believe.

One of the major gifts you receive from Sun in Libra is youthfulness, and this means a lot more than that you will always look younger than your chronological age. By way of an explanation, let me compare our passage through time, from cradle to grave, to the unfolding of a spectrum: the cycles of growth we undergo resemble bands of color that shade into one another so that, by the end of our lives, the full range of our selves is revealed. The point is that we accumulate rather than shed or outgrow selves as we go along, and our happiness depends largely on how well we integrate these various stages into peaceful coexistence, because we cannot, in truth, obliterate any of them. I've yet to know anyone, myself included, who has not found herself at some point in a situation in which she reacts—often to her very great surprise—just as she did as a child, with that same early enthusiasm or frustration or rage or yearning for someone else to say the magic words that will make everything all right again. It has nothing whatsoever to do with how many gray hairs we have on our heads or how many years to our credit; the child each of us once was is still very much alive, but whether she is kicking or not depends on how we treat her. Although this is true for all of us, it is especially true of you. It can be a wonderful gift and, at times, a source of difficulty and confusion, so let's explore it a bit further.

Charm is one of the very positive aspects of this gift. You are able to be completely honest and open in your dealings with others and to express even the harshest realities in a way that does not personally offend—and that is no mean feat. Much of your charm stems from your sensitivity to other people's feelings and your ability to empathize with them and gauge how they will react. Your ability to express yourself graciously is especially valuable in business. It allows you to maintain pleasant relationships, and when it is necessary to refuse or disappoint other people, you manage to do this without unduly discouraging them or hurting their pride.

Your "youthfulness" is also apparent through your ingenuity, inventiveness, and fresh ideas. You have a talent for anticipating what will appeal to the public next, and are usually in the avant-garde of fashion and ideas. You also have a flair for presentation: whether you're touting an idea, a product, or a project, you know how to arouse interest in it and win people over to it pretty swiftly. These gifts can work to your distinct financial advantage, and I suggest that you keep them in mind when you're considering a career.

Another Libran asset is that you are capable of enthusiasm throughout your life and you generate it in others. Life rarely seems stale for you, because even a small dose of boredom will prompt you to search out new ideas, activities, or interests to engage your energies. One surprising factor is that you usually explore a new interest very thoroughly. If you get interested in astrology, for example, you're likely to do a prodigious amount of research, and practice working up charts until you feel you're really able to present a well-integrated picture of someone's personality in a reading. At work, you generally make sure you understand every aspect of the business, including those you're not personally involved in—and what's more, you make friends with people in departments other than your own. I realize that this may not seem like much to you, because you are prompted by your interest in other people and by your desire to understand how things work in a total sense. But you'd be amazed at how many people never concern themselves with anything beyond the limits of their own job and never recognize anyone else's contribution besides their own or those of their immediate colleagues. So what this does for you is to place you in an extremely advantageous position, both in regard to getting your usual work done and in carrying out new projects. People are happy to cooperate with you because you have always treated them as if they mattered, and they'll do their utmost to help you work as efficiently as possible, and to see what sort of innovations would be helpful and how to introduce them effectively.

I hope it is apparent from our discussion so far that Libran youthfulness does not mean that you're simply a cute ball of fluff, here to make life more graceful and charming for the rest of us. It bothers me very much that in all the time that I worked with astrology magazines, I never once read an article that urged Libran women to take themselves seriously. Well, I am here to urge you to do so. The fact that you're charming and gracious is just that: you're charming and gracious, and more power to you in your use of these gifts. You also have ambitions and tremendous capabilities, and every right to pursue these for your satisfaction. If this makes you feel uneasy, estimate how little or how much you would like to take yourself seriously by the degree to which you are attracted to "strong," powerful people. So often we displace onto others what we would like and could have for ourselves. If this is the case for you, then make yourself very familiar with the idea that you can be the person you admire most.

If you are in your teens or your twenties, this may be very difficult for you to believe, because these are the periods in which your youthfulness often feels like a great handicap. Particularly in your teens, you have a considerable amount of trouble perceiving yourself as a distinct identity, even though other people get a clear impression of your personality. Your cloudy perception of yourself can feel pretty awful while it lasts, like those frustrating dreams in which you try to scream and can't make a sound, or try to strike out in self-defense but your arms feel like lead and you make no more impact than a ball of cotton. Naturally, there is no one way in which you'll respond to this. You may react by doing every outrageous deed that springs to mind in order to reassure yourself that you exist. The danger here is that you might cause yourself real damage. You may not respond so drastically, of course; you may choose instead to model yourself after someone you admire a great deal, or you may hope to gain strength by following conventional paths and coping with conventional responsibilities. Apart from the danger mentioned before, there is nothing wrong with these or other methods of coping, and each enables you to perceive your own identity more clearly. Neither is this period all painful struggle, because your sense of fun and your enthusiasm for people and experience come to your aid and help you to a sizable portion of good times.

By and large, your twenties are a very exciting period for you. Naturally enough, you're primarily concerned with launching yourself as an independent adult. Every aspect of this process—from setting up your own home and getting started in your career, to opening your own checking and charge accounts—exhilarates you. The world seems a very glamorous and interesting place, and you're delighted to be part of it. There are moments, of course, when you feel overwhelmed by your freedom and independence, but for the most part you enjoy them tremendously. The one flaw in this intriguing, busy time is, again, the blurred image you have of yourself, irritated by the feeling that you're not really your own person, that you tailor yourself to suit other people's expectations. This is partly true, and it is understandable if you consider this period an apprenticeship in which you are learning a great deal about how things work. It is only reasonable that you pay careful attention to people who have had more experience than you, especially in your business or profession. Indeed, you may tend to value their opinion too highly or to consider them experts on matters quite apart from their real specialties. Take heart from the fact, paradoxical as it may seem, that the sharper your dissatisfaction with yourself becomes, the closer you are to achieving real independence.

This is, generally speaking, the thrust of your transition into your thirties, which is probably the most difficult period you experience. Not that life is a thornless bed of roses once this is completed, but it is rarely again as confusing or marked by so sharp a sense of upheaval. The changes you undergo are essentially private in nature. They do not necessarily mean that you'll change jobs or leave a marriage or enter one. They may involve such large, clearly visible indications of change, or they may eventually result in these, but oddly enough, these really are secondary matters. The issue at stake is finding your own center within yourself and becoming aware that you are your own person. It seems characteristic of such transitions that they begin with an increase of the very things we wish to shed. For example, you may have had occasional bouts of feeling too dependent on others, but this feeling becomes an almost constant state at the beginning of this transition. You tend to lose all sense of yourself and strive even harder for the approval of others. I think that this sort of reaction is actually the way we wean ourselves from old patterns—by intensifying them until they are intolerable and draining them of every last bit of appeal. It's rather like going on a chocolate binge and eating so much candy that you eventually never want to see another piece of chocolate again as long as you live.

It generally works this way for you. You begin by feeling utterly dependent on others, unable to be by yourself and yet lonely in company. This uncomfortable state brings a counterreaction in which you do not have the strength to socialize very much and you lose interest in the activities that usually appeal to you. You don't go in for silent brooding, but you do cut back drastically on your social life, including contact with your relatives. Just meeting the demands of your job may be all you feel able to manage and you find yourself spending your evenings and weekends as quietly as possible. You may do nothing more earthshaking than loll about, reading the newspapers, and watching television, but these intervals of solitude bring some very positive results. For one thing, the fact that you're able to enjoy yourself in your own company restores balance to your relationships. The desperate need for other people disappears and, consequently, you're able to enjoy your friends a great deal more. More important, the time you spend by yourself allows you, at last, to gain a firm idea of who you are, what you need, and what you value. You realize that you survive very well indeed, with or without other people's approval, and that most of the things you've accomplished were done to satisfy yourself, after all. What's lovely about this is that it permits you to take pride in the many skills you've acquired and the amount you've learned and achieved in a comparatively short span of time.

There's no question that you're a great deal more at ease with yourself and the world around you at the close of this transition than at any previous time. Once you've acknowledged that you've learned how to survive—and, in fact, do so very nicely—you're free to direct your energies to other concerns. It's not that you lose interest in your career, but because you're more self-confident about it, you don't need to devote as much time and attention to it as you did before, and you no longer allow it to dominate your social life. Your spiritual needs move to the forefront now, and they play a major role in your life henceforth.

In relation to these, Libra gives you both a need and a flair for order and harmony. Aesthetically, this is expressed in your ability to use color, proportion, and design beautifully, to dress attractively, to make your surroundings interesting and gracious, and to present things to their best advantage. It also makes you exceptionally responsive to beauty in any form, and your appreciation of the arts can be a lifelong source of interest and pleasure for you. Socially, it appears through your tact in dealing with others, and your willingness to work out disagreements through discussion and compromise. You detest violence and loud arguments and have excellent control over your own temper. This enables you to fight very effectively in verbal battles, where your coolness and wit are definite advantages.

Above all, Libra sharpens your need to discern some order in the universe, some larger meaning or pattern beyond the helter-skelter of everyday experience or that which is available by achieving a series of goals such as success in your career, a family, and a home, or whatever. Your search is not necessarily through traditional religions. You may explore nontraditional philosophies, religions, and social theories, or work out an explanation of your own. But however you go about it, you experience a strong desire to expand beyond the narrow limits of the self and to connect with others, with all of life, in a larger, richer bond. It often happens that this desire somehow triggers a release of psychic abilities, and you may find yourself experiencing uncanny moments of preknowledge or of empathy with others. You may also serve as a catalyst in helping other people untangle their problems or arrive at an insight that they've been struggling to achieve.

As I mentioned before, the early cycles during which you are concerned with the self and the transition into the broader, spiritually oriented cycle are the crucial periods for you. Your succeeding cycles are an extension of these, rather than radically different, as far as your inward direction is concerned. You learn both to know yourself better and to extend far beyond yourself, and these seemingly separate drives flow together to help you deepen and enrich your knowledge, create from it, and, eventually, share it with others.

In terms of your energy pattern, you tend toward great bursts of energy and activity, but stamina is not your long suit. You need rest, especially after working all day. It may sound silly, but you'd do yourself an enormous favor if you managed to take a nap in the afternoon or early evening, or even take ten minutes out for meditation at some point during the day when you begin to feel drained. Diversity, however, also refreshes you and you can restore your strength by varying your activities. The worst possible job for you would be one in which you're required to do the same thing all day long. You need to be able to move about, and to have social contact. You're especially active mentally and thrive on the stimulation that talking with other people provides.

On an annual basis, your creative energies are at their peak in spring and fall, and you're probably happiest and most physically relaxed in summer. In fact, warm climates suit you and you often find winter a trial to your spirit, especially since it is the period when your energies are at the ebb point. If you can manage to schedule your vacation during winter, do so, because it is the ideal time for you to get a change of scenery, preferably tropical.

As to your monthly cycle, your Libra transit is an optimistic start. You feel completely comfortable with yourself and you see the positive qualities in people and situations. This is generally an excellent time for smoothing out any snags that may have developed in any project you've undertaken. It is followed by the not-so-euphoric Scorpio transit, which brings doubts and questions in its wake. This period can be helpful in that it raises many questions worth considering. Just remember that there's no need to become unduly pessimistic and that if you find flaws in your plans, you'll also figure out ways to circumvent or remedy them. The following Sagittarian transit is a very upbeat interval. You generally have an even greater amount of energy during this period, combined with a strong, clear sense of purpose that enables you to accomplish a great deal. In a sense, the Sagittarius transits give you the wherewithal to put into effect those projects that still seem worthwhile after the Scorpio transits.

A Capricorn transit is a very plain, solid affair for you. You're in command of yourself and very effective in your relationships with other people and any work you set out to do. It is a particularly good period for getting everything in order, but you need to be a bit careful and not overextend yourself. You don't have the extra energy of Sagittarius, and you should schedule rests even when you feel you don't need them. A new surge of energy comes in Aquarius, but it is primarily mental. You may not feel like lifting a finger physically, and should indulge this "indolence" as much as you can. You are extremely receptive at this time and your transformative powers are also exceptionally strong. Art may be a particularly potent stimulus for you, but whether you're influenced by a piece of music you've heard, a conversation you've had, or an article you've read in the newspaper, the chances are extremely good that you will emerge from this interval with a flock of new ideas. Pisces continues this, but with the difference that your receptivity is to emotional contact with others and to very complex abstractions. This is an interesting but potentially exhausting time in that you feel closer and more involved with other people and also can see the interrelationships among various ideas and the ways to put them into effect. Fortunately, Aries transits provide another more than usually sustained sort of energy and you generally find that you've singled one idea out as your pet and can work on it vigorously. It's a period of singlemindedness; it's not unusual during this time for you to become quite obsessive about things that had been merely interests before.

Understandably enough, the next transit, Taurus, is a slack period. You won't feel up to doing much of anything; if you're lucky, you'll be able to streamline your schedule to accommodate your lassitude. It is even more of a mental than a physical vacation. In fact, in reaction to the high activity of the previous transits, you may counter with a profound indifference to everything and certainly feel in no mood for any mental exertion. It was for times like these that television was invented; ideally, you'll allow yourself to relax and let someone else do the thinking for a while. Gemini is a return to a more balanced state. There is no great mental or emotional fireworks, but it is a very pleasant time for enjoying being with your friends and colleagues and getting your work done.

Cancer transits are times in which you learn and reach a new level of understanding in regard to your intimate relationships and your creative activities. They clarify your direction and are very fine times in which to make plans for your future. You can generally be assured that you're working with ideas and feelings that have been thoroughly assimilated and represent those that are most genuinely attractive to you. It is a quiet, reflective period and one in which you least feel the need for other people, so it might be well to avoid a heavy social schedule during these transits. Leo transits, on the other hand, are perfect for socializing. They feel very much like vacations, perhaps because of the work you've done and the decisions you've made during Cancer. At any rate, your urge to play and generally have a good time is strongest during Leo, and I hope you'll do just that. You also have a good deal of physical energy during this time and particularly enjoy social sports such as tennis or golf. The last transit, Virgo, is also helpful, although in a very different way. It is a time of intimacy, it is generally quieter, and it is also a time in which you mull things over in terms of their most widely felt consequences. It is the transit in which your concern for social justice and improvement generally dominates your thoughts and you are able to view things from a truly long-range perspective.

We should say a word about your concern for social justice, since it is rightfully one of the most famous Libran qualities. It is not a delight in law for law's sake; actually, you loathe seeing the law manipulated to cheat people of their rights or to gain preferential treatment for some at the expense of others. Your feeling for justice goes back to the oldest matriarchal view in which every member of the group, whether it be a small village or a large nation, was entitled to equal rights and equal protection. One of the most fortunate aspects of this concern is that you not only treat other people fairly and decently but you expect them to treat you fairly and decently, too. You may be gracious about it, but you nonetheless persist until a wrong is corrected. You have, in fact, a very long memory for injustices; while you give people every chance to make amends, you make your revenge felt if they should ignore their opportunities.

When you are considering careers for yourself, it might be well to keep these Libran qualities in mind. You have been given an exceptional ability to cooperate with others, to bring forth the best in them, and to endure and work through the hassles that any group undertaking entails. This is especially valuable in politics as well as business, and I personally hope that you make politics an avocation, at least, since you could be such a strong plus for the rest of us.

As I mentioned before, you're able to express yourself without trampling on the feelings of others, even those whose views you strongly oppose. You are able to maintain a warm, personal aura while conducting business—even during the most practical, hard-headed transactions—and this is a highly useful quality in politics, too.

Libra endows you with artistic talent in your own right and with a very strong aesthetic orientation. You enjoy discerning the ideas at work in other people's creations as well as giving shape to your own. Frequently, you are able to spur others to do better work than they've done before: you suggest ideas and supply people with the confidence they need to extend their abilities. This is helpful in public relations work and in any sort of artistic collaboration, such as creating an artists' cooperative. It is important to you that your surroundings, yourself, and your efforts be as beautiful and fine as you can possibly make them, and this does not necessarily mean luxury. One of the reasons you campaign hard against poverty or ignorance is that they are so ugly and limiting. You might consider making your career in one of the art fields or developing your talents for your own private satisfaction. You can gain a great deal of valuable information about yourself through your artistic gifts, and they can help you learn to enjoy your own company and be of tremendous service to you during your difficult times. In short, it is important that you make definite use of them.

You have a quick, active mind and an immense curiosity that may lead you to explore all sorts of subjects and avenues of life. There is no reason I can think of for you to let these gifts languish on the vine. Your wide range of interests is a plus; find out everything you possibly can about anything that appeals to you. Whatever you learn may come in handy at some point in your life or may simply give you the pleasure of learning. Be grateful for these faculties, because they can brighten your life even if you're bedridden or 110 years old.

Without a doubt, Libra helps make you a very attractive person. Your quick wit, your charm, your pleasure in other people's company guarantee that you will never lack friends. You may need to withdraw from them at times, but they like you nevertheless and welcome your return. And there is certainly no danger that you will pine away, your sexual light hidden under a bushel basket. People almost invariably find you charming, and that charm contains a large component of sexual magnetism. A lack of partners is hardly your problem. What may trouble you is a reluctance to settle down with any one person. Your curiosity, your eagerness to know and to try, extends to your sex life, and you're ready and willing to try anything, in imagination, at least, if not in actual reality. As always, you do best when you're on good terms with yourself. Then you're free to really have fun in bed. Your more emotionally oriented partnerships bring the greatest fulfillment for you, especially when you feel at ease enough to express your feelings and are not worried about pleasing in order to be accepted and approved—but you can be pleasing because you like to be.

In light of your preference for cooperation, it is no surprise that you'd rather be living with someone than by yourself. However, given the kind of growing you experience, you may not necessarily stay with one partner for your entire lifetime, unless it has been your good fortune to form a relationship sufficiently resilient to accommodate these changes.

As for children, you like them and can be a very loving, lively companion to them. But here again, your relationship to your children is easy in direct ratio to your comfort with yourself. If you can permit yourself your own need to play and explore, you are able to be remarkably tolerant of your children. When you're busy censoring these needs in yourself, you tend to become very critical of them and view them as artistic productions that you have to mold and shape to some ideal. I suggest that when you find yourself being severe, you treat yourself to a large dose of tenderness and respect, and watch what happens. Without the handicaps imposed by censorship, you have a lot of fun with children, and they enjoy being with you and find it very easy to learn from you.

So would the rest of us enjoy learning from you. You have a great deal to offer, and all the potential to create a rich, exciting life for yourself. Let your compassion extend to yourself first and it will flow outward from you naturally. You have been given the inner conviction that you are a "child of this universe," entitled to access to all of earth's resources, entitled to your equal rights and your chance to do your best with the gifts that you have received. It is a lesson that many of us are slow in acquiring and so we can benefit from your example. Your efforts to make this a reality and not just a longed-for ideal improve the quality of your life and that of a great

many others. Good luck to you—and thanks, for you bring beauty
into the world and brighten it for all of us.

LIBRA VISUALIZATIONS

You possess an extraordinary resource within you: your imagination. Through the power of your inward eye, you can tap into
your innermost self, and into the energies of the universe. The
thoughts you think, the messages you give yourself, the images you
create in your imagination have tremendous power. You can
literally transform your reality to fit the positive images you create
mentally simply by creating those images often enough, and as
specifically and clearly as you possibly can. Through such focused,
purposeful "daydreaming," you can achieve an astonishing range of
goals: practical goals such as weight loss, physical fitness, or money
management; spiritual goals such as enhanced self-esteem, inner
peace, and a deeper sense of connection with other living beings.
For further information on this process, I recommend two books I've
found useful, Shakti Gawain's *Creative Visualization*, and Shad
Helmstetter's *The Self-Talk Solution*.

My primary concern here is empowering you to get in touch
with the Goddess within you, the Eternal Feminine whose creative,
nurturing, renewing energies live within us all. The Great Goddess
is always ready to comfort, to heal, to strengthen, and to guide us
whenever we are in need. Her images come to us from all parts of
our world and from across great stretches of time. By visualizing Her
in our mind's eye, by meditating on Her image, you and I not only
receive help with specific problems and enhanced self-esteem but
also reap the additional benefit of greater esteem for all women, past
and present, and for the wonderful contributions women have made
in creating and advancing civilization.

The images I sketch for you came to me through my research
and through my own meditations. They may work differently for
you than I've envisioned. And, of course, they're not the only
images available to you. I suggest you read Merlin Stone's *Ancient
Mirrors of Womanhood* and Barbara G. Walker's *The Woman's
Encyclopedia of Myths and Secrets* to see what stories, prayers, and

images resonate for you, and use them. I think you'll also find it illuminating simply to gaze within your own mind and see how the Goddess manifests Herself to you. I would be delighted to read your visualization experiences so if you would like to share them, please write to me, c/o the publisher.

How to go about visualization is very much a matter of personal choice: you may sit, stand, or lie down—whichever position you feel you can most comfortably maintain for ten to twenty minutes. You're probably best advised to be in a quiet, darkened room and to keep your eyes closed. Begin by relaxing your entire body. One technique is to imagine a comfortably warm, golden light surrounding you and taking away all tension in the area you're thinking of. Start with your feet and work up to the crown of your head. Once this is done, begin to construct your visualization in your mind.

In times of anxiety—perhaps when you feel pressured to live up to other people's expectations of you—visit the Goddess within you. In your mind's eye, hold the image of the Great Goddess Libera. She holds Her arms out to you, accepting you completely. To Her, you are perfect just as you are, a child of Her spirit. Allow the sense of Her generosity to permeate your soul. Rest in Her embrace, holding the thought that no human being has been given infallible judgment, that even the wisest of us makes mistakes, and that no one else can know the *tao*, the path of truth, for another. Each of us must find her own path. Use your visits to the Goddess to discern your own. As you practice meditating upon the Goddess and you experience the calm and the breadth of Her spirit, you may notice that your thoughts will cease whirling like leaves through the air and will instead float gently. This process, which restores serenity to your soul, may also reveal your own path to you. Do not bother to strain after these insights; let them float gently up into your consciousness. As they pass before your inner eye, simply gaze upon them as if they were beautiful flowers. You need not strive to gather them to you. If they are truly yours, they will remain in your consciousness after your meditation, and they will feel right for you.

There may also be times when you feel oppressed and confined, when you chafe under the restrictions of your life. You literally may not have the money to travel or the time may not be right to take an actual trip. However, you need not suffer. Remember that the Great Goddess Libera is a goddess of mirth, of gaiety, of charm. Take Her hand and float in imagination above the world. Visit the scenes of your life, gazing upon them with the Goddess's smiling eyes and see the humor you may have overlooked on a day-to-day basis. Or, if you feel that you cannot stand the sight of them at this time, visit instead some of the beautiful places that exist on our earth. Float above them like a sun-warmed cloud, drifting languorously through the sky. Drink in their beauty and feel your soul expand.

The Great Goddess Libera is a radiance within you. She is the glint of sunlight, the sparkle of stars. When you feel downcast, meditate upon Her and allow yourself to experience the warmth of well-being, to feel joy well up and bubble within you. The festivals of the Goddess were occasions of joy and freedom for all. In your mind, you may choose to participate in such a festival. Hear the music that delights the Goddess, join the dances that honored Her, join in the games and races where everyone plays her or his best in tribute to Her. Sing and dance and run and have a wonderful time—and emerge from your meditation with your sense of fun renewed.

Transitions are usually awkward times for us all and yours are no exception. For you, they are often marked by a kind of restlessness where you feel unable to be alone and yet lack the strength to socialize, where you, in short, are dissatisfied no matter what your situation is. It may help you to turn your thoughts to the Goddess as the Tree of Life. In your imagination you may even become treelike yourself, in imitation of Her. My dear friend Pamela Williams chose to celebrate Christmas with one tree decorated in the traditional way in her living room for all to enjoy and another more private one in her bedroom, created as a tribute to the Goddess as the Tree of Life and decorated with birds and stars and topped with a silver moon. Whether you choose to work literally with a tree or imaginatively in art or visualization, it may benefit you to focus on your life as a gift from the Goddess. Think of your roots drawing strength from deep within the earth, from generations of ancestors who have created families and civilizations each of us is a part of, and sense how these nourish and sustain you, how essential a part of our planet you yourself are. Think of the trunk of the tree, the strong central portion that supports the branches as an image of the integrity of your self that changes yet remains the same, which grows taller and fuller just as you mature and your understanding deepens yet you are not radically different from who you were. Visualize the branches of the tree, of yourself, as reaching out, adding breadth to your character. Decorate them in your mind's eye with all that you cherish and value, images of those people you love and admire, mementos of events that were meaningful to you, and place among these treasures the gold and silver and precious gems of your hopes, your ambitions, and your values. In imagination, you can almost feel yourself growing; some of that process is private and some occurs in the world of relationships. Allow the reassurance of the Goddess to course within you. You will have and be all that you were, and you may rejoice in your becoming. Feel the strength and flexibility of your central self that can bend under the winds of storms and stand straight and tall when they have passed. Stretch your branches in the soft air and enjoy the beauties of starshine and moonlight, the privacy of fog and mist, the glory of the sun. You are yourself and yet a part of all that is; allow yourself to be nourished and to delight in the process of being all that you can be.

Order and harmony are almost as essential to the Libran personality as air to breathe. At those times when you feel distressed by a lack of harmony in your life, you may use your visualizations of the Goddess to restore your sense of balance. Look within and gaze upon the Great Goddess Ishtar/Ashtoreth, hailed throughout the Mediterranean and Africa and east into Asia as the Mistress of Wisdom, Source of Divine Order, Righteous Judge, Light of the World. Let your spirit be lifted up and soar with the Goddess into the heavens. Observe the orderly arrangement of stars and planets in the immensity of space. Float gently back to earth and contemplate the small world of a flower, how necessary each part is, how beautifully and carefully its petals are arranged, how exquisite is its construction. Visualize if you can the inner world of your own body, the millions upon millions of cells, each beautifully made, each functioning to preserve and maintain your health, your beingness. Return your thoughts to the world around you and contemplate the

procession of the seasons, the Moon in Her phases. Look then at
your life and see if what appears now as disharmony is, in fact, but
a necessary stage in the greater harmony of the whole. Observe the
thoughts that surface in your consciousness to see if they reveal the
way in which you may restore order to your own life.

Whether Libra figures in your chart as Sun or Moon, you are
most probably gifted with psychic insights. The best way to nourish
this gift, in my opinion, is through cultivating respect for these
insights and encouraging them through frequent meditation upon
the Goddess. You are well advised to use fifteen minutes or so of
your daily rest time for such meditation, and I offer you this image
which a friend cut out of a newsletter for me. Unfortunately, the
picture was unsigned so I can't credit the artist, but I give thanks here
to whoever she or he is who created such a beautiful picture. The
illustration shows the Goddess floating through the night sky,
holding a sleeping human in Her embrace. Her face is serene and
thoughtful and Her hair begins as little feathers framing Her face,
then merging into longer feathers at wing level. The silver crescent
of the moon nestles in Her hair. Phases of the moon stream from her
cloak. The human she holds so tenderly is totally at peace; all
worries and anxieties have fled, leaving utter tranquillity. It is one of
the most peaceful images I've ever seen, and I hope it serves you
well.

SCORPIO

October 23– November 22

SCORPIO: The Great Goddess, Dikte, of Crete with Her snakes, who symbolized Her wisdom as well as Her dominion over death and resurrection, and with Her bird, who represented Her as the Holy Spirit. Based on a faience statue, 1600 BC, preserved in the Archaeological Museum, Heraklion, Crete.

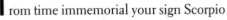

From time immemorial your sign Scorpio has been regarded as the most powerful segment of the zodiac. And not without reason. It speaks to us of the vital matters of sexual union, death, and regeneration. Scorpio's emblems—the scorpion, the snake, the bird—are intimately connected with rebirth and transformation.

Scorpio's power comes from its connection with the world's original deity, the Great Goddess, Mother of All, who ruled the sky, the earth, the depths of the earth, the waters of life, and the fires of heaven and hearths. Her first emblems were the serpent and the bird of Scorpio, present in abundance from the earliest stages of the Neolithic period onward. The ivory tusks of the great woolly mammoths were carved first into figures representing the Great Mother, and then into delicate renderings of snakes and birds. These beautiful carvings have been recovered from the oldest burial sites found yet, and they'd been placed to guide the dead safely into the next life.

Not only have Scorpio's emblems figured among the earliest evidence of human life, but they have been of major significance everywhere in the world. Our own image of Scorpio comes to us from the ancient Egyptians, who named the constellation Selket in honor of the Scorpion Goddess who released Her hordes of scorpions during Egypt's annual sandstorms, and they named the stars entwined with Selket's constellation the "Serpent stars." In Her human form, Selket was pictured as a very beautiful, very kind woman. Her image was painted inside coffins, usually with Her arms extended to welcome the dead to Her loving embrace and to guide them to an even lovelier afterlife.

The fact that the Great Mother could and did bring death as well as life was not seen as a punishment or a cruelty but as a necessary condition of existence, which allowed the cycle of life to continue forever. However, the Egyptians and the other peoples of the ancient world were no more eager to leave this life than we are. Their emphasis was on rebirth; they wrapped their dead in shrouds with frayed edges so that the Goddess as the Great Weaver would grasp the loose threads and begin weaving a new life for the departed soul. To them, the snake represented crucial aspects of the Goddess. In shedding its skin, the snake was seen to imitate the Goddess in its ability to change profoundly yet remain the same, just as the Goddess did in Her nightly manifestation as the Moon. Snakes lived in holes deep within the earth and consequently seemed familiar with both the realm of the dead and the source of oracles. The snake's ability to entwine and wreathe itself around something was viewed as the perfect model of devotion, and not only the pythoness priestesses of the Delphic oracle in Greece but also the Levite priests of the ancient Hebrews wore snake headdresses and armlets to remind themselves to be like the snake in their attendance on the deity. The snake's coolness was also reminiscent of the Goddess; people believed that the Perfect Wisdom of the Goddess was comparable to the cool, subtle light of the moon and not the brash heat of the sun. For this reason, the snake was revered as a wise teacher, and ancient images of the snake often show it as teaching humans or offering them the Goddess's Apples of Immortality.

Throughout the world, even to the small islands that dot the Pacific, the bird represented the Goddess as the Holy Spirit who resides in all of us and who transforms us into spirit when our term as physical beings is completed. Like snakes, birds only indicated the

Goddess's powers, since She did not share their limitations but could go anywhere and be everywhere simultaneously. In New Guinea, people placed figures of the Goddess with legs spread to expose the "gateway of life" along with bird images on their roofs to ensure the safety and prosperity of the families within. In many other cultures, the Goddess as Holy Spirit or Divine Wisdom was most frequently represented either winged or as a dove, or accompanied by them. An ancient Assyrian story tells of the Great Goddess Ishtar, also called Nu'a, who became enraged at the evil and warfare on earth and unleashed a mighty flood, but then lamented that She had drowned Her children. She sent Her dove to see if the waters had abated and when it returned bearing an olive branch signifying dry land had reemerged, She set about repopulating the earth. Our dove of peace bears an exact likeness to this ancient messenger. The Celts of Europe, the Ainu of Japan, and the peoples of Asia Minor all revered oak trees because doves, symbolic of the Goddess, nested in them.

Doves were the most popular but they were by no means the only bird emblem of the Goddess. The owl symbolized Her wisdom. The raven and the vulture were Her agents in death. The goose, too, was associated with the Goddess. In North America, Indian women formed special Goose societies and our genial Mother Goose, usually depicted in Welsh costume, was once even more exotically garbed in the flowing draperies of Asia Minor and the Mediterranean or the colorful patterned cloak of the Celts. But, whether She was hailed as Aphrodite, Venus, Ishtar, Ashtoreth, or Astarte, She stood or sat upon the strong back of the goose and flew through the wide spaces of Her domain. And the Phoenix of Scorpio represented the resurrected soul each of us would become.

So here you are, connected to the most powerful segment of the zodiac, represented by the death-dealing forces of the scorpion, the serpent's wisdom and devotion, and the spiritual transformation of the phoenix. In ancient times you would have been under the guardianship of the Goddess Hecate, who rules the dark of the moon and the potential of that darkness for mystery—for creation, destruction, and regeneration. Scorpio is neither an easy nor a simple

influence. Yet its great rewards of passion, knowledge, and achievement are worth every bit of its complexities.

If you wish to read this information in terms of your Moon
rather than your Sun, you'll need to shift your thinking from your
identity, your will, your essential self—the way you manifest being
you in the world—to focus instead on the inner you, the emotional
you—your self at the deepest levels of your unconscious. Your
Moon not only has to do with your feelings but also includes those
things you take for granted in your self—those things you assume
everyone else feels or is like, since they are so essential to your
personality. Your Moon gifts might not be the most obvious features
in your personality. They are ever present but elusive qualities you
know intimately and yet can't quite put your finger on. The Moon
also has to do with what went on in your family of origin, your
home, your background. It concerns all those things that give you a
sense of emotional security.

Specifically, Moon in Scorpio gives you a powerful connection
with the past, both your own personal past and our collective
history. This contributes to your need to know, to explore, to
investigate, to penetrate mysteries so that you can synthesize the
information you have gathered into a meaningful whole. In this
conjunction, the past serves as a wonderful resource. It does mean,
however, that you're not likely to be the first one on your block to
own the latest in electronic gadgetry, and may prefer to reread
eighteenth and nineteenth century novels than to venture much into
modern literature. A Scorpio Moon is perhaps most apparent in
your emotional life, endowing you with intense, passionate, long-
lasting feelings. As you might expect, it will take some doing to gain
control over them in a balanced way so that you neither suppress
them and deny yourself their richness nor are at their mercy. Moon
in Scorpio will also manifest itself in the feminine side of your
nature in personal magnetism, a flair for the dramatic, and a
tendency to be self-reliant. In addition, you are likely to have a vivid
imagination and a powerful intuition, gifts to take seriously and
nurture carefully.

You may find that if you mention you have strong Scorpio

influences working in your horoscope, people will look at you with renewed interest, primarily because of Scorpio's sexual reputation. I don't know what they expect—perhaps, that you'll demonstrate "passion incarnate" on the spot. You, however, are under no obligation to try to be sexy all the time in order to live up to your Scorpio image. More often than not, your sexuality is a very present, very quiet force that might best be compared to a current of electricity coursing through you. In fact, you may not be very comfortable in casual conversations about sex. And it's almost a certainty that you tend to form single, intense attachments and are not terribly interested in playing the field.

One thing is sure—your sexuality is far more complex than party chit-chat would imply. In the first place, it is very much with you from the time you're about two or three years old, and you probably began to have fantasies and to masturbate from that early age on. Whether this was comfortable for you or not depends to a large degree upon your parents' or guardian's attitudes toward sex, and this is something over which you have very little control. If you have a child with strong Scorpio influence in her chart, I'd recommend you take a relaxed attitude toward her sexuality and exert only those controls necessary for public decorum and to prevent her from hurting herself. As for yourself, you may have grown up at a time when you would have been considered a little demon for masturbating or showing any interest in sex, since children were supposed to be asexual until adolescence. More careful observation of children at all their early stages, plus information from other cultures, has proved that this was a Victorian wish rather than a fact of human behavior. However, if your family was distressed and upset by your behavior, you may well have been bewildered by impulses you couldn't control and you may have suffered a loss of confidence in yourself. The negative self-image you may have formed as a child can be repaired as an adult, and you have the resources to cope with and balance out these early attitudes.

It's possible that you will react by championing sexual freedom in any or all of its aspects. You may find, however, that when you first begin full adult sexual activity (which is generally in early to mid-adolescence) that idealistic fervor does not necessarily work out all that well in bed, and those earliest experiences may not be particularly gratifying. Another obstacle to your own pleasure may come, strange as it may seem, from your sensitivity to others and your desire to please. You may fake satisfaction rather than risk making your partner feel diminished or inadequate. This mistaken courtesy stems from the widespread fallacy that sex is something we do to or for each other rather than with each other. It is certainly a courtesy that does nothing for you except, perhaps, make you feel as if there's something wrong with you because you didn't have an orgasm. Ultimately, it doesn't do a whole lot for your partner, either. The result of successfully fooling your partner is that you'll privately regard that person as a dupe and a shlemiel. Needless to say, the sooner you ditch your "good manners,"the more fun you'll have. And Scorpio women do enjoy themselves, without a doubt, once they get going!

Naturally, your sex life is very much tied up with where you're at in your developmental cycles, and therefore it's a shade difficult to treat it as an absolutely separate topic. Please bear in mind that much of what I have to say applies also to other spheres of your life and excuse me if I seem to be scuttling back and forth. At any rate, during your first thirty to thirty-five years, you may be drawn to people who are especially attractive physically or who possess powers and abilities, particularly in respect to coping with the world at large, that you may feel you lack. Privately they may not be quite as strong as they appear, and may need "mothering" or indulgence or call it what you will. They may also be incapable of having a really intimate relationship. There's no question that such people will give you a host of legitimate reasons to complain about their behavior and will tax your understanding to the limit. But let's go on the premise that no matter how barren or heartbreaking a relationship may seem, we remain in it because it does offer us something we need. That something may be just that it's familiar and we're afraid of change—which can be a very big fear. Or it may be that it allows us to feel privately "strong," which we hope will compensate for our painful sense of inadequacy in work or social situations. This generally proves to be a less than stellar arrangement. It does not really relieve our unhappiness with ourselves to keep a running account of somebody else's shortcomings or to ask that someone else be effective in our stead. We remain burdened with our fears and pressured by our sense of the unexplored, unused potential within us. And we tend to lose sight of the genuinely positive aspects of the relationship. Let me assure you that the sooner you concentrate on being effective in your own right and experience the confidence that this generates, the sooner you'll feel good about yourself and be able to select your partners more wisely.

This relates particularly to partners whom you find madly attractive, yet who frustrate you because they ward off real intimacy no matter how long you remain with them. These relationships resemble an awkward dance; you advance lovingly and your partner retreats; your partner then reconsiders and advances to you, but you've withdrawn in hurt feelings and anger, and so it goes, and it doesn't amount to a great get-together. Now, some people do thrive on the eternal quest, and a pattern like this one would add spice to their lives. But that's rarely how it affects you. Generally, it reflects your own ambivalence toward intimacy: you may desire it intensely and yet feel afraid and unready for it. The chances are good that you are hoping to win your partner's acceptance and approval in the expectation that such approval will make you feel terrific about yourself. For better or worse, our psyches just don't work that way. Somebody could sit down and spend from now until next Whitsuntide reassuring you about what a lovely person you are and yet they wouldn't be much help. You can't believe it until you learn it for yourself.

Granted, you may have absorbed negative ideas about yourself in childhood. Apart from sexuality, you may have been considered "different" or "peculiar" or "special." Whether the terms were flattering or otherwise, you may have felt set apart. You were probably able to play very happily by yourself and may have spent a great deal of time alone, compared to other children. Your capacity for privacy might in itself have been viewed as peculiar. Your ideas, your intense enthusiasm, even your hobbies, may have provoked strong reactions from your family. In addition, there may have been some chaotic circumstances to deal with, such as frequent changes in your family's residence or fortunes. All of this generally adds up to great private strength and considerable self-doubt. Your adolescence may bring some relief in that it's usually a more sociable period for you. You have more friends, although they, too, may be considered offbeat. That's relatively unimportant compared to the fact that you do find kindred spirits and can begin to counter the image of yourself as a uniquely weird example of the human race. Your courage surfaces in this period and you'll try much that is new for you, even take risks or enter experiences that would intimidate others. You also gain some confidence in your talents, your ability to survive and to make friends, and like most of us, you may also devote a great many private moments to imagining yourself as the toad of the universe. In light of the thousand-and-one imperfections you see so clearly in yourself, you suffer from the idea that your friends are simply being charitable, since no one could really like someone as "unworthy," "ugly," et cetera as you. Needless to say, these evaluations do not mirror reality.

Your twenties are often a radical contrast to your childhood. Your urge for privacy is often sacrificed to a prodigious appetite for social contact, and you may be extremely reluctant to be alone. Naturally, this shows up in your sex life, and you're quite likely to have several serious affairs interspersed with brief encounters. It may seem as if there's hardly breathing space between relationships; one no sooner ends than you're launched into the next. Given the realities of our times, I advise you to be positively paranoid about sexual hygiene and protection, or to channel these energies into less dangerous pursuits. If instead you marry early, that marriage may not be a lifelong union, and a rush of sexual experiences will probably follow its termination. There's a good chance that if you marry before or during your twenties, you will do so from mixed motives, among which may be the desire to try a new experience and, even more, the need to satisfy a social expectation. Such motives do not generally make for permanent relationships, but that's not to say that the relationships you have mean nothing to you or do not have anything to offer you. Both your affairs and (if you'll pardon the assumption) first marriage offer you a great deal, and you certainly give them your all.

By the way, the word *casual* is rarely appropriate for Scorpio.

You may dress casually, but that's about it. You bring intense, profound loyalty to your closest relationships and your emotions are deeply engaged, no matter what cycle you're in. To expect yourself to be casual about these is about as likely to succeed as asking yourself to grow wings and fly. In regard to your sexual relationships, you are able to gain a great deal of self-knowledge from them, though such insights are more readily available in retrospect. Nevertheless, your experiences are a great help to you, especially during those times when you temporarily withdraw from the sexual field.

These withdrawals are connected to the major transition of your mid-thirties, which has to do with establishing a better balance between your need to socialize and your need for privacy. Your situation is practically the direct opposite of Libra's. Libran people tend to be as other directed as you are inner directed; their need for a social context is as strong as your need for a private context, and their job is, generally, to develop a stronger sense of their inner center while yours is to develop your ability to extend outward more comfortably toward others, minus the fear of losing yourself. Which goes to show you that everybody's got problems.

As I said before, your twenties are a very social period for you. You're still able to be happily absorbed working on your own, but you distrust this almost as much as you enjoy it; generally, you permit yourself this sort of pleasure only if it's in response to work or school requirements or done primarily for somebody else. These times are, nevertheless, small oases and they do refresh your spirit, as they always have and always will. But the need of this decade is to supply you with the social experience you may not have gotten earlier; since you enter things with intensity, you may well go to an extreme in believing that you can't function independently.

By your early to mid-thirties, you've had enough of this. You're fatigued by your efforts to mold yourself to suit others, especially since you keep popping out of the mold no matter how hard you try and it just makes you feel like a failure. You're particularly weary of sexual relationships in which you're forever chasing after the elusive carrot of approval. You may be profoundly tired of some of your old ways—the "Last-Minute Lulu" routine, for example, in which you put off work to the last possible minute and then must summon up enormous amounts of energy and work frantically to meet your deadline. You can still do it, perhaps, but it's an approach that's lost its charm. You no longer see it as a challenge, but as a tedious, hectic business that leaves you no time to enjoy the work at hand or other projects you might also like to do.

Say a prayer of thanks for your exhaustion. The chances are excellent that it will usher in a transition that will enable you to live the remainder of your life with a richness, interest, and depth beyond anything you anticipated. The transition itself is by no means easy, and you may wisely choose to enter therapy to get some help in sorting things out. It may start out with all hell breaking loose, and in the initial period, you may well feel numb or cry so often that you feel as if you've exhausted your life's quota of tears. It is, throughout, a very inner-directed time and, paradoxical as this may sound, you'll be better off to place yourself within a stable social context. This is not the moment to go freelance. However, if you've been out of the job market for a while, it is an excellent time to reenter it or return to school. You'll benefit by having some basic structure imposed on your time and you need to anchor yourself to some steady, preferably simple means of remaining in contact with other people. Keep the outward form of your life as simple and clear as you can possibly manage, since you'll have plenty to contend with and explore in your private thoughts. The sexual aspect of your life during this transition will probably be minimal, since there's very little energy available for such emotional commitments. It's possible that you will go through a series of casual encounters, but these probably won't do much for you at this point.

This transition takes about two to four years to complete, and the first year is the most difficult. During that time you have just about enough energy to cope with basic survival. Once that arduous phase is past, however, your energy begins to revive and it is generally directed to work or education. For example, let's suppose that you've returned to work after being at home for a considerable time. You may have grabbed any job available to start out with, which is absolutely fine, because the major point to make to yourself is that you can get a job and that you are more than competent at it.

Once that's established, you're able to start looking around for work that might suit you better in salary, say, or environment or responsibilities. The crux of the matter here is that you are starting to evaluate from the viewpoint of what suits you, what is compatible with your temperament and needs. It may start out small and it may not seem all that earthshaking, but in fact, as you begin to take charge of your life and give up trying to change yourself to suit others, you'll find that strength and excitement course through you more and more often.

Similar reactions occur if you've decided to return to school. As soon as you see that, indeed, you're perfectly able to handle your assignments and that being older than many of your classmates is neither a discomfort nor a disadvantage, you'll sense a difference in yourself. For the first time in your school experience you'll be actively conscious of trying to get what *you* need for yourself instead of simply meeting the requirements. In the past you may occasionally have had opportunities to initiate a project or do a paper on a topic that commanded your interest and enthusiasm. Work was then a pleasure, and these occasions probably shine forth as the highlights of your school experience. But you may have seen them as sheer good luck. The difference now is that you will be more and more aware that there are questions and subjects you wish to explore, and you will actively try to adapt your course work to fulfill these needs to whatever extent possible.

You learn an enormous amount during this transition: how to study, how to research, how to organize, how to ask for help and from whom, how to deal with people, how to pace yourself. This list could go on and on. The most important thing born of this time is the awareness that you have your own personal work to do, and that it is profoundly important to you. As this strengthens, you may run into some flak from others who resent that your attention is not always available when they want it. That does have to be worked out. But it is an absolute mistake to consider giving up your own work entirely. Without it, you feel incomplete and you're restless in your relationships with other people; obviously there's no advantage to that. With it, however, you gain a sense of wholeness and the release that comes from meeting some deep, inner responsibility. From that vantage point you'll be better able to create a workable balance between your emotional commitments to others and those to yourself.

As you emerge from this transition, your energies will be strongly focused on work. In fact, the contrast between the first part of this phase and the last is absolutely amazing. You may work and go to school; you may have a full-time job and freelance or take on a part-time job. Fortunately, you have tremendous stamina and regenerative powers because you place very heavy demands on your physical strength at this point, and you need a hardy constitution to get you through. The work you are doing is likely to be connected to major interests but not yet fully, personally yours. For example, opportunities may open to you or you may be invited outright to participate in a project because of particular skills you have, but these are not yet the things that you design and execute completely on your own. Don't misunderstand me—I'm not knocking this in any way, shape, or form. If nothing else, these things almost force you to take yourself seriously and to acknowledge gifts that you've pooh-poohed as nothing. And their value as an apprenticeship for your own projects is beyond reckoning.

The cycle from your mid-thirties to your mid-forties is one in which you strengthen yourself through experience and then launch into the work dearest to your heart. From them on, you can enjoy being alive in a way you've never before experienced. Despite the tedium that any work entails, it is minor compared to the fascination, the sense of purpose, and the satisfaction it holds for you. Curiously enough, your work gives you real control over your sexual drive. You can now convert it to creative energy when you need to or choose to and, of course, you can use it in the good old tried-and-true ways, too. Your relationships with other people also benefit. The fact that you no longer ask or expect others to supply the impossible—to wit, a sense of direction, purpose, and an acceptance of yourself—enables you to appreciate the very real support and love that people can give one another. And once the issue of your work is settled—or rather, launched, and with it the respect for yourself that makes it possible—you will again be interested and able to form emotional relationships besides those you retain with your relatives and close friends.

I am going to leave the subject of your cycles at this point. For one thing, I feel that it would be presumptuous and disrespectful to try to lay your life out for you as if it were a map. For another, I think the most crucial area has been covered—that once you work your way through to respecting and enjoying your power, you'll be more than able to take on the ups and downs and roundabouts that life presents. So let's move along to more specific gifts that you receive through Scorpio.

You have, first of all, a very strong sense of fate, which deepens as you get older. Most of us are hard put to explain the universe and its workings, but you are very much aware that it is working. Whether or not your spiritual orientation is framed in one of the traditional religions, it is very present in childhood and adolescence, and it reasserts itself very powerfully from your mid-thirties onward. The seemingly coincidental yet fateful connections among people, events, locations, or issues make a deep impression upon you and you are equally struck by the recurrence of themes both in your private life and in history. For example, it may happen that an activity or a topic surges up as a powerful claim on your attention in your thirties and forties, and you suddenly remember all the ways and times it has appeared in your life before. It may have figured as a brief but intense interest, and then as something about which you periodically, randomly, gathered more information. You may also be aware of the tributaries to this interest, the skills and experience you've gathered along the way that have met in your current project. I cannot say what practical use, if any, this has; only that these discoveries are somehow thrilling, that they help to reconcile you to yourself, that they strengthen your sense of being part of a larger pattern, however incomprehensible, that frames your life and gives it richness and stability.

Scorpio is connected with death as well as with sex, with the end and the beginning of life. This may account for your interest in the opposites in life, of which you are keenly aware and which you try first to analyze and then to synthesize into a coherent whole.

Death itself is not an easy subject in our culture, and until you arrive at your reconciliation stage, it may give you a great deal of trouble and heartache. I will pass on to you these often useful suggestions, which may help you during your early thoughts about death. You can, to some extent, use death as an index to your feelings about your life. Suppose there's been no death among your family and friends, yet you find yourself thinking incessantly about death and lay awake at night feeling the earth spin through space, hurrying you toward the end. Take it as a very strong signal that you are very unhappy and dissatisfied with your life, and changes are absolutely mandatory. None of us could stand the strain of living as if each moment and day were our last; we need some feeling of stability and continuity, however illusory it may prove to be. Neither can we afford to ignore the fact that our moments and days will come to an end, and therefore we might as well spend that time being as true and respectful toward ourselves as possible. And that doesn't necessarily mean any great, grand thing. I remember one Sunday when I had just started to regain the ability to enjoy myself in my own company, and I was busy with my stamp collection. It was a beautiful, crisp, sunny day, a day that anyone would want to go outside to enjoy. I felt guilty at not being like "anyone" and suddenly fear and disgust washed over me with thoughts of, "What if I were to die tonight? What if this were my last sunny afternoon and here I am, not taking advantage of it?" The point was that it also would have been my last afternoon to fool with my stamps, which I obviously preferred doing. But as soon as I wandered off into comparisonland with reflections on how much better other people used their time and what an unimaginative sod I was, the only thing I managed to do was spoil my own pleasure. That's an example of how death can be used negatively.

Although we don't usually think of death's positive aspects, they are there. Once the awareness of mortality makes itself felt, it can add another dimension to living. You're not as likely to be shy about your affection and regard for those close to you. You may choose to speak directly of your love and respect for them, and share your appreciation for what they add to your life. You may choose to get out of an intolerable situation rather than persist in your Scorpio way. You may more easily accept the fact that you often meet your needs in nontraditional ways. The example that suggests itself in regard to this is your strong need to mother and nurture. Obstacles may prevent you from satisfying this in the traditional pattern. You may be able to have a child and unable to bring yourself to team up legally with anyone, but you may have the wherewithal to have and raise your child or children on your own. You may, for physical or circumstantial reasons, be unable to have children, but you may still be able to satisfy that need, either by adopting as a single parent, by marrying and adopting, or by marrying and becoming a stepmother. Another alternative is to be in close relationships with other people's children, either as a teacher or as an aunt. Then again, you may convert that need into creative energy directed toward issues related to the transmission of culture and wisdom. What you don't need to do is sit around and berate yourself because you don't fall into the standard category of mother.

Scorpio also gives you strong intuitive powers and insight into other people's feelings and motivations. When you're feeling negative about yourself and the world, these may be experienced as suspicion and distrust. Generally, they help you balance your intensity in that you can remain aware of other people's needs and feelings no matter how pressing your own concerns and enthusiasms are. May I offer herewith my standard precaution to protect yourself from the temptation to be noble and self-sacrificing? And may I also urge that the next time you're ready to make a joke at your own expense or berate yourself for a fault or a mistake, you consider for a moment whether or not you'd be that caustic or critical toward a friend? No? Then why not extend a little mercy toward yourself?

Another Scorpio gift, which is something of a mixed blessing, is your tenacity, or loyalty. This definitely characterizes your relationships and can be a disadvantage at certain points. You will hang in there with people and situations, even if they make you miserable. No doubt you're able to extract every last drop of value from these situations, but you also drain every last drop of poison. You may also hang on to patterns of response and behavior until they're absolutely threadbare. In part, this is because you are conservative by nature, though you may be unconventional in your style and ideas. I'm not speaking about politics now, but about your urge to conserve or preserve those things such as family, which you regard as essential to the wholeness and continuity of the natural and social world.

Your tenacity is a distinct advantage in connection with your creative energy or your pursuit of particular goals. You are able to persist despite setbacks and fears. When you go through a slump in enthusiasm for your goal, you can shift to taking satisfaction in persistence itself until your interest is regenerated. This is especially helpful as a counter to your impatience. One of the early barriers to your creativity is your wish to dispense with the apprenticeship period and proceed immediately to the masterpiece stage. Some of that is simply fear tricked out in a grand disguise, but your wish to create will hound you worse than your fear. Eventually you'll take the risk of being less than perfect, and your persistence not only will help you realize your goals but allow you to learn that the process of creation is as satisfying for you, if not more so, than the ultimate result.

I suppose *tenacity* is another word for "willpower," and let's clear up right here that it may not be available in equal strength for all things. It will vary according to mood, circumstance, and degree of interest a project holds for you. For instance, you may try repeatedly to crochet or sew, and end up with a lot of yarn or fabric and unfinished projects in your house. You may try to write or paint and, lo and behold, you have the stamina to do so. It could work just as easily the other way around, of course, and it clearly depends on which activity satisfies you best. By the same token, if you're eyebrow deep in a long-term, demanding project, don't be surprised if you can't diet successfully or this isn't the golden moment to give up smoking.

Your energy also fluctuates in terms of the kind and amount available at particular times. Generally speaking, Scorpio gives you physical strength and you may be tempted to be prodigal with it. Even though you're capable of doing for yourself, learn to ask for help with heavy tasks: don't carry packages that would stagger a packhorse, for instance, and try to limit your work when your energy level is low. An important component of your strength is your ability to recuperate; this, too, you'll need to learn to use wisely. The fact that you're able to spring back comparatively quickly after a bout of partying, or sustained hard work, or illness does not mean that you should continually overdo and expect this gift to bail you out. Every gift has its limits and a variety of ways in which it can be used. Your regenerative capacity, for example, is not limited to the strictly physical aspects of your life, but can be extraordinarily helpful in emotional, intellectual, and spiritual spheres as well. In these areas it's likely to help bring you more lasting, interesting results than would getting through a hangover swiftly, for example. Your power can help you survive a bitter experience and emerge intact. It allows you to transform your experience into insight and wisdom, which, in turn, help give direction to your life. It can deepen your compassion and the degree of intimacy in your relationships. In short, it's not to be trifled with.

Your energy definitely alternates between active and passive periods. You generally pattern out to three- to five-day periods in which you do a lot, followed by two- to three-day periods in which you can hardly bring yourself to complete the normal daily round. During these latter days, you may feel impatient with yourself, and fidget and complain inwardly because you're not accomplishing anything. You might as well forget the impatience, because that's the way it works. Make yourself a batch of popcorn, grab a mystery, and enjoy yourself—and get used to the idea that you have intervals in which you blank out. It may help to realize that these times are essential, especially for any creative activity, because you are quite busy unconsciously, sorting things out and reflecting on them.

On a monthly basis, a Scorpio transit seems a bit like a standstill: you know you're thinking, you have an intense feeling of concentration, but you're not quite sure what it is you're thinking about. Sagittarius brings a lovely sense of release. Your direction becomes clear and your energy is in harmony with it. Capricorn and Aquarius are also generally positive; Capricorn offers you a sense of balance in your life and gives strong help in organizing things, which you can probably use, since Scorpio frequently tends to alternate between chaos and order. Pisces and Aries transits are difficult, and they may frighten you with their cold quality and with the potential for anger they seem to inspire. You may feel numb, as if you didn't give a damn about anything or anyone in the world, and that is upsetting. Or you may feel ready to do battle with the world, and that's not too comfortable, either. Personally, I've learned to treat transits like these with great respect, and to interpret them as signals of a powerful need for privacy, which it's best to heed. Taurus is a good transit because it's such a nice, sociable time and a bit of a relief after the others. Gemini is also generally positive in that you're able to communicate easily with others; if you have to win anyone's support for your plans, this is an excellent time to do so. You're usually reflective and quiet in a Cancer transit, but this is most often a tranquil, quiet time with no hassles about it. Leo brings an upsurge in energy directed toward mundane matters rather than grand schemes; it can be a great time to organize your files or clean out your closets. A Virgo transit is better for organizing projects and making long-term plans, since it clarifies and broadens your view of life. Libra transits, pleasantly enough, are lovely, lighthearted intervals; they are especially good times for socializing and feel like well-earned rewards after your periods of hard work.

In your annual cycle, your highest level of physical energy usually occurs from late October through late December, and you'll be on the go a great deal of the time. Your pace eases up during the late December to February stretch, but this is your time of greatest creative energy in relation to generating ideas and plans that you will eventually carry through. Your tempo throughout the rest of the year is fairly even, though you may experience a brief, often bewildering or agitated time around April. August and early September bring a definite drop in physical strength, and that's when you'd like nothing better than to be near water. It doesn't make much difference whether it's an ocean, a river, or a lake, just so long as you can swim, row, canoe, or simply sit around looking at the water and listening to it.

The gifts you gain from Scorpio are especially suited for teaching, religious work, research, writing, and theater arts. You're imaginative and inventive, with a flair for the dramatic and, periodically, a very real need for excitement. This last can work for you or against you, so it would be wise not to stint yourself on nondestructive outlets for that kind of energy. Make sure you shake off your routine every once in a while and go out to the theater or make a party for yourself. Otherwise, you may be prompted to create a crisis just to get some drama back into your life. Your interest in human nature, your compassion, and your respect for people's confidences suggest that psychiatry and psychotherapy may also be careers for you to consider. Archaeology and anthropology will probably interest you even if you choose not to enter either as a career. In fact, your interests in general are diverse, and you're likely to be busy all your life with various hobbies and enthusiasms. Retirement will present few difficulties for you, and you'll be quite as happily and usefully engaged during that more leisurely cycle as you were in your working years.

Your Scorpio heritage gives you a powerful concern for the people you love, and a sense of responsibility toward them and your society. However private your path, you have a clearly etched vision of how things should be. You try to promote the humane and the generous, and to do battle against the injustices in this life. It is important to you that you live your life with honor. Your personal code may differ in many respects from other people's, but it is strongly felt and you abide by it scrupulously. Your error, in fact, may be that you judge yourself too sternly. Your own desire to learn generates a great deal of enthusiasm—in yourself and in others. The knowledge you share and the pleasant or new experiences you provide for others help satisfy your need to be of use and to make a contribution. May you learn the lesson of Scorpio—that your way of being human is as fine and as worthy as the next person's—and may you develop your gifts and use them as they were meant to be used: to celebrate the grand adventure that this life is.

SCORPIO VISUALIZATIONS

You possess an extraordinary resource within you: your imagination. Through the power of your inward eye, you can tap into your innermost self, and into the energies of the universe. The thoughts you think, the messages you give yourself, the images you create in your imagination have tremendous power. You can literally transform your reality to fit the positive images you create mentally simply by creating those images .often enough, and as specifically and clearly as you possibly can. Through such focused, purposeful "daydreaming," you can achieve an astonishing range of goals: practical goals such as weight loss, physical fitness, or money management; spiritual goals such as enhanced self-esteem, inner peace, and a deeper sense of connection with other living beings. For further information on this process, I recommend two books I've found useful, Shakti Gawain's *Creative Visualization*, and Shad Helmstetter's *The Self-Talk Solution*.

My primary concern here is empowering you to get in touch with the Goddess within you, the Eternal Feminine whose creative, nurturing, renewing energies live within us all. The Great Goddess is always ready to comfort, to heal, to strengthen, and to guide us whenever we are in need. Her images come to us from all parts of our world and from across great stretches of time. By visualizing Her in our mind's eye, by meditating on Her image, you and I not only receive help with specific problems and enhanced self-esteem but also reap the additional benefit of greater esteem for all women, past and present, and for the wonderful contributions women have made in creating and advancing civilization.

The images I sketch for you came to me through my research and through my own meditations. They may work differently for you than I've envisioned. And, of course, they're not the only images available to you. I suggest you read Merlin Stone's *Ancient Mirrors of Womanhood* and Barbara G. Walker's *The Woman's Encyclopedia of Myths and Secrets* to see what stories, prayers and images resonate for you, and use them. I think you'll also find it illuminating simply to gaze within your own mind and see how the Goddess manifests Herself to you. I would be delighted to read your visualization experiences so if you would like to share them, please write to me, c/o the publisher.

How to go about visualization is very much a matter of personal choice: you may sit, stand, or lie down—whichever position you feel you can most comfortably maintain for ten to twenty minutes. You're probably best advised to be in a quiet, darkened room and to keep your eyes closed. Begin by relaxing your entire body. One technique is to imagine a comfortably warm, golden light surrounding you and taking away all tension in the area you're thinking of. Start with your feet and work up to the crown of your head. Once this is done, begin to construct your visualization in your mind.

There will be many times when you need to be comforted, and whether it is from pride or the need for privacy or fear that your strength will be dissipated, you often do not turn to others to satisfy this need. At such times, then, I suggest you invoke the image of the Great Mother to come to your aid. Personally, I often see Her as Mary, Mother of God, Mother of All, and in my mind's eye, She gently smooths my hair or puts Her arm around my shoulders and I sense Her reassuring me that all will be well. You might also see her as the Great Winged Isis, who enfolds you in Her downy embrace and rocks you gently, or flys you away temporarily from the exasperations of the daily routine.

The Winged Goddess also imparts a wonderful sense of protection and strength, and you might think of Her when you are feeling shy or anxious in a social situation. In your imagination, see Her straight and tall, Her gaze level, equal to anything, Her strong wings outstretched, sheltering you. As you look upon Her, feel Her strength and equanimity pass into you, filling you with courage, freeing you from self-consciousness and enabling you to turn your attention to others.

When responsibilities weigh heavily upon your soul and you feel your burdens too much to bear alone, turn to the Goddess, who will lift you to sit or stand beside Her on Her goose. Its wings spread and lift you swiftly into the sky, and you may look without fear at the world flowing beneath you. Go as swiftly or as slowly as you need to; allow your spirit the refreshment of distance and perspective. Allow yourself to feel light, almost weightless, borne as a feather in the wind. When you are ready, the Goddess will bring the goose to a smooth, gliding halt and you will step off onto firm earth again, with no dizziness, no loss of balance, renewed in your strength.

Although change and transformation are very much Scorpio's business, your transitions are by no means easy matters. There is often quite difficult work involved in a transition and the temptation frequently is to duck out of it. I should know, having spent a goodly portion of time procrastinating or dodging what must be done, and so I would like to share with you a visualization that came to me quite unbidden and which has been an enormous help to me; I hope it will help you, too. This image came to me unexpectedly, in broad daylight, as I was walking to my friend Judith Werner's house, where we were to discuss the updated chart she, an astrologer, had done for me. The image was so compelling, so breathtaking, that I hurried to the nearest park bench to sit down and "look" at it. In my mind, I was in a very dark cave. I knew it was in Crete and that it was one of the many underground shrines to the Great Goddess Dikte. Before me, much taller than I, balanced on its gleaming coils, was poised a great golden cobra. I could not "see" the cobra exactly, but I had the impression that it was bejeweled with emeralds, rubies, diamonds, and gold. It did not speak but looked unblinkingly at me with its golden eyes, and the message passed to me that change is not only inevitable, but necessary, and that the refusal to change is a kind of death. I felt as if I were naked, aware that the Goddess knew me to the last particle of my being, knew that in my heart of hearts I was twisting and turning and trying my utmost to avoid the tasks of change. It was a very strange sensation. There was no hint of criticism or anger or ridicule, no chastisement of any sort. There was only the calm presentation of the fact of life and the opportunity to see myself as I actually was. I had the distinct impression that what I did with this opportunity was strictly up to me. As the picture faded from my mind's eye, I felt the wonderful peace of courage flow within me again, along with a growing excitement. Naturally, I could hardly wait to tell Judith what I had seen, but more than that I felt a sense of adventure about the future and a readiness to greet it, whatever it might hold. This is not to say that things have gone smoothly from that point on. They have not. And there are still many times when I resent or fear the changes that life brings. But now I know where to go for help and inspiration, and I invite you to do likewise.

There is a tendency in Scorpio personalities to overload your agendas, to take on too many things at once or to attempt to accomplish a complex project in too short a time. You are tempted to this by your intense enthusiasm and your belief that you have unlimited strength. The result very often is that you finish the project or whatever utterly exhausted, with your enthusiasm and strength in tatters, creeping through your paces fueled only by sheer dogged persistence. Of course, it would be infinitely better if you simply learned not to do this, to ease up on your schedules, and to apportion activities over longer periods of time. However, going on the likelihood that you and I will make this error from time to time, I suggest that one way to renew your spirits and help you feel human again is to visit the Great Goddess Hecate in your imagination. Hecate was the elder aspect of the Goddess as Trinity; She was the Crone—the Grandmother—and Her special period was the dark of the moon, which gave respite to the hunted, privacy to lovers and cloaked the world in the soft mystery and serenity of darkness. In your mind, visualize the velvet darkness of Hecate. There is no moon in the sky—just the faint silver glimmerings of the stars. The air is hushed; even the birds are still. Perhaps you will walk with her through a forest, listening to the soft rustlings of the trees and the occasional scamperings of the small animals who may safely play in the darkness. Perhaps you will sit with Her on a flat boulder still warm from the day's heat, next to a lake whose surface gleams blackly in the night, whose small waves quietly lap the shore. You may rest in Hecate. Lie down and put your head in Her lap and She will smooth away your cares and worries. Allow the peace of Hecate to still your soul and wash away your weariness. Become aware of the larger scheme of things and place your concerns in proper perspective again. When you are ready to leave, give your thanks and gently return yourself from this visualization, resting quietly for a few moments after you have opened your eyes.

If you have a Scorpio Sun or a Scorpio Moon, the chances are good that, from time to time, you will be gripped by the fierce talons of jealousy, especially in your youth, when your sense of your own worth may be a bit shaky. Let me first assure you that all of the other signs also experience jealousy; it is not confined to Scorpio's domain and it is not even a characteristic of Scorpio. What is peculiar to Scorpio is that jealousy is an intense, all-invasive, and horrible experience, and it is very difficult to free oneself from it. However, let me also assure you that help is available. The following visualization was suggested to me by the excellent tape *Loving Your Self: Songs & Meditations* by Louise L. Hay and Jai Josefs. For this exercise, we use your element, water. Imagine yourself standing on the shore of a great calm sea, the waters of life. There is water as far as you can see and the world looks as if it were newly born. As you look, the Great Goddess Aphrodite rises from the water in all Her beauty and glides across the gentle waves toward you. As you watch Her, become aware that She is very pleased with you, that She loves you and regards you as a wonderful manifestation of Her spirit. She holds a vessel out to you for you to have. Imagine the vessel in as great detail as you can: look at its size, color, shape. However large it is, it is not too heavy or awkward for you to hold. She invites you to fill your vessel from the waters of life, to take as much and as often as you wish. Notice now that you are no longer alone. The shore is crowded with people—people you love and like, people you know, people you have seen or merely have a passing acquaintance with. Each one holds her or his own vessel and is also invited to take her or his fill. Each one, like you, fills the vessel of choice and yet the ocean stretches endlessly before you. There is enough for all of you. The portion that you take suits you and is in no way inferior to that of anyone else's. The others now vanish and you are once again alone with the Goddess. Become aware that you may return whenever you need to and that there will always be this abundance to draw from, that you will always be loved for your essential self, and that you will always have all that you really need. Feel your jealousy weaken and shrink. Let it ebb out of your being to be absorbed by the sand and evaporate in the sun. As it leaves, you will feel light and joyful again, cleansed by the healing waters of the Goddess, warmed by Her radiance, and restored to an awareness of your own worth.

There are times when Scorpios get very serious, even grim, and need to lighten up. I've found water imagery very helpful in these situations and would like to share two such scenarios with you. In the first, you are again standing near the ocean of life, this time weighted down with all your heaviest thoughts. Far off in the distance, coming nearer and nearer, is the Great Goddess standing on or riding a dolphin as if it were a horse. Other dolphins swim beside Her. Sometimes they disappear from view, diving deep below the waves. Then they leap from the waves in great silver arcs, drops of water spinning from them gold and silver in the sunlight. You are filled with a longing to join them, knowing that, no matter how deep you dive or how high you leap, you will be completely safe. They glide up to you, smiling their wonderful, kind, silly dolphin grins. The Goddess invites you to ride the dolphin next to Her and you climb onto its strong, smooth back. Off you go, as swift as thought, through the emerald and turquoise water. You dive deep, the sunlight turning the world beneath the waves a beautiful golden green so that you may see all the colors and treasures within the ocean. You speed to the surface and leap high in the air, to look at the world shining gloriously before you. You are a child again and play to your heart's content. When you are ready, the Great Goddess Aphrodite and Her dolphins swim you safely back and deposit you on the shore again. They smile their good-byes to you, but there is no sadness in their leaving, for you are welcome to join them whenever you wish.

In this last visualization, which I've mentioned for Cancer, I invite you to imagine that you are an otter and that the sea in which you play is the Goddess Herself from whose waters of life we are all born. The rocks by the shore form a natural slide for you to play on. You climb up and slide swiftly down, delighted with your speed, delighted to dive deep below the water and see the fish and other creatures there, none of whom will hurt you. You surface and float on your back, your paws clasped on your stomach in complete contentment. You are buoyed up and completely supported by the Goddess as Water. You may relax and watch the clouds floating by overhead and the birds wheeling through the sky. You may stay alone, enjoying your privacy, or be joined by your children or other loved ones. If others join you, you can play tag or race each other or simply float together, rocked gently by little waves, feeling utterly happy and carefree.

SAGITTARIUS
November 22– December 22

SAGITTARIUS: The Great Goddess, Artemis, looking very much like the Amazons who worshipped Her. Drawn from many sources, notably a vase painting, 460 BC, of *The Death of Penthesilea* at Antikensammlungen Museum, Munich, and a Greek amphora, seventh century BC, preserved in the Leningrad Museum.

The true symbol of your sign, Sagittarius, is the Amazon warrior-huntress on horseback, armed with bow and arrows, and carrying the double-bladed lunar axe of the Great Goddess jutting through her bejeweled girdle. She represents the untold numbers of real women throughout history who fought and hunted, who ran races and excelled in sports, and who acquitted themselves with great honor and skill in those activities we've come to regard as masculine. She represents the Celtic women of Europe, who were not only highly trained in military skills and athletics but often led their armies and were more ferocious in battle than their men, according to Roman reports of them. She is also the Teutonic women of ancient Germany and northern Europe, who received a complete outfitting of armor and weapons as part of their marriage gifts and who obviously used them, judging from the number of female skeletons found buried at ancient battle sites.

In her image, we also salute those medieval women left behind while their men went to fight one holy war or another, who led the meager forces at their disposal in defense of their homes against marauders. She is all the young women thoroughout pre-Hellenic Greece who wrestled and ran and proved their strength and athletic prowess in contests that later became the Olympic games but started out as trials to prove who was worthy to be Moon priestesses, dedicated to the service of the Great Goddess. And she stands for such great religious figures as widely separated as the Navajo's great invincible warrior, The Maiden Who Becomes a Bear and Egypt's armed Goddess, Sekhmet.

More important, she is the image of those very real Amazons of Asia Minor and Africa and their Goddess Artemis/Diana, who is linked in a variety of ways with our conventional symbol for Sagittarius: Chiron the Centaur, the jovial archer who was half-man and half-horse. In the original religious story, the Great Goddess Lato, who was Original Darkness from whom all were born, gave birth to Her daughter Artemis, the Moon. In a later version put forth by patriarchal Greeks, Lato gives birth to twins, Artemis the Moon and Apollo the Sun, and both female deities are far outranked by the male Apollo. The divine twins then go on to educate Chiron the Centaur, who, in turn, educated many Greek heroes and was rewarded by the Greek father god Zeus, who transformed him into the constellation Sagittarius.

However, Chiron resembles Artemis in so many respects that it seems highly likely his image was simply superimposed on the earlier feminine image as more acceptable to the god-worshipping, father-right groups who conquered Goddess-worshipping communities. Artemis was often worshipped as a triple-person Goddess: Mother, Daughter, and Crone, or Grandmother. She was both the Great Huntress and the Protector of Animals. Young girls dressed as bears in festivals held in Her honor; elsewhere, deer, wolves, lions, and of course horses were considered Her sacred animals. She was the Protector of Women in Childbirth, the Healer, the Giver of Swift Merciful Death.

In communities such as the military state of Sparta, where Her worship continued up to the fifth century BC, the life of women was markedly better than in the neighboring patriarchal Greek city-states. Spartan women enjoyed a far greater degree of freedom and equal rights than, say, their Athenian sisters. All female children were permitted to live, but male babies were kept alive only if they were strong and healthy. Spartan girls were well fed and well trained in athletics, military skills, and home management—in contrast to Athenian girls, who were cloistered at home, skimped on their food, and all too frequently died in childbirth. Spartan girls wore short tunics with slit skirts that gave them maximum freedom of movement, quite unlike the long, restrictive costumes of their neighbors. Patriarchal Greeks thought their fashion highly immodest, since it exposed either one or both breasts. However, this baring of breasts was a form of reverence to the Great Mother Goddess whom the Spartans worshipped, in whose image Spartan women believed themselves created.

Outstanding among the many other people who worshipped Artemis are the Amazons, groups governed by and consisting mostly of women who have virtually disappeared in the mists of myth. And yet there they are in art and in historical accounts, dressed in short tunics or, in colder territories, in long trousers and cloaks, but all wore leather armor and high, supple leather boots embroidered with stars and all carried leather shields shaped like the crescent moon and the double-bladed lunar axe of their Goddess. They were excellent horse-women and ferocious fighters, yet they governed the people they conquered so well as to earn their complete loyalty, which was more than Rome could boast of. The thirty cities that Zeus supposedly granted Artemis out of fond indulgence were but a third of the cities known to be Amazon strongholds in Turkey and pre-Hellenic Greece. They usually ruled by a triumvirate of queens: one queen responsible for general administration; one for the arts and sciences; and one for military planning and leadership, and guarding the frontiers.

They treasured honesty and personal freedom above all things and fought fiercely against the rising tide of patriarchy that would transform women from free, independent beings into property owned by their husbands. They particularly hated the patriarchal Greeks. According to Athenian accounts, they laid seige to Athens for four months before finally being driven off. So bitter was the memory of that defeat that many years later Queen Penthesilea brought her elite corps to aid the Trojan king, Priam, against the Athenians, even though Priam himself was a former enemy. Amazonian battle sites, shrines, and burial mounds trace a path from Libya in North Africa across Greece and penetrate far north of the Black Sea. The Amazons fought valiantly but they did not succeed in turning back the historical clock; their defeat was probably due to their limited numbers and to the strains and pressures that their radical style of life imposed. The fact remains that they did try, and we may honor their memories because it would be a sad thing indeed if the subjugation of women were accomplished without a female hand raised in self-defense.

What a magnificent heritage you have! Among your spiritual foremothers you may count Amazon queens with lovely names like Penthesilea, Hippolyta, and Antiope—flesh-and-blood women who preferred to wage war rather than submit to oppression. Their impact upon western Europe and northern Africa was so profound that even when they were finally defeated, their conquerors continued to commemorate them in art. At any rate, the qualities that enabled your foremothers to take great risks and achieve so much are bequeathed to you, and chief among these gifts are foresight, compassion, and a love of freedom and action.

If you wish to read this information in terms of your Moon rather than your Sun, you'll need to shift your thinking from your identity, your will, your essential self—the way you manifest being you in the world—to focus instead on the inner you, the emotional you—your self at the deepest levels of your unconscious. Your Moon not only has to do with your feelings but also those things you take for granted in your self—those things you assume everyone else feels or is like, since they are so essential to your personality. Your Moon gifts might not be the most obvious features in your personality. They are ever present but elusive qualities you know intimately and yet can't quite put your finger on. The Moon also has to do with what went on in your family of origin, your home, your background. It concerns all those things that give you a sense of emotional security.

Specifically, Moon in Sagittarius colors your emotional life with warmth and spontaneity. You are likely to be quite open about expressing your feelings, especially affection and love. A Sagittarian Moon endows you with a responsive imagination and strong intuitive powers. You are quick to perceive how others feel and to empathize with them. You are independent in the sense that you loathe restrictions and limits, but a Sagittarian Moon almost certainly guarantees you are sociable and flourish best in the company of others. You are deeply attached to your family and friends, and rarely view these relationships as restrictive since they are so vital to your well-being. Moon in Sagittarius is expressed in the feminine side of your nature in all sorts of delightful ways. It imparts a buoyant quality to your personality. You tend to be vivacious, enthusiastic, and endowed with a lively sense of humor. You enjoy presenting yourself to best advantage and take good care of your appearance. You will go to great lengths to help others, especially those you care about, and you pay attention to the little details about them, giving freely of your compliments, your encouragement, and your assistance. You have a natural gift for making others feel wonderfully interesting and important, and I can think of no surer way to win friends and influence people. In addition, your Moon in Sagittarius gives you great courage in any effort on behalf of those you love. You will move mountains to get the information, the assistance, the opportunity, whatever is needed, to help your nearest and dearest. Be sure to enlist this incredible energy to further your ambitions and satisfy your needs as well.

Let's begin our discussion of Sun in Sagittarius with the passion for liberty, since it underlies all other qualities you possess, and it would be wise to take this into account in all your decision making. It doesn't mean, by the way, that you're a flibbertigibbet, incapable of making deep commitments to other people. On the contrary, you form very strong attachments and are fiercely loyal to the people you love. The love of freedom affects the nature of your relationships. You're not cut out for playing the submissive-little-woman game, nor are you particularly keen on bossing other people around as if they had no minds of their own. Your relationships with others, whether they're friends, lovers, employers, employees, or children, tend to be partnerships of equals, however much your respective responsibilities vary. For example, you don't expect children to have the self-control or be able to cope with the same responsibilities and problems as an adult, but you nonetheless regard them as individuals who are entitled to their human rights and respect and consideration, and you treat them accordingly. Your employer, for instance, may have more control over the work situation than you do, but that doesn't cloud the fact that she or he is another fallible human being, and you are not too likely to go cringing around your job in terror of your boss.

This independence of spirit can be a useful guide in evaluating situations. If you're having trouble with someone or with a job, or if you're considering entering a new situation, check whether or not it infringes upon your sense of yourself as a free, equal human being. Some jobs are still structured in such a way as to hamper you in salary or in opportunities for advancement, simply because you're a woman. It may be wiser to avoid working in that type of setup or, if the job is sufficiently appealing to override that drawback, to strive within the job against the bias toward women.

It is also recommended that you avoid making your life among humorless people who take themselves in dead earnest. Stuffy, pretentious behavior and very formal situations tend to activate your sense of the ridiculous. You're likely to be spurred to mischievous remarks, to clown around—to do anything, in short, to puncture the pompousness. By the same token, you're not particularly comfortable with people who strive continually to be fashionable in their appearance or in their opinions. Your own activities and tastes are geared very much to your own personal responses and needs, rather than to how you can trade on them as social coin. It may happen that if you've been exposed to a lot of people who treat themselves as if they were steamer trunks and each new book they've read or play they've seen is a new label to slap on as an advertisement of their chic, you may go to the opposite extreme and prefer never to say a word about your own experiences.

Naturally, this independent spirit affects your personal philosophy. You flourish best in an atmosphere of physical and intellectual freedom and, conversely, see little merit in censorship and restraints. You enjoy exploring new ideas and can do a thorough, enthusiastic job of research, provided the ideas can be adapted to practical application. My Sagittarian mother took a business refresher course at a center that also offered job training to handicapped people. During her time there, she not only managed to do splendidly in her work but, by investigating legislation affecting the handicapped, enabled many of her new friends to apply for medical benefits they hadn't known they were entitled to. For me, her action on behalf of her colleagues illustrates two powerful Sagittarian characteristics: the outraged response to injustice and ignorance, and the need to translate that response into effective action. It's a terrific combination, and since ours is far from a perfect world, there's no shortage of opportunities for you to use this gift. Here's to it! And here's to your success in the battle of your choice!

As a fighter, you're not easily discouraged. Once you've set a goal for yourself, you're able to persist in its achievement. More important, you can be flexible in your approach. If one technique doesn't work, you'll try another, and this willingness to experiment works to your advantage in that you learn a great deal in the process. I don't mean that trials and errors are easy for you to bear, because they're not. You do get very impatient, but although this is uncomfortable for you, you can generally convert that impatience into positive effects. You not only try different solutions to a problem, but you'll invent new ones. You also view problems and tasks with an eye to streamlining and simplifying them so that they may be handled as quickly and efficiently as possible. I've found advice from my Sagittarian friends enormously helpful in tackling complicated problems. They've helped me distinguish between the essentials and the frills, and to set up priorities; usually they have suggested several swift techniques for resolving the matters at hand.

On the home front, your impatience prompts you to accomplish your necessary tasks with maximum speed. You may be very competent at housework, but the chances are strong indeed that it's not the love of your life. If you dote on cleaning your home or love and excel at needlework, you may thank something else in your horoscope for these interests and talents. The gifts you receive through Sagittarius are more happily expressed in tackling big jobs such as laying tile, building shelves, or wallpapering a room. You can become extremely skilled at carpentry, home repairs, and interior design; you might wish to consider these as the basis for a freelance business you could operate from your home. As I mentioned, unless there are strong influences to the contrary in your horoscope, you're not particularly inclined to make homemaking your sole, full-time occupation. Besides a basic lack of interest in many of the tasks involved, you're a very sociable person and your need for companionship may not be satisfied by your children, although you love them dearly.

In light of these factors, it may be wise to make homemaking a part-time area of your life. The ways this can be done are myriad. You can pool with other parents in your neighborhood so that each of you gets some absolutely private time per week. If you can afford to, you can hire babysitters, or do as one friend of mine did: she provided room and board to a college student in exchange for child care several hours a week. Or you can work, part time or full time, depending on your preference and situation. That statement may strike you as sounding rather grand, especially since 51 percent of all mothers work and the majority do so out of necessity. The point to keep in mind, really, is that whether it's by choice or necessity, you're not a villain if you leave your children in competent care while you're away from home. There's been a lot of propaganda to the effect that we're depriving our kids if we don't spend every moment with them. It's equally valid, if not more so, to say that if you arrange responsible, sympathetic supervision, your children have gained more people to love and relate to, and you have not only gained the freedom—and the money— essential to you but also have the very valuable benefit of the obser- vations of other adults in relation to your children.

As I have learned from three of the women closest to me—my mother, my sister, Lili, and the sister of my heart, my dearest friend, Rosalee Abrams—a strong Sagittarian influence works to make you an excellent parent—or teacher, or guide to children in any capacity. In addition to your consideration for children's basic rights and your ability to perceive children as distinct personalities, you have an extraordinary ability to nurture. Your own sense of fun enables you to select toys and games and to initiate and guide activities that really delight children. As a parent, you are likely to be unstinting in your concern for your children's happiness and intellectual as well as emotional and physical growth. You will tend to discount the efforts involved in taking your children on trips to museums and other cultural events appropriate to their level, or to the activities that will foster their skills in sports, dance, art, music, or socializing. Your need or wish to work outside your home in no way diminishes or contradicts your ability to be a kind, considerate, generous, and loving parent.

Sagittarius generally endows you with talent and skill in several areas, and you are able to handle more than one major activity at a time. In fact, you probably prefer doing so, and this is made very much easier by your flair for efficiency. Please don't read this as an encouragement to be Superwoman, that amazing being who juggles home and career with the greatest of ease and caps off her day as the unruffled hostess of a dinner party for twelve. As far as I'm concerned, there isn't a gold star big enough to make that sort of effort, and the loss of self it entails, worthwhile for any of us. I'd much rather instead that we learn to ask for help with running the home from all of the people who share our homes. If, for example, a five-year-old can put the dinner napkins on the table, can you imagine what wonders the older members of the family are capable of? In regard to your versatility, it's not a question of proving how much you can do or how splendidly, but of arranging to do those things that give you pleasure and satisfaction without killing yourself in the attempt.

One talent you can put to good use in practically all spheres of your life is your ability to manage money intelligently. You have a knack for constructing a realistic budget—realistic not only in terms of meeting obligations and building assets but emotionally realistic as well, in that you do not impose limits that are too difficult to live with. This enables you to take care of responsibilities and save, without making life insufferably dreary or inviting a big splurge as a reaction against constraint. You share with Aquarians the ability to get excellent value for your money and to be alert to genuine bargains. Big-name labels and chic stores do not impress you in themselves and you're not likely to be paying a 50 percent markup to seem fashionable.

This skill with finances is by no means confined to domestic matters, and it might be worth your while to learn as much as possible about stocks and bonds, accounting, real estate, insurance, taxes—anything, in short, having to do with money. If you're at home and can't work, or choose not to, you might direct your volunteer efforts toward being a club treasurer or learning everything you can about the legal and financial end of running a home. That experience can serve you well when you do decide to work outside your home. And let's face it, there's hardly an area of life today that is not involved with money—and that includes charities, churches and synagogues and temples, and certainly politics. It's been thought to be terribly cute for a woman to be utterly baffled by the enormous task of balancing her checkbook. Yes, indeed—very feminine, very charming—and very powerless. If our great-great-grandmothers were around to witness any of us going through an eye-fluttering routine like that, they'd give us a swift boot in the rear and tell us to smarten up. No one who wants to open a business, or go freelance, or manage her family's budget, or advance in a career, or launch a community project can afford to be cute. As women, we're the best judges of what's feminine, and there's no reason for us to cooperate with images that limit our effectiveness. My advice to you is to start reading the financial pages of your newspapers and magazines, subscribe to the *Wall Street Journal,* take a course in money management, and back up your native ability with as much experience and information as you can lay your hand to.

Another talent you have that ties in well with your financial shrewdness is the ability to promote and administer enterprises. These can range from community-oriented projects such as setting up a library, a reading program, or foster care for the elderly to political and industrial ventures. You name it. Sagittarius can plan it, run it, get funds to back it, and have a terrific time in the process. A Sagittarian Sun is bound to give you a phenomenal talent for strategy, and you may as well put that to good use, because it won't go away if ignored or thwarted; it'll simply divert itself into seeing schemes where there are none and running your personal affairs as if you were Napoleon plotting army maneuvers. Obviously, it's a large talent and it needs plenty of room and worthwhile goals. Many of the things you think are just plain idiotic about the way the world is run can be changed—by you. Ally yourself with the causes and projects that appeal to you, and I'll bet that after you've served your apprenticeship and learned how things have been done, you'll be getting into the planning yourself.

Your strategic gifts are closely related to the gift of foresight, which is also characteristic of Sagittarius. In the classic pose of the Amazon Artemis, like that of the traditional centaur archer, She moves forward while glancing backward. Sagittarius learns from history, but moves on—learns from the past without brooding over what's been done and without ignoring the present and the future. As a matter of fact, Sagittarius sharpens your intuition, and you generally have very accurate fantasies and dreams. Without going into the whole field of psychic experience, let's say that you're able to learn the essentials in human behavior from your past experience and to project them very accurately into the future, and you will often be able to predict outcomes in personal relations, business ventures, and politics.

Personally, I think that you should pay very close attention to your dreams and fantasies. These are, after all, messages to ourselves that come from deep within ourselves. I'm not especially fond of the Freudian school of dream interpretation, which seems to impose a rather arbitrary system of symbols—and values—upon our experiences. I've found the Gestalt technique more useful, myself. It's discussed rather fully in *Gestalt Therapy Verbatim*, by F. S. Perls; briefly summarized, it consists of going through each dream from the alternative viewpoints offered within the dream—of being the other things or people you've dreamed about and recovering their messages, which are frequently bizarre in their presentation. For example, if you have a dream about a car, you might try to be the car instead of the dreamer; as you imagine yourself as the car going through the dream's action, you may very probably learn what you meant by that car. This may or may not work for you. At any rate, I suggest that you make it a practice to note your dreams—for a while, at least—and see if you can become familiar with your own symbol system.

The attention you pay to your dreams can serve as an excellent balance to your drive for action. Many times you subconsciously know the consequences of a relationship or an action, but are so hell-bent on doing something that you ignore your inner signals. This is especially true in regard to people, because one thing Sagittarius gives you is insight into other people's character. You know when people are insincere or trying to impose on you, and when you allow yourself to recognize this, you're usually able to divert their attempts to take advantage of you very gracefully, indeed. Ill feelings are actually kept to a minimum when you acknowledge your inner feelings and, for that reason alone, you should heed them. The two major obstacles to your paying attention to your own observations are your ardent wish that the person or the situation involved be what you wanted, or your belief that she, he, or it is your only chance at what you want. Let's look at the first of these delusions. Despite our zealous efforts to the contrary, wishing isn't going to make it so. There are some folks and some situations that are just plain bummers, at least in relation to ourselves, which is all we have to go on in this life. And these sorts of investments, which represent a lot of effort and tears and feelings of worthlessness, ultimately are nothing but hindrances to getting what you do want. Now the second unhelpful belief. In reality, you'll have plenty of options—and plenty of surprises—in your life, and you can get what you want.

I know this is all very easy to say and hard to act upon. And I can't tell you what a pleasure it is to be sitting here at the typewriter, recollecting in tranquillity, instead of being in the middle of one of those difficult situations. May the Goddess be kind to me and help me not to succumb to another of those dead-end routines. May She be kind to you, and help you to listen to your own inner voice, which can tell you the story a whole lot more accurately than I can. Needless to say, your intuitive powers sharpen the more you exercise them. What may begin as a high incidence of lucky hunches can develop into a real shrewdness in predicting the outcome of events—not a bad skill to have if, for example, you were playing the stock market!

Given your preference for a busy, active life, it's fortunate that you also have a high energy level and a great deal of endurance. Your energy, of course, has slumps—everyone's does—but you find it difficult and bewildering when these set in. In the same way, you tend to react to illness as if it were a personal affront and you can be careless about your health. Your distaste for sickness is so intense that you are often tempted to ignore problems in the hope that they will simply disappear. This impatience generally extends to members of the medical profession, whom you tend to regard with great distrust. While it is true that these people are not magicians, and there is a great deal yet to be known about treating disease, it is still not the wisest course to dismiss them entirely. You can, however, check a doctor's credentials before selecting her or him as your physician. And you can most certainly make it clear that you expect complete, candid information as one adult to another. There's no reason why any of us should permit that medical mystique designed to enhance the physicians' status to deprive us of honest information. We don't hire physicians to act in the place of our parents, to call us "dear girl," or to soothe us with misleading tidbits such as that removing an ovarian cyst will cause "a little discomfort" when, in fact, it usually means we'll have considerable pain for quite a few weeks. That sort of thing does not really soothe us; it leaves us unprepared for the realities of our situation and causes us to doubt and distrust our own reactions. Granted, we don't need that and we don't need to put up with it, but nevertheless, you could try to be a little less cavalier about your health and goad yourself to check out difficulties early rather than later.

As I said before, you're a physically active person, and the periods when you slow down generally puzzle you. On an annual basis, your peak period is late fall and early winter, followed by generally even, medium energy levels during spring and summer. Early fall is the low point of your year; it feels hard for you to "rev" up and you may be astonished at how exhausted you feel. Remember that these slumps are not peculiar to you; we all experience them, and there's little to be gained by pushing yourself contrary to your natural inclination, unless you absolutely must. It actually works to your advantage to accommodate the slack periods by tending only to absolute essentials. I know that this is especially irritating when you're in the middle of a big project. It's a Sagittarian trait to launch an undertaking all fired up with energy and enthusiasm, and to have the expectation that this high level of interest and energy will last for the duration. It often doesn't, because we're not static beings, but there's no need to bemoan your lassitude or to worry that you'll never stir again, because you assuredly will. If you can treat your slow times as little vacations, you will be rewarded by renewed physical and creative energy.

On a monthly basis, a Sagittarian transit of the Moon starts you off feeling most comfortable with yourself, because it usually charges you with great physical and mental energy. It's a period during which you're rich in ideas and have the physical wherewithal to carry them out. The Capricorn transit maintains this happy blend of energy and is particularly helpful in regard to organizing your work, becoming aware of the details involved in a project, and planning how to handle them. Aquarius is also very positive, although your physical energy drops a little from the Sagittarian high. It's a good period for overall review and for research, and it usually brings a sharp increase in your already excellent ability to make long-range plans. The Pisces transit that follows is rather difficult, in contrast. There's generally a marked slump in physical energy and you may find yourself feeling irritable and pessimistic. I see this as a period in which you need to relax and have more privacy. To your great relief, the next transit, Aries, brings another strong rush of physical energy. You are inclined to be more than usually sociable during this period, and it would make for the best of all possible worlds if you could arrange your entertaining schedule to mesh with Aries transits. Taurus is a very workable transit; it stimulates your pleasure in being outdoors, and you need only watch out that you're not forced to be housebound during this period. Gemini transits generally emphasize your desire to be with and do things with the people closest to you. You're not particularly keen on socializing, per se, but you do enjoy excursions with your family and most intimate friends.

Cancer transits are very difficult for you. They are particularly bewildering in that you tend to feel as if you've lost interest in everything, and they are usually the periods in which your physical energy is at its lowest ebb. They are do-nothing times when you need to be particularly careful not to push yourself beyond your strength. They don't last forever, and they might be more bearable if you treat them as recuperative periods, which seem to be what they are. You'll feel very much your usual self when the Leo transit rolls around; the only thing you need to watch out for then is that, in your relief at being active and alert again, you don't take on so much that you wear yourself out. Virgo transits are milder in that your energy level is medium rather than high. But they're comfortable times in which life seems to be rolling along quite smoothly and you are able to take things very much in stride. Their extra benefit is that they, too, are excellent periods in which to review the past and make long-term plans. Libra ushers in a more frivolous interval. You're not likely to be interested in anything too serious, but you'll have plenty of energy for lighthearted activities. They form a nice balance to the Scorpio transit, which concludes your cycle and which is definitely a serious period for you; not that it's grim, by any means, but it is a time when you're more concerned with serious issues and are best able to reevaluate relationships and plans.

Your energy is the sort that needs to be balanced between physical and intellectual outlets. Strictly intellectual work, particularly if it's sedentary, makes you intensely restless and brings on the sort of fatigue not easily or completely refreshed by sleep. It would be well for you to provide yourself with outlets for your physical energy. There is certainly no dearth of activities to choose from: backpacking, hiking, swimming, tennis, a hard bout of housework, gardening, karate lessons; the list could go on and on, and of course there's no need to confine yourself to one activity only. The point is, you need variety and physical activity; it only remains for you to choose the things you like to do and then do them. Sports or projects that require real physical effort are particularly good in that they absorb your attention while you're involved with them, and therefore they offer you a real rest from your other concerns. Just as some people review a problem before they go to sleep and then wake up with the solution, matters most frequently straighten themselves out in your thinking after you've diverted your attention from them with a rousing bout of physical exertion.

In terms of your larger cycles, the issue that you consciously and unconsciously are working out is the matter of voluntary versus involuntary dependence on other people. Throughout your life, you are a friendly, open person who prefers companionship to solitude. In your youth, however, it may be difficult for you to reconcile your desire for independence with your attachments to your family and friends. Since your attachments are very strong, you may feel swamped by them, as if you're living primarily in response to other people's expectations. The fact that others see you as an independent being, fully equipped with your own tastes and opinions, is very little comfort while you are experiencing yourself as a superdependent person. This state of affairs generally starts to ease up in your late twenties and early thirties, but, like all transitional periods, it can be a bewildering time. You may find that a lot of anger and distrust surfaces during this period and that much of that stems from the necessity to put some psychic distance between yourself and the people you're closest to. There's no denying that these feelings can be very frightening, especially since they can rouse the fear that your relationships will disintegrate entirely. It certainly is a period in which you may feel on guard much of the time, to prevent encroachments on your self. Hard as it is, it's worth it, and when you consider the alternative, there really is no other course. You're not likely to want to subside silently into a sense of dependency, which you'll only resent and, what's worse, disrespect yourself for. Better to press on, to say no firmly instead of giving in to yes when you don't want to, to keep your personal affairs private and not feel compelled to give an account of yourself when asked. The rewards for your efforts are immense: you not only clarify—to yourself—who you are but you usually find that your relationships with the people you really love are much richer and deeper precisely because they are on a voluntary, adult basis. And once you are free from the burdensome misconception that you must live to please others, you are able to seek out those relationships that genuinely support and nurture you on an adult level.

In line with this, there's a marked improvement in your sexual relationships once you've attained a strong, clear sense of yourself. Let it be said that, with a strong Sagittarian influence, there are very few times indeed when you're without a partner. You have a basic nonchalance about sex, a recognition that it figures as a strong need and that your partner must be a loving, affectionate, loyal companion. However, the problem is that you may find yourself with a talent for choosing the "wrong" people—people who deny you, who make you feel even more helpless and dependent, who aggravate rather than help matters. When you've sorted out your own identity, you no longer labor under the idea that unhappiness and suffering are staples in any love affair. You can arrive at the delightful realization that not only do you want to be happy with your partner but this is a perfectly reasonable expectation and it is possible to find someone you are really compatible with. Once that idea has hold of you, you will not settle for anything less. The courage to be yourself, which may be the hardest task any of us face, enables you to take another great risk: to love someone else deeply and to share your life as you've longed to, in genuine intimacy.

Your optimism also matures. There's little left of wishful thinking; your personal victory builds instead a great reservoir of courage and spirit to see life realistically and yet to concentrate on its positive aspects. This bears no relationship whatsoever to some simpleminded Pollyanna routine. It is founded on tremendous discipline and conscious choices to direct your energies toward the real joys and satisfactions your relationships and work offer. It also means that you are very likely to take great risks, deliberately. Although you have a very strong sense of adventure, this doesn't mean that you live like a daredevil, leaping from one peril to the next and stirring up melodramas when life seems tame. It does mean that you may embark on commitments or actions that others regard as too difficult or too chancy, once you've decided that the hazards involved are outweighed by the emotional and intellectual fulfillment possible.

One result of this is that you are frequently an inspiration to other people—and you're probably not aware of it. Your own enthusiasm freshens other people's hopes and encourages them to see life in terms of its options rather than its limitations. Your courage spurs others to find and use their own. Your sensitivity and insight enable you to give profoundly of yourself to the people you care for, which you need to do, and in turn teaches them a great deal about human nature. The gifts you receive from Sagittarius are not static quantities; they gain in depth and range as you grow older. You will continue to have much of great value to share when you are an elder in your family and in your community. Your battles will be for your own independence and then to win just treatment and the right to self-determination for others. You may not have to ride into actual battle as your ancient grandmothers did, but you can be a great warrior in your own right—one of whom they would be very proud.

SAGITTARIUS VISUALIZATIONS

You possess an extraordinary resource within you: your imagination. Through the power of your inward eye, you can tap into your innermost self, and into the energies of the universe. The thoughts you think, the messages you give yourself, the images you create in your imagination have tremendous power. You can literally transform your reality to fit the positive images you create mentally simply by creating those images often enough, and as specifically and clearly as you possibly can. Through such focused, purposeful "daydreaming," you can achieve an astonishing range of goals: practical goals such as weight loss, physical fitness, or money management; spiritual goals such as enhanced self-esteem, inner peace, and a deeper sense of connection with other living beings. For further information on this process, I recommend two books I've found useful, Shakti Gawain's *Creative Visualization,* and Shad Helmstetter's *The Self-Talk Solution.*

My primary concern here is empowering you to get in touch with the Goddess within you, the Eternal Feminine whose creative, nurturing, renewing energies live within us all. The Great Goddess is always ready to comfort, to heal, to strengthen, and to guide us whenever we are in need. Her images come to us from all parts of our world and from across great stretches of time. By visualizing Her in our mind's eye, by meditating on Her image, you and I not only receive help with specific problems and enhanced self-esteem but also reap the additional benefit of greater esteem for *all* women, past and present, and for the wonderful contributions women have made in creating and advancing civilization.

The images I sketch for you came to me through my research and through my own meditations. They may work differently for you than I've envisioned. And, of course, they're not the only images available to you. I suggest you read Merlin Stone's *Ancient Mirrors of Womanhood* and Barbara G. Walker's *The Woman's Encyclopedia of Myths and Secrets* to see what stories, prayers, and images resonate for you, and use them. I think you'll also find it illuminating simply to gaze within your own mind and see how the Goddess manifests Herself to you. I would be delighted to read your visualization experiences so if you would like to share them, please write to me, c/o the publisher.

How to go about visualization is very much a matter of personal choice: you may sit, stand, or lie down—whichever position you feel you can most comfortably maintain for ten to twenty minutes. You're probably best advised to be in a quiet, darkened room and to keep your eyes closed. Begin by relaxing your entire body. One technique is to imagine a comfortably warm, golden light surrounding you and taking away all tension in the area you're thinking of. Start with your feet and work up to the crown of your head. Once this is done, begin to construct your visualization in your mind.

There are so many wonderful images of the Great Goddess for you to work with that it is hard to select among them. Let us start with your need for freedom and the fact that life, being what it is for most of us, is bound to have you chafing at your restrictions from time to time. At such moments, you may call forth the image of the Goddess as the Great Mare, known as Macha in Ireland and Epona in Celtic Europe. Among the Goddess's many powers was that of shape-changer. She could appear as a human woman or as any shape She chose—in this instance, a horse. In your need for freedom and movement, She will stand still for you and allow you to mount Her. And there you are, in your mind's eye, utterly safe and yet mounted on the most powerful, swiftest horse in the world. The skill of the Goddess will transfer to you, and even if you have never ridden before, you are now completely at ease on horseback. Ride where you will. Perhaps you will race across the Great Plains when that land was young and unsettled, stretching out before you as miles upon miles of golden grass. Perhaps you will race across the moors of Britain, or the warm sandy stretches of North Africa at the foot of the Atlas Mountains, or across the vast steppes of Russia. Wherever you choose to go, you are filled with the exhilaration of speed as the Great Mare flys like the wind across boundless, sun-drenched space. You are completely free, the whole world lies before you, and all sense of restriction falls away from you. As you come to the end of your visualization, the Goddess slows to a walk and brings you to the site of your choice to dismount. You slide off Her back easily and are once again on solid ground. Perhaps She changes before your eyes into the Great Goddess of the Celts, standing tall before you in richly embroidered cloaks of deep blue and purple, Her hair rippling in silken waves to Her ankles. Her eyes may be gray as the mist, blue as the sky, brown as the earth, green as the ocean. She smiles upon you, brushing your hair from your face, and then She is gone. You remain, refreshed as if your soul had bathed in the purest waters of a forest spring, ready once more to live within the framework of your life.

Sagittarians are celebrated for their candor, but there are times when you regret this gift and would prefer to restrain your words. In situations where the old adage "least said, soonest mended" applies, call to mind a vision of the Great Goddess of India as the Divine Mare, who holds in Her mouth the fires of anger and passion and in Her mercy lives deep within the sea to avoid scorching the earth and destroying the creatures of the land. Imitate Her and in imagination sink beneath the waves to cool the hot words that come flooding to your lips. Let them pour forth into the water to sizzle and cool. Then reemerge, restored in your ability to choose what you say and to communicate in the least destructive way possible.

There are times when even the generous spirit of Sagittarius shrivels in the withering blasts of jealousy and envy. When you are besieged by such feelings, when it seems that what others possess is better or more than yours, and you lose your awareness of the richness of your own life, turn to the Welsh Goddess, Rhiannon, for help. Rhiannon rides a magical white horse and carries the Magic Bag of Abundance. She lifts you up beside Her to ride through Her enchanted island where nature is at its most beautiful. Her horse moves gently through forests and beside beautiful streams, and you are soothed by the peacefulness all around you and filled with a sense of Rhiannon's great love for you as a child of Her spirit. You come to a lovely meadow where deer graze quietly and rabbits play in complete safety. Rhiannon lifts you down to sit among the flowers, and She takes the Magic Bag of Abundance and invites you to open it. You loosen the strings so that the sack falls open. And there before you is a vision of the riches of the world, all the love and health and beauty as well as material goods—as much and more than you have ever imagined. You see that there is more than enough for you, more than enough for everyone, and you quietly look among these treasures, realizing which ones have real meaning and value for you. You see also your own life and all that is valuable to you. As you examine what you have and what you want, you become aware that you will not be stinted in life. You may have as much as you really want. The Goddess does not favor others over you; you are equally Her child and She offers you the gifts best for you. Allow your spirit to expand within you, supported by love and by your awareness of the abundance of life, and all the possibilities that life holds for you.

From the Celts comes yet another image that may serve you when the tasks before you seem too much for your strength. It is then you might visualize the Scots' Goddess, Caillech Bheur, who sometimes appeared as the Great Gray Mare but at other times as the Old Woman Who Moves Mountains. This Crone, or Grandmother, aspect of the triple-personed Goddess was credited with building Stonehenge and other Neolithic stone monuments to the Goddess. The Scots believed that She carried the huge stones in Her apron. Surely She will walk with you, holding your hand in Hers that has accomplished so much. Perhaps, in your mind's eye, you will visit Stonehenge, standing in awe before the great stones that dwarf us humans. Perhaps you will see the outline of the Goddess as the Great Mare on England's chalk cliffs. It may be that Caillech Bheur will gift you with a vision of your human sisters who, from the beginning of time, worked in so many ways to create our civilization. Perhaps, in the serenity that comes from a walk with the Goddess, you will be blessed with ideas of how to cope best with your task, how to simplify it, how to inspire others to help you. At the very least, you will feel uplifted in the knowledge that the Goddess has added Her strength to yours and is ready to assist and guide you whenever you need Her.

When you are weary of routine and long for adventure, you may choose to envision the Roman and Celtic version of the Goddess Artemis, Diana the Silver Huntress, who as the Moon skims along on Her silver feet through the night sky. Imagine yourself bathed in silver light. Diana reaches Her hand to you and lifts you up into the heavens, to run by Her side through black and silver clouds and shimmering stars, far above the sleeping cities of the earth. The world below you seems small and yet infinitely precious. You stretch and leap and run with joy, as fleet as the swiftest deer, as silent as the jaguar, as radiant as if Diana had transformed you into moonbeams. Return from your meditation with the sparkle of this vision still within you.

Your Sagittarian independence of spirit may bring difficulties to you in the form of pressure from others to conform to their ideas of how you should be and what you should do. It is essential for all of us to be true to ourselves, and this is particularly vital for you. At such times in your life, it may help you to envision the Great Goddess Artemis, who teaches us to value our personal integrity and freedom. Images of Artemis have the added power of your element, fire. You may choose to meditate upon Her as Diana bearing the Torch of Enlightenment. You may choose instead to join, in imagination, one of the great festivals in honor of Artemis. It is early evening. You stand before the Temple of Artemis, waiting your turn to receive your lighted torch, consecrated to Artemis, from one of the priestesses. You claim your torch and join the procession that wends its way up the mountain. People walk quietly; like them, you too are quiet, serious, and yet filled with great joy. Night closes in and the only lights now are the silent stars, the pale young crescent moon, and the flames of the torches. When you reach the top of the mountain there is a leveled space, at the center of which is a great bonfire. Like the others, you bring your torch to the center and add it to the flames, watching as it flares up in the mightier fire. You look around you; across the plains, on other mountaintops, great bonfires are also burning. You are aware of yourself as a distinct individual yet part of the many who value honesty and knowledge and personal freedom. Your thoughts and prayers swirl up in your mind like sparks from a fire. Perhaps you see your personal path more clearly, perhaps you draw courage from those who have made their own way before you and those who do so even now, or perhaps you become aware of the ideals of the Goddess as a warmth glowing within you. However you choose to partake of the Enlightenment of Artemis, you return from this visualization cheered and revitalized.

CAPRICORN

December 22–January 19

CAPRICORN: China's Kuan-Yin, Goddess of Mercy, portrayed with twelve hands to represent the gifts She gave to humanity each month of the twelve-month solar-lunar year. Based on an eighteenth-century Chinese wood carving and on an eighteenth-century scroll painting, preserved in the Wellcome Institute of Medicine, London.

Your sign, Capricorn, has a very beautiful story to tell us and its message contains the key idea of the zodiac. It is an ancient story, dating back to 3000 BC at least, when people throughout the world worshipped the Great Mother, or Great Goddess. We humans have always tried to capture everything, even the most complex abstract ideas, as precisely as possible in words, and so we gave many names and titles to the Goddess in our efforts to honor each of Her attributes and powers. Every object or living creature that reminded us of Her in some way was also used as a symbol for Her. That we developed the skill to see patterns within the stars and make a map of the night sky was a tremendous accomplishment, and we weren't about to use just any old image for those patterns. Instead, we identified the constellations with images that already had enormous religious significance for us. Each sign of the zodiac, then, is an important symbol commemorating particular gifts we received from the Great Goddess. But it was Capricorn itself which celebrated the Goddess as Gift Giver, as the source of all life and all our blessings. The particular blessing emphasized in Capricorn was the Goddess as Healer, and the priestesses who served in Her name as our world's first doctors, surgeons, pharmacists, and medical teachers.

Originally, Capricorn appeared in the earliest zodiacs of ancient Egypt and Babylonia as a creature consisting of the body of a fish with the torso and head of a goat. In ancient China, Capricorn's symbol was, first, the crescent horns of the moon in their lunar zodiac, and then the dolphin in their solar zodiac. However, goat, fish, dolphin, moon—all began as symbols of the Goddess and Her bounty. To learn more about the fish-dolphin image, see Pisces; for information on the moon, consult Cancer.

Since the name Capricorn means "the Horn of the Goat," let us focus here on the Goat as symbol. It was the totem animal of priestesses devoted to the medical arts, whose mountain shrines to the Goddess served also as hospitals, surgeries, pharmacies, and medical colleges. They chose it, no doubt, because the nimble, surefooted, brave little animal lived in mountainous terrain. Another reason was that it is a milk giver and, like the cow which women had also tamed, symbolized the milk of the Great Goddess, which She sent in the form of dew and rain. Its horns represented the crescent phases of the Goddess as Moon.

The story traditionally told of Capricorn comes to us from Hellenic Greece after the Greeks had reorganized themselves into patriarchies and male gods had either replaced or overshadowed the Goddess. According to "classical" myth, the god Zeus was the child of the god Kronos and his sister Rhea, "She of the Sacred Oak." Kronos not only was an incestuous old crank, but he lived in terror that one of his children would one day overthrow him, a problem he solved by devouring them as soon as they were born. Unhappy Rhea determined to outwit him and when Zeus was born, She hid him and swaddled a stone in his stead, which Kronos promptly gulped down. Rhea then whisked baby Zeus off to the mountains of Crete where he was raised by a compassionate goat named Amaltheia and her sisters. She fed him a diet of milk and honey, and Zeus flourished under her care, growing up to be a powerful young god who then returned home, killed his father, and set himself up as the "Father of the Gods." In gratitude to Amaltheia for her kindness to him, he fixed her image among the stars as Capricorn. And as Robert Graves points out in his *Greek Myths*, "He also borrowed one of her horns . . . which became the famous cornucopia, or horn of plenty . . . always filled with whatever food or drink its owner may desire."

The facts are that Zeus originated in Crete as a very minor deity. Amaltheia and her sisters were not goats at all, but medical priestesses who served the Great Goddess Rhea/Aegea, whose title "She of the Sacred Oak" refers to Her powers as healer. One reason oaks were sacred was that they supported the mistletoe plant used in religious rites and medicinally as a cure-all in virtually every order of priestess-healers. This plant was known to Greeks and Africans as *asclepius*, "that which hangs from the sacred oak." Ironically, under patriarchy, Asclepius became the "Father of Medicine," and acquired as his symbol the staff entwined with serpents that belonged originally to the priestesses. He was also given a nearly brand-new life story: that as an infant he was nursed by goats on a mountain renowned for its medicinal plants, and that he grew up to be skilled in surgery and the use of drugs. The Goddess Athena was so pleased with him, so touched by his compassion for others, that She gave him two phials of the blood of the gorgon Medusa. The blood from the left, or feminine side, was so powerful it could restore the dead to life; that from the right, or masculine side, could destroy anyone or anything. From then on, Asclepius was an exemplary doctor, assisted in the routine, unimportant tasks by his daughter Hygeia, or Health.

Like the Capricorn story, this illustrates how the new religion borrowed features of the old and converted them to its purposes. The Amazonian Gorgons of North Africa worshipped the Great Goddess Athena/Aegea/Hygeia. Her name Hygeia honored the wonderful cures She brought about through the efforts of Her priestesses. From Her name Aegea, we get the Aegean Sea and our word *aegis*, meaning protection and guidance. The *aegis*, however, was first a goatskin apron worn by medical priestesses. It was trimmed with cowrie shells—which resemble the vagina and reminded people of the sacred "gateway to life"—and with thongs to represent the serpents—symbolic of the Goddess's dominion over inner earth, the realm of the dead. The *aegis* was also a goatskin shield painted with the awe-inspiring face of Medusa, Her hair the thirteen snakes of the lunar year, Her eyes bulging, Her tongue protruding—a face that supposedly could turn men to stone. This shield warned people that they were in the presence of a person, or medical facility, or city under the protection of the divine power of the Goddess.

Zeus is not the only one who owes a debt of gratitude to Capricorn. Our word *medicine* originally meant "knowledge of the wise woman"; across the ancient world, from what is now Great Britain in the West to Japan in the East, people were indebted to those wise women healers who set broken bones, revived people from comas, cured illnesses, helped women in childbirth, anesthetized those in pain, and performed complex, delicate operations with consummate skill. The medicines they developed are still useful today and were in fact unrivaled until this century, when we developed sulfa and antibiotics. The sacred Horn of the Goat, used as a holy vessel for religious beverages and liquid medicines, symbolized the compassion of the Goddess and Her endless gifts to us grateful humans. Needless to say, you receive a very, very rich heritage indeed through Capricorn.

If you wish to read this information in terms of your Moon rather than your Sun, you'll need to shift your thinking from your identity, your will, your essential self—the way you manifest being you in the world—to focus instead on the inner you, the emotional you—your self at the deepest levels of your unconscious. Your Moon not only has to do with your feelings but also includes those things you take for granted in your self—those things you assume everyone else feels or is like, since they are so essential to your personality. Your Moon gifts might not be the most obvious features in your personality. They are ever present but elusive qualities you know intimately and yet can't quite put your finger on. The Moon also has to do with what went on in your family of origin, your home, your background. It concerns all those things that give you a sense of emotional security.

Specifically, Moon in Capricorn endows you with a highly creative imagination. It also prompts you to be reserved in your emotional responses. Only your very closest family and friends will be permitted into your confidence and allowed to know how you really feel. On the surface, you appear even-tempered, courteous, and friendly, all of which are the result of the almost ever-present discipline you exert over your feelings. Underneath this cheerful exterior, you are warm-hearted, sentimental, and tender. You are not only wary of your softer side but also downright harsh toward yourself when your efforts don't succeed as you think they should. Meditation can be a considerable help in rescuing you from the gloom and melancholy that engulf you. Your Capricorn Moon is expressed in the feminine side of your nature through a combination of qualities, some of which may bring you into conflict with our traditional definition of what's feminine. For example, your Capricorn Moon endows you with a strong component of ambition, a desire to succeed and stand well in the world's judgment. Although ambition is finally being acknowledged and increasingly accepted in women, it's never been listed with "sugar and spice and everything nice" as one of our basic ingredients. You may be tempted to project this onto others, such as your partner or children. Resist this temptation with every ounce of the considerable discipline at your command. Another quality that may be difficult is a certain zest for competition, for winning by your wits, and this, too, will repay your efforts to give it scope in your life. You are also gifted with the ability to endure, to make the best of things, to be steadfast in your relationships and in times of trouble. More "socially acceptable" feminine traits are your desire to help people in need, especially in times of illness, and your pleasure and generosity in offering hospitality, particularly cooking for others. Exercise caution with your tendency to place other people's needs before your own.

The first gift—which to my mind is never sufficiently stressed in discussing Sun in Capricorn—is the tremendous creative energy it bestows upon you. In those areas that interest you, you are rarely satisfied to remain at a basic level of competence, but will push on to gain further skill and information and, especially, to begin to create on your own. Joan Williams, my friend Pamela's mother, was a Capricorn who beautifully illustrated this capacity. Not only did she have a great interest and talent for music but she carried her many hobbies to a level far beyond the amateur. Her embroidery could easily be displayed in England's Royal Academy of Needle Arts. She mastered the art of knitting to such a high degree that she was able to devise her own patterns, and her original designs were sought after at craft fairs. She was fond of birdwatching, and if she heard a song she didn't recognize, she would first get out her binoculars to see the songster more clearly and then turn to her books on birds to identify him, happy with a new song and new knowledge. My friend Caroline Pintoff also comes to mind as an example of this Capricorn trait. When she became interested in sewing as a hobby, she first learned the basic skills and then went on to study pattern making to master the principles of construction and then translated her own ideas of fashion into actual garments.

Like Sagittarians, you find abstract ideas most attractive if they can be transformed into concrete realities and solid accomplishments. It is a necessity for you to feel that you've made some mark on life, that you have in some way—private or public—extended your talents to serve larger concerns than personal gratification. You must make and do and learn and create, and your activities gain a special dimension if you feel that they will make life better for other people as well as yourself. Your creativity is linked to many other things, among them the need to live an exciting life. Excitement for you, however, is not just a matter of having a night on the town or partying, although these are welcome in their place. You have little tolerance for humdrum routine and, fortunately, are a self-generating, resourceful person. You're not likely to sit around waiting for external events to combine into patterns that interest you. When things get dull, you'll initiate projects of your own. It stimulates you to confront the challenges of new ideas or problems, to develop fresh projects based on old skills, or to set out in quest of new skills to implement your ideas.

What I found most impressive about the creativity linked with Capricorn is that it is connected to a series of traits that work to make those personal ventures very effective. For example, as I'm sure you've read before, you have an amazing capacity to organize and to exercise authority. Well, what does that mean? A great deal more than neat closets or simply getting the particular job done. It means that you have at your disposal the very things that will best help you realize your ideas. In effect, you will not be working against your temperament, as so many of us have to do, in order to achieve what you wish. People often labor under a simplified notion of what creativity is all about, as if it's simply a matter of having an idea and, lo and behold, it's now a fact. No idea, no matter how fascinating it is in itself, is so easily or glamorously translated into reality. There are always less-than-fascinating details to tend to; there is frequently a great deal of hard work and not all of it is necessarily absorbing.

The act of creation is, in a certain sense, a process of establishing order from chaos. Imagine how it is for a writer of fiction. Think of the parade of characters that present themselves, the events and complications that could spin off, the amount of selection that a writer must exercise. Any creative act involves deciding what to proceed with and what to leave out, and how to marshal your materials so that you can accomplish what you set out to do, but yet not be so rigid that you learn nothing new as you go along. Obviously, this involves a fine balance between knowing when to control and when to be receptive. You know how to sketch out a scheme of work from start to finish and then portion its separate parts into smaller units. This skill enables you to use time well and to tend to details and small tasks during your spare moments. You also are able to delegate responsibilities so that your time is freed to concentrate on accomplishing the work you really want to do or feel must be done by you personally. Your organizational gifts become stronger the more you exercise them, and you can eventually make plans or execute projects on a really grand scale, perhaps because you know how to keep your plans from becoming overwhelming.

One Capricorn friend of mine is an excellent example of this combination of creative and organizational talents. She started out as a music teacher in a public school and began to create new opportunities for herself and her students to use their talents. First she introduced a corridor show of Christmas caroling, which became an annual tradition; then she went on to organize talent shows and special programs. These efforts were not only hugely successful but they also encouraged her to branch into children's theater in her after-school hours. She researched how to apply for federal funds for the arts and was able to promote her project into semiprofessional status; it provided a valuable training ground for talented children and gave even the strict amateurs a much needed outlet for their energies. I remember that she would sit down for a coffee break and manage to sketch out a program while relaxing with the rest of us; from her I learned that one could take care of details at odd moments, so that even a large task need not loom as beyond one's scope.

Your need to create, to shape and direct your energies into tangible results, makes you more than usually alert to see opportunities and utilize them to the utmost. It is your natural inclination to assess activities and situations in terms of their future potential, and you prefer those that are dynamic rather than static. Capricorn has been described as overwhelmingly ambitious, and perhaps that's how it works in some horoscopes. It seems to me, however, that the motive for that ambition is to extend your knowledge and capabilities, and if that can bring you material rewards as well—why not? More power to you!

This seems a good place to review the premise of this book: that we, too, are dynamic rather than static beings. Your Capricorn influence is not going to work the same way every day or be of the same strength throughout the month and year. There'll be plenty of times when you'll feel very *un*creative or when you couldn't care less about managing anything more complex than having a good read on the sofa. We all experience such fluctuations, and you can imagine that if you are putting a tremendous amount of energy into the process of creation and into organizing matters so you can realize your plans, it stands to reason that you will need time off, since these drives demand a lot from you.

In terms of your annual cycle, your high point is winter and early spring, dropping to a lull in late spring and balancing into a steady, smooth flow during the rest of the year. The low period can be boring for you in that you may feel fatigued and fidgety simultaneously. You may want to do something or, more likely, want to be interested in doing something, and just not be able to get yourself going. If possible, try not to force yourself, and cooperate instead with the sense of physical lassitude. I firmly believe that if we obey our inner signals, these periods can work to our very great advantage. Slow down then, if it's at all possible, and let yourself just mosey around for a while. For all you and I know, these periods may be the time when the experience you've gained during the past year is coming together in a new way for you in much the same way that our dreams sort out daily experience, and you can emerge from the interval feeling revitalized, as if from a special kind of sleep or dormancy.

On a monthly basis, you're most likely to feel in harmony with yourself and the world when the Moon transits the earth signs—your own Capricorn, and Taurus and Virgo. The water transits—Pisces and Scorpio—also affect you well, although Cancer may be a bit tricky and may encourage negative thoughts. Otherwise, these transits evoke a sense of excitement and you are most aware of the spiritual dimension in your thoughts and plans, and of the deeper significance that ideas hold for you. Fire transits—Aries, Leo, and Sagittarius—are generally very positive; they call forth new ideas or a strong sense of purpose and satisfaction in the work you're doing. Air transits are not particularly easy; you may feel very frustrated and irritable on Gemini days, and have an uncomfortably sharp sense of your own and other people's shortcomings. It may not be a bad idea to try to grab a little more privacy for yourself or to give in to the distractions prompted by Libra. These are certainly not ideal times to make any important decisions, and since everything feels as if it's going awry anyway, why not grump off to a movie instead?

The directions your energies can take are enormously varied. It is almost certain that theater arts will figure in your life. You will have a very keen appreciation of entertainment, and very possibly you will work in connection with music, dance, acting, movies, television, or in a related field. Given Capricorn's background, it's no surprise that you may also be drawn to the healing arts: medicine, surgery, pharmacology, psychology, and psychiatry, and may be both a practitioner and a researcher. Interestingly enough, another facet of your organizational talents is your ability to understand how organizations and institutions work, and how to work with them. For this reason, there's hardly a sphere of modern life that is not accessible to you. Should you wish to, you can direct your energies to government, politics, labor, industry, or business; that pretty well covers the major powers in our society, doesn't it? You're not frightened of power, and it interests you to learn how it's distributed, gained, and manipulated. Your coolness in this respect can serve to advance the plans you cherish and can give you the opportunity to wield considerable power in your own right.

Since our society would vastly benefit from the substantial participation of women, I'm not about to urge you to hide your lights under a basket. Do let them shine! Learn all you can and give yourself every chance to exercise your knowledge. It always strikes me as peculiar that success in nondomestic concerns is thought unfeminine; we could hardly find more feminine women than the women who preceded us four thousand years ago, and yet they were completely at ease in running governments, supervising education, negotiating treaties, inventing, studying—you name it and they were doing it. Why, then, should we be limited? If anything, you'd think our more numerous conveniences and our longer life span would free us to be even more fully engaged with the lives around us.

This brings us to another strong influence exerted by Capricorn: you are concerned about the preservation of yourself and of your society. Characteristically, this is grounded in solid reality first and then moves to more abstract levels. You will take care of the basic business of promoting and ensuring your own good health and that of the people in your family. You have a respect for food and rest as the very simple yet necessary means by which so much else is achieved: good looks, the energy to do what you want and to enjoy the doing of it, and above all good health. You manage to eat well and wisely without making a big deal about it, and to the extent that you're responsible for other people's nutrition, you treat that as a serious trust without spoiling the menu by constant reminders about all the good the food is doing. One of the things I've always envied is the Capricorn ability to be genuinely enthusiastic about genuinely healthy foods and to eat moderately, with great pleasure. And I've often had a Capricorn friend to thank for my decision to put aside my bag of potato chips and join her in eager anticipation of a salad. Another enviable reward of this attitude is that you do not run to fat as we potato-chip eaters so often do. Your own good looks and good health are the best testimonial for your commonsense approach; you are apt to be lean and hardy, and your vigor and endurance remain with you throughout your very long life.

As I've mentioned, you guide others toward a more positive pattern by making it attractive to them rather than by beating them over the head with its virtues. This characterizes your pursuit of other concerns as well. You have tremendous compassion for other people and a very real appreciation of personal quirks and individuality. What some interpret as a devotion to the status quo seems to me to be a tolerance, acceptance, and downright enjoyment of the splendors and oddities of human nature. You take people as they are and respect them as individuals in their own right. This does mean that you focus first on *what is*, but it certainly is no handicap toward striving for improvements and changes in conditions. It's simply that you don't set yourself up as the right hand of the divinity and try to impose your idea of what people *should be*. This seems the best of all possible attitudes. There's nothing more provoking than to be treated as some cardboard figure, to be dampened and pressed into a new shape to serve an ideal. No doubt it's very nice to feel that one has the right to pronounce judgment and to dictate what others should be like, but it's most tedious to be on the receiving end of these gracious enlightenments.

Your compassion for others tends, then, to be directed toward preserving their dignity and helping them, even subtly, toward a position of greater strength. Outwardly, your manner is matter of fact—which is to say that you don't find it necessary to win gold stars for how sympathetic you are. You do, however, expend a great deal of energy in trying to help other people help themselves. You work from a very vivid idea of how uncomfortable they must feel, and concentrate on creating or clearing the path to opportunities for them to realize themselves.

This is a very forward-looking attitude. Your efforts are focused on supporting and extending people's strengths. You know how hard it has been to form families and societies, and therefore you are not willing to toss these achievements aside as one would discard a plaything of the past. Yet you concentrate on making things better while not dwelling on past or present miseries. This is true, also, of the Capricorn brand of courage—a courage I find prodigious. The closest I can come to describing it is to liken it to the Oriental approach to life, which presumes a great deal more discipline and a far more active concern for the larger community than is our Western custom.

You will go to considerable lengths to ferret out the positive aspects of the most difficult situation, to cast an amusing light on past dangers, or to face future fears with the most cheerful view. This may be because you are aware of the other people involved with you. In a sense, there's a danger in this; since you live in a society that encourages women to disregard themselves and put others first, you are encouraged to abuse your strong sense of responsibility. Therefore, use caution in this regard. You personally might prefer a world that operates on the feminine sense of responsibility and concern for others, since the individualism that ignores the presence of others and the need to cooperate with people is an adolescent fantasy at best. However, you and I are in a transition period when our society is beginning to learn that social living and morality are more than the good sheriff going off to confront the evil villain. And while we are in transition, what do we do? By pretending to have no self, we do no one any good—least of all ourselves. Yet, in trying to guard against this, we are often maneuvered into uncomfortable postures where we may have to insist upon ourselves more than we like, more than seems appropriate. I can say no more on this except that this is, indeed, where we are; let's hope that the kinder view wins out; in the meantime, be extremely careful about self-sacrifice.

We may as well pick up at this point on the strictly personal spheres of your life. Through Capricorn, you are able to work independently and to enjoy a single life. Your preference, however, is to be engaged on a more extended scale, even in your private arrangements, and you would rather be with a partner or within a family or some similar group. Your appreciation of physical reality applies, of course, to your sexual life, and you accept and are often amused by the very real and somewhat less than glamorous aspects of romance. This is not to say that you make light of your intimacy or make your moments of passion the topic of casual conversation. You keep these things very private indeed, but nonetheless you can be ribald and terribly funny about the ill-timed burp or snore.

When you are without a partner, you share the Sagittarian ability to put yourself in the way of adventure instead of contenting yourself with sporadic daydreams, as Scorpios tend to do. This, of course, depends on whether or not you are interested in finding a partner at the time. We have come to the opposite extreme of the Victorian view in regard to sex. The notion that we are totally disinterested and unresponsive to sexual pleasure has been replaced by the idea that we are always responsive and that sex is our most absorbing concern. There must be a balance somewhere between these two views, and it will be a great relief, socially, when we arrive at it. It happens that there are times when we are not madly interested in romance. There are certainly fluctuations in desire and response within the closest relationships. At any rate, there is no need for you—or any of us—to apologize for those intervals when you are single and would rather be sleeping alone because your energies are so totally directed elsewhere. This kind of reaction is quite likely to occur when you've ended a relationship or when you've entered upon a very ambitious, very demanding project. It seems psychologically logical that you would need to limit your emotional involvements during such periods.

This may also happen during transitional periods, particularly in your early thirties; again, it makes inner sense because you are necessarily self-involved at this time. All transitions entail a lot of sorting out within ourselves, but the bridge between your twenties and thirties is your most thoroughgoing period of reassessment, and from this you make some of the major decisions of your life. It tends to be a bewildering time when you feel as if you're thrashing out first in one direction and then in another, dissatisfied with the whole lot. The passions you may experience are likewise fleeting, and if you are in a long-term relationship, you may find yourself bafflingly cool. Naturally, you will try to deal with this with the best grace you can summon up, but be careful to be patient and compassionate toward yourself. It hardly helps to harass yourself for all your shortcomings when, in truth, you are struggling to realign your experiences and needs. Somehow, it makes me think of children when they're exhausted. Have you ever seen a child who's been trooping around all day, shopping with her parent or out for some exciting treat? At day's end, that little girl may be screaming and whining, unable to take another step, maddened from sheer fatigue. Who would recommend punishing her at such a point? Clearly she needs to rest, to be quiet, to have less rather than more stimuli. As adults, we rarely abandon ourselves and have a screaming, crying fit on the sidewalk. But we may be getting many signals that the time has come to ease up for a while, to treat ourselves gently so that we may deal with and assimilate what we've encountered so far before moving on to new experiences and directions.

Interestingly, in regard to partnerships you tend to be attracted to people who are more similar to you than different. You may both be somewhat shy, but bolster each other's social confidence instead of intensifying the shyness. You are also most comfortable and content with people who share many of your interests, and while it's not necessary for you to spend every leisure moment in each other's company, it's important that you have a good portion of activities you enjoy in common. This, by the way, provides a very nice balance to the often solitary nature of your own career. Your work may, of course, differ, but you're likely to choose people who are at least at your intellectual and achievement level. This makes for a delightful relationship insofar as it is a partnership of equals. The one danger is that you may decide to subordinate your career and ambitions or your deepest interests. Although this may work fine in the first intensity of a relationship, it promises very souring resentment as a long-range plan. You don't need anyone to be successful for you and you're not likely to choose a fragile reed as a partner, someone who'd be devastated by your success. It would be wiser, then, to work out some other compromise, if necessary, than abandon your own work.

In other respects, your similarities work very much to your mutual advantage and enhancement. Your most fortunate, long-lasting partnership generally starts when you're in your thirties, and you bring to it great loyalty and affection as well as the more passionate sensual responses. You may not be very demonstrative publicly, but your private life is an altogether different matter. In this relationship, there is a strong sense that you are a team and that the closeness between you is a source of strength. Your love and concern and pleasure in your children—those you have or those you gain through marriage—does not infringe upon your adult relationship. Consequently, that transitional period when your children launch out on their own does not have the particular difficulty of having to renew your acquaintance with your partner.

Capricorn inclines you to be circumspect in expressing your

feelings, especially in public. This is an advantage in respect to your creative energies and your organizational abilities. It does not mean, however, that you are unemotional, nor does it happen that the power to control your emotions erases them. They are there—and it's recommended that you try to balance your life so that they may be released, particularly through talking things out but also through sports or acting.

Capricorn enables you to see and make the most of your opportunities, to extend your knowledge and experience beyond the traditional frontiers. It most certainly enables you to learn from your experiences—not merely data, but solid human wisdom. You definitely grow wiser as you mature, and the chances are that you will travel in the latter part of your life. Your approach to cultures other than your own is unconventional in that you tend to be less interested in sightseeing and more concerned about particular human conditions. It may be that you'll look into the status of women, or the treatment of orphaned and abandoned children, or the type and distribution of medical care. Whatever your focus, you come away with a great deal more than lovely images of foreign attractions, and often have imparted valuable information in turn.

You have a rich heritage through Capricorn, a history of fine achievements that occurred in every section of our globe, and you most certainly have the personal wherewithal to enrich that tradition in your own life. You can opt for family life and gain the rewards of a close union, or you can choose to go it on your own, with the emotional support of close friends, and gain the rewards that come from a deep commitment to your personal work. Guard yourself against worry and the tendency to push yourself to the point of exhaustion. And enjoy your gifts. They can bring you immeasurable pleasure, and they will almost assuredly benefit the rest of us as well.

CAPRICORN VISUALIZATIONS

You possess an extraordinary resource within you: your imagination. Through the power of your inward eye, you can tap into your innermost self, and into the energies of the universe. The thoughts you think, the messages you give yourself, the images you create in your imagination have tremendous power. You can literally transform your reality to fit the positive images you create mentally simply by creating those images often enough, and as specifically and clearly as you possibly can. Through such focused, purposeful "daydreaming," you can achieve an astonishing range of goals: practical goals such as weight loss, physical fitness, or money management; spiritual goals such as enhanced self-esteem, inner peace, and a deeper sense of connection with other living beings. For further information on this process, I recommend two books I've found useful, Shakti Gawain's *Creative Visualization*, and Shad Helmstetter's *The Self-Talk Solution*.

My primary concern here is empowering you to get in touch with the Goddess within you, the Eternal Feminine whose creative, nurturing, renewing energies live within us all. The Great Goddess is always ready to comfort, to heal, to strengthen, and to guide us whenever we are in need. Her images come to us from all parts of our world and from across great stretches of time. By visualizing Her in our mind's eye, by meditating on Her image, you and I not only receive help with specific problems and enhanced self-esteem but also reap the additional benefit of greater esteem for *all* women, past and present, and for the wonderful contributions women have made in creating and advancing civilization.

The images I sketch for you came to me through my research and through my own meditations. They may work differently for you than I've envisioned. And, of course, they're not the only images available to you. I suggest you read Merlin Stone's *Ancient Mirrors of Womanhood* and Barbara G. Walker's *The Woman's Encyclopedia of Myths and Secrets* to see what stories, prayers, and images resonate for you, and use them. I think you'll also find it illuminating simply to gaze within your own mind and see how the Goddess manifests Herself to you. I would be delighted to read your visualization experiences so if you would like to share them, please write to me, c/o the publisher.

How to go about visualization is very much a matter of personal choice: you may sit, stand, or lie down—whichever position you feel you can most comfortably maintain for ten to twenty minutes. You're probably best advised to be in a quiet, darkened room and to keep your eyes closed. Begin by relaxing your entire body. One technique is to imagine a comfortably warm, golden light surrounding you and taking away all tension in the area you're thinking of. Start with your feet and work up to the crown of your head. Once this is done, begin to construct your visualization in your mind.

Since you tend to be an energetic type, you may become irritable when your energy is at low ebb. It is often difficult for you to relax, and you chafe at not being able to do all that you'd like to do. I suggest you use your element—earth—for help in adjusting to the slower pace our bodies impose on all of us periodically. Why not treat yourself to a visualization of the Great Goddess Freyja of Scandinavia? Fly off in imagination to the forests of Finland or Sweden, where Freyja walks or rides in Her chariot pulled by cats as dark as midnight. It is winter. The boughs of the fir trees are laden with snow. The rowan trees, whose red berries eased the pain of childbirth, are sheathed in ice. When you look through their bare branches, it seems as if the moon is caught in a crystal web. The snow gleams silver in the moonlight. It is firm beneath your feet, and as you walk, you listen to it crunch and feel yourself sink a little into the softer snow underneath. The Great Goddess Freyja, usually so elusive, walks by your side, holding your hand to guide you through the woods. A great feeling of peace passes from Her to you. You become aware that like the earth sleeping under Her blanket of snow, you too need rest. You sense that this quiet time has its own beauty, its own reward; and you return from this visualization feeling calmer and ready to let this slower interval unfold naturally and enjoy the pleasures that it brings.

When you need comforting, and we all do at times, you might choose to visit the Goddess of Mercy, Kuan-Yin of China, a Goddess so beloved that the Buddhists could not eradicate Her from the minds of the people and had instead to adopt Her image into their religion. Sometimes Kuan-Yin was depicted as having twelve arms, and in each of Her twelve hands She held one of Her gifts that She gave humanity in the course of the solar year. You may see Her as you wish, with twelve arms or two. Her face is radiant with the compassion She feels for us. Her eyes see the hurt within your soul, and Her mercy flows within you like a gentle healing balm, easing your pain. You are loved and accepted exactly as you are. Become aware that you are perfect just as you are; that you are being what you were meant to be. Rest quietly in the love and mercy of the Goddess, and return from this visualization feeling restored.

Capricorn influences you to create and to preserve that which is created, so there will be many times when you feel the tug and pull of ideas in your mind. To clear the path for these ideas to come forward easily, I suggest you meditate upon the Goddess. You might choose to see the quiet image of China's Shing-Moo, or Perfect Intelligence, who resembles the Christian Mary, Mother of God. You may prefer to focus on the Kiowa Indian Goddess, Pasowee, or Buffalo Woman, who taught Her people about medicine and architecture. Watch Her in your mind as She moves about, absorbed and happy in Her work. Still another image you might choose to concentrate on is the slim, beautiful Goddess Isis, of Egypt. Perhaps She hands you the Heavenly Horn of the Goat, brimming with Her sacred wine that will allow you, in imagination, to experience the still center of the cosmos, the order and timelessness of our universe.

There come times that make our spirits quail within us, when we feel as if we do not have the strength to cope with what life presents or when we feel somehow threatened and uneasy. When such times visit you, you have an array of mighty Goddess images from whom to select a guardian. You may call to your mind the Amazonian Athena, bearing the goatskin shield emblazoned with the fierce image of Medusa. Under Her aegis you are completely protected. Feel the knots of your fear and bewilderment loosen, and your thoughts grow calm within you. Allow Athena to guide you; She will share Her strength with you and renew your courage.

You may instead wish to meditate upon the Great Goddess Hera, whom people worshipped in Anatolia, Mycenaea, Crete, Greece, and Africa long before the idea of Zeus had even been thought of. Mighty was Hera in battle, and mighty were Her accomplishments. As Mother Earth, She fed us when we were simply gatherers of Her bounty, and then She taught women to grow food, to make pottery, to design and build houses, to make medicines, to create civilizations. Many were Her names and many the temples raised in Her honor. In meditating upon Her, draw not only upon Her strength but upon Her breadth of vision. Allow your thoughts of Her to range over time so that you may regain your own sense of perspective and deal with your current situation in a balanced way.

The intimate connection between Capricorn and the Goddess as Healer is bound to manifest itself in you in some important way. It may be that you will be gifted with healing powers or that you will choose to enter the medical profession. The very least it will give you is a sense of responsibility for your own and your loved ones' health. Pay attention to this influence; you are fortunate to have it. When you feel the urge to have a candy bar instead of fruit, or would rather watch television than exercise, call to mind the Great Goddess Hygeia. In your mind see Her before you, radiant with health. She smiles upon you fondly, and in Her smile you see yourself, eager to indulge yourself "just this once." Yet by Her presence you also see that, by and large, you create your own health and that it is your responsibility. Your vision of Hygeia not only can strengthen your resolve but may allow you to maintain the discipline that health requires with a sense of joy, a vivid image of the rewards that such discipline will bring.

Life brings all of us moments when we are envious of others or our own lives seem bleak and meager. Capricorn provides you with a wonderful image to combat this insidious mood. Think of your constellation—the Horn of the Goat—shining among the stars. In your mind's eye, see it grow brighter and larger, becoming a great shining cornucopia spilling over with the gifts of the Goddess. We take so many of these gifts for granted that we've forgotten they are gifts: our food, our homes, our families and friends, our country, all the beauties of the earth we live on. Become conscious of these gifts and see them in the framework of history, ranging in your mind across the centuries and looking at the treasures we've accumulated, at the glories of nature and at the splendid arts humans have created. Look then at the treasures of your own life and see them with new eyes as if you had just received them. Feel your spirit expand with your awareness of the bounty of the Goddess; rejoice in your gifts and use them well, in the spirit of generosity in which She bestowed them on you.

AQUARIUS

January 19– February 19

AQUARIUS: A young priestess holding the sacred vessel that symbolized the Great Goddess as the Waters of Life and Wisdom. Based on a Greek amphora, 520–510 BC, preserved in the British Museum, London, England.

Y our sign, Aquarius, has undergone some curious changes in the course of its history. Like every other sign of the zodiac, it originated as a religious image commemorating gifts received from the Great Goddess, whom people everywhere worshipped as their central deity. In this, our first religion, we saw the universe primarily in feminine terms, as the continuing creation of the Great Mother, whose names, powers, and domain were boundless. The Egyptians tried to convey some idea of Her scope in their pictures of the Goddess Nut, whose body arched over the earth to form the vault of heaven. Naturally, She controlled the celestial waters, which included the sky itself as well as rain and dew. As Mistress of Heaven, She was drawn as the Sacred Water Jar, symbolizing Herself as the source of the waters of life and wisdom.

Then as now, the Nile River was crucial to Egyptian life. Each year it overflowed its banks to deposit a rich layer of soil that made agriculture a possibility in the midst of the desert. In the course of time, the Egyptians had figured out when the flooding would occur. They had also personified the Nile as Hapi, a handsome youth who was one of the Great Goddess's many sons and, of course, subordinate to Her. Their coding for the Nile's flooding was a pictogram of young Hapi with the Great Mother in Her form as Divine Vessel, and the water that poured forth was Her gift of life.

Neither the Greeks nor the Romans, whose stories we've inherited, gave a rap about the Nile since it had no bearing on their lives. They didn't bother with the image of the young man with a divine vessel until much later. As a matter of fact, the Greeks originally pictured Aquarius as the young Goddess Hebe, the Daughter aspect of the Triple Goddess Hebe/Hera/Hecate—or Daughter, Mother, and Grandmother, or elder wise woman. It wasn't until later, when the Greeks switched to patriarchy and promoted Zeus to "father" of the gods, that Hebe was demoted from being the divine source of water and wisdom to merely the cupbearer of the gods. She was not to enjoy even this position for very long. A new story circulated, based on a misreading of earlier matriarchal art, showing a portion of the sacred kingship ritual in which a young man won the right to be the queen's consort for a period of time—originally one year, then nine years, then multiples of nine. One scene that often appeared on vases showed a beautiful youth, Ganymedes, holding a bowl and about to pour a libation to honor the spirit of his predecessor. Usually the queen is also pictured, watching him perform the necessary rites. Sometimes, however, the scene shows an eagle swooping toward the genitals of Ganymedes. The eagle, like other birds, symbolized the Goddess as the Holy Spirit. In this scene, the Goddess as Eagle confers Her divine power on the youth and sanctifies him as the royal consort.

The Greeks reworked this scene into a highly popular story supporting homosexual love. In the patriarchal version, Ganymedes is a Trojan youth of such compelling beauty that the great Zeus himself falls passionately in love with him. Disguised as an eagle, Zeus swoops down and kidnaps Ganymedes and carries him off to Mount Olympus. Zeus then installs his new lover as the cupbearer of the gods, and compensates Ganymedes's heartbroken family with rich gifts and the promise that their son, now immortal and forever young, will shine in the sky as the constellation Aquarius.

The Romans imported this story into Italy, where it was reinforced by a real-life romance between the Emperor Hadrian and his young lover Antinous, who drowned tragically in the Nile during their sojourn in Egypt. The emperor was inconsolable. Cyril Fagan reports in *Astrological Origins* that, "He enrolled [Antinous] among the gods, caused numerous statues of him to be made, founded the Egyptian city of Antinopolis in his honor . . . erected a temple to him at Mamtinea [and] finally, in A.D. 132, he placed him in the starry skies right below the constellation of the Eagle." The Eagle (or Aquila) is the companion constellation to Aquarius, the Roman name meaning "male waterbearer."

Our concern is less with the sex life of our assorted ancestors than with the rationales attached to it. In matriarchal societies of Asia Minor and preclassical Greece, male homosexuality was accepted, but the rationale for it differed radically from the later Hellenic view. In Goddess-worshipping societies it was understood as a strong desire to identify with the Great Mother, to become as much like her and her human counterparts as was possible for a man to be. Under patriarchy, the emphasis shifted from the male worshipper who elected to identify with the Goddess to the male, usually older, who sought love and pleasure from a youth. The story of Zeus's passion for Ganymedes was gratefully seized upon by men such as Plato and the poet Thamyris, who were sexually drawn to younger men. This story not only justified certain sexual choices but it had additional political benefits as well. If a man is simply imitating the "Father of the gods" in his love for a younger man, his passion is both sanctioned and positively ennobled. In fact, in classical Greece it was elevated into the loftiest ideal of human love. And if the most perfect love was that of one man for another, where did that leave women? The answer is, pretty much at the bottom of the heap, denied social and political rights, barred from intellectual and economic life, and belittled even in terms of our biological abilities. Where once we had been esteemed as almost magical beings who, like the Great Goddess Herself, could bring forth life from within us, we were demoted to being mere receptacles for men's all-powerful seed. You will forgive me, I hope, if I am a little leery of so-called classical Greece and Rome as the source of our images of ourselves.

I confess I prefer the older, matriarchal view. Then, the sacred vessel of Aquarius represented the sheltering womb and nurturing breasts of the Great Mother. It also signified Her creative wisdom from which She drew forth the wonders of this world. Women were believed to share the Great Mother's wisdom and creative faculties to an extraordinary degree, a view backed up by their solid achievements. Among the outstanding intellectual leaders of the ancient world were the nine Muses, who are known to us as goddesses of inspiration but who were probably an order of priestesses in mountainous Thrace, a country renowned for extremely sophisticated astronomy, gold mining, mechanical sciences, and colleges. The ritual names for the priestesses who developed and taught the arts in these colleges were: Terpsichore, who gave us dance; Clio, of history; Urania, of astronomy; Thalia, of comedy; Melpomene, of tragedy; Erato, of love songs and erotic poetry; Polyhymnia, of sacred music; Euterpe, of flute music; and Calliope, of heroic poems.

In addition to the nine Muses of specific arts, all of our highest ideals are personified as women and have been known by feminine names from the dawn of history. In expressing such concepts as liberty, mercy, wisdom, soul, intelligence, peace, and honesty in feminine form, we are appropriately honoring the people from whom we received these ideas. For it was our earliest foremothers who taught us not only how to survive but how to be human beings, and the precepts by which they guided us toward civilization remain the finest ideals toward which people can aspire.

If you wish to read this information in terms of your Moon rather than your Sun, you'll need to shift your thinking from your identity, your will, your essential self—the way you manifest being you in the world—to focus instead on the inner you, the emotional you—your self at the deepest levels of your unconscious. Your Moon not only has to do with your feelings but also includes those things you take for granted in your self, those things you assume everyone else feels or is like, since they are so essential to your personality. They are ever present but elusive qualities you know intimately and yet can't quite put your finger on. The Moon also has to do with what went on in your family of origin, your home, your background. It concerns all those things that give you a sense of emotional security.

Specifically, a Moon in Aquarius endows you with a well-developed imagination and an adventurous spirit, a readiness to learn about and to try the new and the unconventional. It also cools your emotional responses and fosters a greater concern for ideas, events, and issues. It's not that you are cold-hearted and unfeeling. On the contrary, you are likely to be of a friendly disposition, easily liked and respected, and to be seriously concerned about world hunger or earthquake victims or people suffering anywhere, so that personal feelings seem rather trivial matters to you. An Aquarian Moon also promotes a rather detached attitude toward your past. You may very well reserve your deepest feelings and allegiance for the family you create rather than for your family of origin, and may prefer to have little contact with your original family. Moon in Aquarius is expressed in the feminine side of your nature through an emphasis on the intellectual, the logical, the idealistic, and you are drawn to people who offer intellectual companionship. It is also apparent in your unselfishness, which you may need to guard against, and your involvement in broad, humanitarian concerns. You are a tender heart who will feed and shelter all the stray animals in the neighborhood, and who will work tirelessly to improve education, to foster the arts, to support any cause designed to make the world better. An Aquarian Moon also strengthens your ability to read other people's character accurately, and it creates a need to explore the nature of reality.

Respect is the first gift you receive through an Aquarius Sun. I place it first because it is difficult for most of us to achieve and understand, yet its presence makes life infinitely more gracious and honest. Even in your youth, when you may be short on self-confidence, your self-respect is already well developed. You see yourself as a blend of strengths and weaknesses and accept yourself as such. You develop your own standards rather than accept them wholesale from other sources, who are no better qualified than you to determine what you should be and how you should live. This may be as natural as breathing to you, but you'd be amazed at how hard it is for others. Personally, I'm very grateful to my Aquarian relatives and friends for their help, much of which came simply from the way they conduct their lives.

You tend to have strong likes and dislikes, and you certainly give voice to your opinions, but you don't try to force other people to accept these as their own or to shape themselves to a pattern of your designing. You neither kowtow to others nor demand that they bow to you. One feature I especially love is that you don't go through a lot of contortions to suit others, no matter how grand their status might be. If the queen of England were to walk up to you, you'd remain your natural self and probably have a pleasant, interesting conversation with her. And just as you deal with people on your own terms and respect them as they are, you expect the same in return and do not permit yourself to be repressed or bullied by someone else. This takes a lot of needless mystery out of your relationships. Since you share your opinions and speak up when you feel your rights are being infringed upon, other people know where they stand with you and also feel free to express themselves. Consequently, there's little hidden resentment, and the adjustments and compromises that human relationships naturally call forth can take place in an open atmosphere.

You also have the ability to listen to criticism from others without feeling as if your essential self is being destroyed when someone notices a possible flaw. However, you do not abandon your standards in the face of another's judgment. You hear people out, evaluate what they say, and then, on the basis of whether you find their remarks justified, either defend yourself against unjust criticism or heed what has been said.

Aquarius also predisposes you to sociability. You are congenial and enjoy sharing activities and working with others. This is very much enhanced by the fact that you are equally at home in your own company. Your life tends to be very busy so that you do not, in fact, get to spend much time alone, and you cherish your private moments when they come. The great benefit to enjoying yourself alone, apart from the pleasure it brings in itself, is that you do not seek out other people simply to protect yourself from solitude, but because you genuinely enjoy being with them. The inner freedom that comes from self-respect and self-reliance enables you to take great pleasure in your relationships and to give of yourself generously. You have friendships with a great many different types of people, and yet the bonds between you are based on interests and values you share in common. You don't expect to be all things to all people nor do you demand this in return. Therefore, it seems comfortable and natural to you to have a variety of friends, each of whom calls forth different aspects of yourself. You tend to seek close ties with people who enhance your sense of emotional well-being and who are intellectually stimulating. Ideas and ethics are extremely important to you: you prefer people who share your values, even if these are framed in differing contexts of belief. It is very likely that you may join or support one or more organizations that promote the causes you cherish.

As in your friendships, people feel honored to have you as a member of their group or as a working colleague. I don't mean by this that they greet your approach with a fanfare of trumpets, which would embarrass you, or that they treat you as a being apart, which is a lonesome reward for merit. However, you are generally recognized as a person of great worth and ability, and you are valued very highly, without the usual accompaniment of spiteful envy. In part, this freely given esteem is due to your own balanced outlook. You are usually much too busy, interested in living life and tending to your own business, to be terribly concerned about seeking attention for no other purpose than to be in the spotlight. Ironically, the very fact that you don't make a habit of butting in with unasked-for advice seems to encourage people to seek out your opinions. The trust others place in you is well founded. You are honest and sincere; people are assured that you're not trying to curry favor or to please them with empty words. You think things through, so that people are sure the opinion you offer represents a real effort to give your best attention to the matter under consideration. In addition, you are able to give advice without crowding the seeker out of the picture, and to state your view while still leaving the other person plenty of room to take up your suggestions or not. Personally, I find this extremely refreshing. Matters are kept very much on the level of one free and equal adult to another, and there's none of that tiresome, constricting business of being treated like a child.

The one problem it might be well to guard against is stinting yourself in terms of full recognition of your strengths and abilities.

It is a truly lovely experience to know someone who does not puff up
with self-importance and who is capable of genuine humility.
However, humility can drop into underestimating yourself, a lack of
confidence that you're especially liable to in your youth. You get
very little help from your society in this regard, which makes things
considerably more difficult. The sad but true historical facts are that
women have had to campaign very long and very strenuously to gain
the rights we have, and even these are not yet complete. You are not
yet in a situation that encourages you, as a matter of course, to think
highly of yourself and to value your abilities. The prevailing
attitudes toward home and family are some measure of the esteem in
which we are held. It strikes me as peculiar that this particular job
should be categorized as trivial, and I marvel that so much emphasis
is placed on the tiresome, monotonous aspects of homemaking
when, in reality, there isn't a job in the world that doesn't have its
full share of tedious business. We do not have to regard homemaking
as the be-all and end-all of our existence, unless it pleases us to do
so, but neither do we have to shun it like the plague. We, as women,
are not trivial and neither is any job we undertake, whether that job
figures as our major career or occupies only one or two decades of
our working life. My hope for you is that you will have close,
strongly supportive friends to help you recognize your worth and
talents during those periods when your self-confidence ebbs. And
that you use your excellent reasoning powers in your own behalf to
defend yourself from accepting a negative evaluation of women
involving very limited views on the range of our capabilities.

It is probable that you will marry fairly early and get started on
your family while you're in your twenties. This is a strongly felt
need, and very definitely an active choice on your part. However,
since it arises during or just after your ebb in self-confidence, the
one may color the other. It's important to sort this out for yourself
and recognize that you are, indeed, taking care of vital business
rather than abandoning your talents and ambitions because you
"don't really have the talent" or you "could never be such and
such," et cetera. You can see the dangers in that kind of thinking: it
belittles the private sphere, which you actually value and enjoy; and
it doesn't do a whole lot for you in regard to the public sphere of life,

either. In short, it's one of those charming situations in which you can't win for losing. This is not only unnecessary, it's unrealistic. The fact that you'd prefer to have your family early doesn't mean that everything else must grind to a halt. There's no reason not to prepare for work you believe you'd eventually enjoy doing. Your family, like every other one, will grow up; a time will come when you're not as deeply involved at home as you were and would like to return to work. And despite the propaganda to the contrary, there are very few careers that cannot be interrupted for a considerable while and then resumed. Employers used to make a great stink about hiring women, claiming that we were unreliable because we'd marry and get pregnant and then desert the job. Very little attention has been paid to the fact that men shift jobs almost as often as women, and that unless there's a depression or some such circumstance that puts jobs at a premium, there's no guarantee any employee is going to stick around. At any rate, I hope the point is made that you needn't curtail your preparations, or apologize and deprecate your choices as to how you proceed with your life.

Aquarius inclines you toward partners who have strong talents of their own and who are pretty colorful personalities. You need someone who is capable of giving a full commitment to your relationship and whom you find interesting and stimulating intellectually as well as emotionally compatible. To outsiders, you may often seem cool and detached because you shy away from public demonstrations of affection. Privately, however, you are very warm and affectionate, and very much attached. The relationships you enter tend to be long-term commitments rather than casual affairs that end quickly. You are faithful and honest yourself, and while it is possible for you to understand infidelity—that is, understand how someone might succumb temporarily to an attraction for someone else—you have no respect for it whatsoever. To you, it means betrayal and lies and sneaking about, behavior for which you have nothing but contempt. You may retaliate with affairs of your own, but these are not all that helpful in that they aggravate the disappointment and coldness that have touched your heart. In such a situation it might be better to terminate the relationship, go through your period of grieving, and start again, with yourself intact—easy to say, I know, but difficult in the doing. Best of all would be to avoid people who have demonstrated that they are incapable of the loyalty you need. Life generally portions out enough hard times as it is, so that you don't need to invite difficulties and bitterness by ignoring your own vital needs.

You are attractive, owing as much to your candor and friendliness and to being very much your own person as to physical good looks. Your attractiveness is not simply a function of youth; it remains with you throughout your life. There's very little reason, then, to worry about whether other people will find you sexually desirable. Instead, you can concentrate your thoughts on your likes and needs. Your ability to have men as well as women friends gives you a broad experience of human nature; this can serve you well in determining if a person is only superficially attractive or has the depth of character and breadth of interest to which you can truly respond. Perhaps this sounds terribly cool and rational—and let's admit that when it comes to falling in love, there's very little of the cool and rational about it—but when it comes to deciding to stay with someone, you generally do know if you share the same values, if you enrich each other or battle all the time, and other little items that provide strong clues to how you'll do together in a long alliance. You give tremendously of yourself and you can gain immeasurably from a partnership, so it is well to choose your lovers carefully. Avoid those arrangements in which one gives all the time and the other takes. The best thing that relationships of this sort offer may be a sense of one's greater generosity of spirit—pretty slim pickings considering what you can gain from genuine intimacy.

Your ability to form strong, close bonds is a tremendous advantage. It provides an emotional richness that supports rather than interferes with other aspects of your life, and it makes it a great deal easier for you to accomplish what you desire. The one drawback, if it may be called that, is that just as you do not enter lightly into relationships, you do not leave them easily, either. Separation or divorce are extremely difficult, even when you believe that this is the best course for both of you. The death of someone you love is a truly profound loss and may influence you toward keeping future relationships on the most superficial basis. I remark upon these unhappy possibilities because I believe we are led to expect—and hope—that the pain of grief will pass swiftly when in fact it takes most of us quite a bit of time to recover from our losses, and the process is gradual rather than one quick, easily articulated experience. Since you are not a person of shallow feelings, be gentle and patient with yourself if grief should befall you.

To return to more cheerful matters, however, your private family life can afford you a great deal of pleasure and satisfaction. The chances are that you will have few rather than many children, and that you will do your utmost for them. One excellent advantage that you receive through Aquarius is that you think of yourself as a guide instead of as a molder of your children's personalities. From infancy on, you see them as distinct individuals and respect them as such. You try to help them understand themselves and encourage them to develop their potential, whatever that may be. This is not to say that all is easy and ideal. Children can be exasperating, to say the least, and there may be many a moment when you'd like to throttle them. You don't, however. Teaching them to be considerate and fair is especially trying to you, since these values are absolutely basic to your temperament and you feel their absence very keenly. You may feel that they'll never learn, but they will—and probably more from your own example than from all the conscious effort you expend. The most pleasant feature of motherhood for you is that your children do not bore you. Perhaps because you don't imagine them as little lumps of clay to be patted and pushed into predetermined shapes, you are free to respond to them as unique beings with their own interesting views and insights. Consequently, you have a great deal of fun together, and the years of their growing up are not all fights and hullabaloo, although there'll be times when it feels like it.

It is likely that you will regard most experiences in life as a proving ground for yourself. You yearn to excel, and you have the gift of taking as much pleasure in the processes involved as in the results. As a student, you rarely content yourself with meeting the routine obligations, but develop special, independent projects of your own or become active in extracurricular activities. If your time is limited by having to work, you strive to maintain an excellent average. In your youth, you have plenty of impulses to speak up, but you may be shy about bringing attention to yourself. Try to get yourself to jump in anyway; you'll hasten the business of getting over your shyness and classes will be a lot more interesting for you if you're not always choking back your contributions. Part of the process of becoming a first-class citizen is learning to respect your own thoughts: listen to them, take note of those little interior mental comments, and share them. I'd bet you anything that you've heard someone pipe up with a remark and said to yourself, "That's just what I was thinking!" You may even have experienced surprise on recognizing your own thought. That surprise generally stems from a conviction we've had for so long that we don't even know it's there—that what we think isn't worth listening to or remarking on. Nonsense; it just takes practice. It may happen every now and again that you say something less than scintillating. So what? That's everybody's lot, even the most gifted speakers. The ground isn't going to open up and swallow you. You won't be branded for life if every remark isn't brilliantly relevant. But most of your thoughts are very much worth sharing. And you will be happily surprised at how your voice gains in timbre and assurance the more often you use it to contribute your opinion—and you will gain in assurance and self-confidence. There's no telling what delightful results will follow from these powerful ingredients.

Your desire for personal excellence is a gift designed to broaden and enrich your life, and it's a spur to develop the considerable talents in your possession. Please don't misunderstand me; I'm not talking about trying to be Superwoman at all. That's using your energy and gifts against yourself, as far as I'm concerned, and it's premised on a very sad feeling that one has to justify one's presence on this earth by the number of jobs accomplished. Working instead on the assumption that you and I are very welcome on this earth because of who we are personally rather than what jobs we do, let's look at your gift in terms of the pleasure it can bring you. It spices up your life by encouraging you to try new things, learn new skills, go beyond the basics.

At home, for example, you make sure that you get all the basic skills down pat and then branch out to innovations and specialties.

You may become skilled at doing home repairs, including electrical work and carpentry or refinishing furniture. You may choose to become an accomplished needleworker and you are almost certain to have a flair for cooking. The thing that never ceases to amaze me about Aquarian talents is how effortlessly they are exercised. While most of us are wont to puff and toil and groan in preparing a dinner party, you Aquarians seem to whiz through the process with the greatest ease. You'll use the occasion as a chance to try something new, and everything generally winds up delicious and elegant.

Since it is my conviction that what this country needs is an Aquarian woman for president, it follows that I would not suggest that you spend all your life at home. Your gifts can most definitely flourish in the public sphere of life just as well as in the private. If you've been away from work for a long time, don't discount the skills you've acquired at home or in community service and functions. These skills and experiences can point the way toward the field you'd like to enter, or they can be converted into independent business ventures.

The range of Aquarian interests and talents is truly staggering. Look at what you have to draw upon from yourself: you have a predilection, if not a decided preference, for law, philosophy, science, music, art, the social sciences, psychology, and literature. You are talented at administration and, in fact, may be called upon to straighten out your family's business affairs from time to time. You combine logic and intuition in your approach to ideas and problems; you are able to go beyond the narrowly rational type of thinking. Your respect for science and for the occult—or, to put it another way, for the known and the unknown—allows you to be open to new insights and ideas. You are remarkably lacking in arrogance. You tend to be especially attracted to those ideas and efforts that promote the sisterhood and brotherhood of peoples. Like your ancient grandmothers, there's hardly a field of human endeavor to which you cannot turn your hand and mind if you choose.

In regard to your energy pattern, you feel most competent and self-confident when the Moon transits your own Aquarius and the other air signs, Gemini and Libra. Libra transits are particularly positive for you. Transits through the fire signs—Aries, Leo, and

Sagittarius—are generally advantageous and give you an intensified sense of purpose and well-being. Transits through Virgo and Taurus may be difficult, in that you may feel listless, even bewildered, but a Capricorn transit is usually a more positive experience; while it means a low energy level, it is a good time to make plans. Pisces transits may encourage you to be more than usually intuitive, but the other water signs—Cancer and Scorpio—are rather plain, ordinary days for you.

Your energy tends to group itself into several hours of sustained effort followed by the need for a period of quiet and calm, and it would be wise for you to try to keep your evenings as restful and relaxed as possible. You are certainly able to relax if you have the time to do so, and it is especially helpful as a way to increase your stamina.

On an annual basis, the high point of your cycle occurs in late winter and early spring, with the low in early winter. You might be said to have more stamina than energy, which keeps you on a fairly even basis for most of the year but can tempt you to overwork yourself in the day-to-day scheme of things. When my dear Aquarian friend Leona Dallis was an executive secretary in an extremely busy law firm, she often worked a lot of overtime as well as her usual heavy load. She would then come home to a battery of tasks that could knock you out on a day off. Of course, she should've relaxed. But like so many of us, she had to take care of many of these things so her home wouldn't go absolutely to pot because she held a paying job. It's hard to know what to suggest because, in truth, we still have an awful lot to do, despite all of our appliances. Apart from hiring help, which few of us can afford, I suppose we should get into the habit of asking for help from the people who live with us—and we should also strip our tasks down to the absolute essentials, and share our ideas with each other, since no one as yet has come up with the definitive answer to this complex problem.

One last point in regard to your cycles is that your energy tends to focus and come to full strength from your late thirties onward; therefore, it's particularly important for you to guard against our society's views on age or, rather, youth. If we were to believe the propaganda, all people over twenty-five should rush like lemmings to the nearest cliff and hurl themselves off in a fit of uselessness. To say that this attitude is foolish is to dignify it beyond its just deserts.

Like most of us, you find transitions rather difficult. Change makes you nervous, and you may lose sight of the fact that you have a distinct flair for making friends. Although you don't set out to ingratiate yourself with people, you are friendly, open, and responsive, and people are drawn to you very quickly. The newness of a job or a situation—that uncomfortable period when you feel as if you don't know anyone—does not last very long, and therefore you should not hesitate to make a change on that basis. The time prior to making your decision is the hardest. Whereas some people positively dote on debating "should they or shouldn't they?" it's a trial for you, and you may find yourself feeling nervous and bewildered, crying easily and given to very grim moods. Give yourself a break during such periods. Turn to your friends for comfort and support, go out for dinner and drinks and a few laughs, ease up on your schedule, gain a few pounds. And try to keep things easy for yourself the first few months after you've made a choice. If it's a new job, you will undoubtedly be very busy learning your work and starting to get an idea of what's involved in the whole operation, since one Aquarian talent is learning the totality of a situation.

Of course, it's not possible for all of you Aquarians to be president—at least not simultaneously. But I do hope that you use your extraordinary gifts for your own and our collective advantage. You have the rare ability to reconcile a practical, realistic outlook with a profoundly humane idealism. It gives you great satisfaction to learn how things work and to achieve excellence in whatever you choose to do. Our history is like coral, building slowly, steadily, to form a mighty reef. You are poised on the topmost layer, and whether your life is conducted in the private or the public sphere, you are building for the people to come through those things that most satisfy your own soul. When you're discouraged by thoughts that you're too old to start a career or develop a talent, remember Grandma Moses, who began her painting at seventy-eight. When you feel that you're limited as a woman, remember your Aquarian foremothers who led the world toward so much because, like you, they loved to learn and to share and had a vision of a finer life for humanity. Yours is usually a long life; that must be because you have so many gifts to use and so much to teach others. Enjoy your time on this earth and remember—we look to you.

AQUARIUS VISUALIZATIONS

You possess an extraordinary resource within you: your imagination. Through the power of your inward eye, you can tap into your innermost self, and into the energies of the universe. The thoughts you think, the messages you give yourself, the images you create in your imagination have tremendous power. You can literally transform your reality to fit the positive images you create mentally simply by creating those images often enough, and as specifically and clearly as you possibly can. Through such focused, purposeful "daydreaming," you can achieve an astonishing range of goals: practical goals such as weight loss, physical fitness, or money management; spiritual goals such as enhanced self-esteem, inner peace, and a deeper sense of connection with other living beings. For further information on this process, I recommend two books I've found useful, Shakti Gawain's *Creative Visualization*, and Shad Helmstetter's *The Self-Talk Solution*.

My primary concern here is empowering you to get in touch with the Goddess within you, the Eternal Feminine whose creative, nurturing, renewing energies live within us all. The Great Goddess is always ready to comfort, to heal, to strengthen, and to guide us whenever we are in need. Her images come to us from all parts of our world and from across great stretches of time. By visualizing Her in our mind's eye, by meditating on Her image, you and I not only receive help with specific problems and enhanced self-esteem but also reap the additional benefit of greater esteem for all women, past and present, and for the wonderful contributions women have made in creating and advancing civilization.

The images I sketch for you came to me through my research and through my own meditations. They may work differently for you than I've envisioned. And, of course, they're not the only images available to you. I suggest you read Merlin Stone's *Ancient Mirrors of Womanhood* and Barbara G. Walker's *The Woman's*

Encyclopedia of Myths and Secrets to see what stories, prayers, and images resonate for you, and use them. I think you'll also find it illuminating simply to gaze within your own mind and see how the Goddess manifests Herself to you. I would be delighted to read your visualization experiences so if you would like to share them, please write to me, c/o the publisher.

How to go about visualization is very much a matter of personal choice: you may sit, stand, or lie down—whichever position you feel you can most comfortably maintain for ten to twenty minutes. You're probably best advised to be in a quiet, darkened room and to keep your eyes closed. Begin by relaxing your entire body. One technique is to imagine a comfortably warm, golden light surrounding you and taking away all tension in the area you're thinking of. Start with your feet and work up to the crown of your head. Once this is done, begin to construct your visualization in your mind.

You have great stamina and, as I mentioned earlier, you may be tempted to push yourself too far and make too many demands on this resource. To avoid this, set aside some time each day for meditation. A wonderful image for this purpose comes from your element—air—in the form of the Great Goddess as the Eagle. Imagine yourself seated upon Her back. Feel Her power, which supports you in total safety. She lifts you high into the sky so the earth below dwindles into a speck. You are free—warm, comfortable, secure, and yet absolutely free. The Goddess will take you wherever you wish. If you feel playful, She will swoop toward the earth so that your hair streams behind you in the wind and then climb sunward once again. If you yearn for rest, She will glide smoothly through the sky, over any part of the earth you choose so that you may look over Her great wings and enjoy the scene below. When you are ready to return from this visualization, the Goddess will gently return to earth so that you may climb down and watch Her as She soars alone into the air and disappears from view. Take a little extra time to come out of this visualization so that you experience no dizziness.

When you need to be comforted, you may turn to the Goddess Mawu, who was worshipped in Africa, the birthplace of humanity. The Dahomey people, like so many others, believe that we live because the Goddess has loaned each of us a piece of Her spirit. We are all truly sisters and brothers, sharing in the one great soul of the loving Mawu, and for this reason Mawu teaches us not to fight and kill one another. The Great Mawu will lift you up as if you were a little child and carry you, in imagination, to see the wonderful things She has brought forth on this earth, and distract you from your pain. You may look upon the beautiful waters of Her lakes, rivers, and seas. Look also upon the splendid mountains shining in the sunlight. They resemble the breasts of the Great Mother in their outward form and Her womb in their secret caves. Gaze upon Her trees rich with fruit, upon the grasslands whispering in the breeze, upon animals basking in the warmth of the sun, and the birds flashing like small rainbows in the sky. Allow the warmth of Mawu's love to soothe your soul, to heal your aching spirit, to remind you that we are meant to love one another.

Your Aquarian influence will bless you often with ideas and insights. To encourage these gifts, it may be helpful to meditate upon the symbol of your sign, the Goddess as the Divine Vessel. You might choose to dwell in imagination on the art of pottery making itself, whose secrets women learned so many thousands of years ago. You might see yourself choosing the clay you will work with and forming it carefully into the shape you desire. Like your foremothers, work silently in respect for the spirit within the clay and for the creative spirit the Goddess loans us. When you have completed the form, let it fire in your mind's creative energy, and then offer it to the Goddess within you to be filled with the inspiration you need.

You may choose instead to see the Divine Vessel as the Chinese Sacred Cauldron, the source of oracle. Look deep within the cauldron. Perhaps its surface ripples and reflects like water, gleaming in the moonlight; perhaps its surface swirls like smoke or the mists rising from the mountains at dawn. Simply gaze quietly and let the images come to you as they will, or not at all, for that, too, is appropriate.

You may choose to focus on the Goddess Herself, and I offer you the image of Seshat of Egypt, who created writing and numbers, and the implements of writing: the papyrus scroll, the ink, and the pen. It was Seshat who is credited with inventing architecture and with writing down our good and bad deeds on the leaves of the Tree of Life. It is She who advises us to enjoy life and to make our good deeds many, for our actions are our true possessions. Dwell upon Her perfect image in your mind; think of Her gifts and what those gifts have made possible. Allow your mind to open to Her creative energy, to activate your own creativity.

When you are having trouble coming to a decision or you need help understanding your dreams, you may turn for help to that most ancient Goddess, Nidaba of Sumeria. The Great Nidaba often took the form of a cobra, so you may see Her in woman's form or as a great snake, whichever you prefer. The Sumerians gave thanks to Nidaba for the gift of writing and of wisdom, for interpretation of dreams, and guidance in making decisions. You may visit Her in Her Holy Chamber or walk through the star-strewn skies with Her, for it was She who arranged the stars into patterns that we humans could recognize. Her message will come to you in the silence and silvered darkness of your mind.

When you lack confidence or feel insignificant, you might benefit from visiting in your imagination your human counterparts from so long ago who served the nine Muses, the tripled Triple Goddess. Travel back in your mind thousands of years to ancient Thrace, the site where modern Turkey now stands. You are at the base of the mountains, outside a walled city. The gates are flung open and you are welcomed within. The city is laid out in the pattern women chose so long ago, with the Temple to the Great Goddess in a large circular space at the center and the streets arranged in radials from that circle, in imitation of the Goddess as the Wheel of Life, endlessly repeating the cycle of birth, life, death, rebirth. Become aware that you are at a great center of learning; notice that people from many different areas have gathered here to study with the priestesses. Today, however is a festival in honor of the Goddess, and you are invited to join the circle of women, to join hands with them and dance your joy, bare feet beating out the celebration rhythms against the hard-packed earth. The music of flutes and of women's voices fills your ears. The songs to the Goddess give thanks for all Her gifts, for the many wonderful skills

She has given women, for the many splendid things we have achieved in Her name, for the beautiful ideals She has inspired in us. Feel your spirit soar with pride at all that has been accomplished and all that is being done now. Allow the strength of that great heritage to course through you so that when you return from this visualization you are able to appreciate that you, too, have value and that your contributions, whatever they may be, are worthy of respect.

When you feel jealousy or envy, or somehow scrimped on life, see in your mind's eye the beautiful young Hebe, a silver vision in the night sky. She holds the Sacred Water Jar, the heavenly vessel of women's wisdom from youth to adulthood to old age. In the names of Her Daughter Self, Her Mother Hera, Her Grandmother Hecate, She pours the waters of life and knowledge in an endless stream from heaven to earth. The gifts of this vessel twinkle like stars: they are ideas, insights, intuitions, and deliberated judgments. Thus has She poured out for us from the beginning of human time. Thus She continues to pour. There is more than enough for all of us. There is more than enough for you. Allow your spirit to rejoice in Her abundance.

PISCES
February 19–
March 20

PISCES: The Great Goddess of All Waters, based on a facade from a Celtic church in Cinuos-Chel, Upper Engsdine, Switzerland, and on comparable renderings of the Goddess from Japan and from Spain.

Your sign, Pisces, is a profoundly feminine sign and it has always exerted a powerful fascination. Astrologers have tended to regard it as both the most sublime and the most dangerous sign in the zodiac, leading either to the highest spiritual development or to utter degradation. Unfortunately, traditional interpretations tend to be pessimistic. In one sentence you may be congratulated on your creativity or emotional depth and compassion, but the very next may picture you awash in tears or strong drink, a creature of moods, incapable of independent decision. It can get very bewildering, especially if even your positive qualities are presented in terms of their potential for disaster. No doubt these cautions are well meant, but they are based on our culture's distrust of the feminine. This distrust was born of propaganda that started a few thousand years ago, when male gods began to replace or overshadow female gods. For several hundred years now we've been taught that feminine powers and qualities are either destructive or inferior, a view that seems like fact only because it's been repeated so often. If we want to really understand Pisces, I think we'd better scrap this point of view and return to square one, when astrology began as an outgrowth of a worldwide religion based on the worship of the Great Goddess.

Let's start with the femininity of Pisces, and what that meant. For most of human history we humans have regarded women as almost magical beings, because our biological powers linked us to the three liquids crucial to life: water, blood, and milk. It was observed that women seemed to have a special relationship to the moon, that we bled once a moon, or month, and stopped this monthly bleeding when a child was growing within us. We also knew that our children lived first like little fish in the waters of our wombs, and that we somehow miraculously produced milk to feed these children when they were born. These observations gave rise to the belief that water, blood, and milk were feminine, part and parcel of women's magic. In our efforts to make sense of the universe, we reasoned further that the universe itself was essentially feminine and that women's powers mirrored the infinitely more wonderful powers of the Great Mother.

Women's biology set off this train of thought but women's achievement reinforced it. Like the Great Goddess, we not only created, nourished, and sustained life, but we also took raw materials and transformed them into new and wondrous, life-enhancing creations. Just think of what was involved in our mastery of food production alone. When we taught ourselves how to plant food and not just gather it, we revolutionized human life. We also figured out how to use fire, create pottery, fabric, clothing, medicines, heal illnesses, perform operations, design and build houses, and on and on. In the ancient prayers of thanks to the Goddess we see the reflection of women's many accomplishments ranging from the concrete and practical to abstractions such as law, religion, science, and philosophy. Perhaps this all sounds like bragging but, believe me, what I've given here is only a partial list of the results credited to women's magic. To sum it all up, *feminine* referred to the processes of creation and transformation.

Your Pisces symbol—two fish, head to tail to form a circle— was meant to convey the original idea of creation. The fish represent the multitude and variety of life the Goddess created, and the circle they form symbolize the Original Womb of the Goddess from whom all life was born; Her endless cycle of birth, life, death, and rebirth; and the opposites She reconciled into the wholeness of life. Sometimes the Goddess Herself was pictured as a great fish or as a dolphin, sometimes as a voluptuous woman with a single or double fishtail instead of legs. The mermaid, now trivialized in folk and fairy tales, was once the ancient Celts' most beloved image of their Goddess of the Waters. They pictured Her with thick, flowing, abundant hair to emphasize Her magnetism and the range and intensity of Her intellectual and emotional powers. She was always shown with bared breasts, sometimes cupping them, as a reminder of Her generosity and desirability. In Her mermaid form, She was the supreme creatrix and nourisher of life, and the personification of all desire, dream, and idea. She, the ultimate mystery, was the keeper of all mysteries, who simultaneously challenged, lured, and guided us to explore the secrets of our world and the possibilities within ourselves.

Let's look briefly at the women of the ancient Celts to expand our ideas of femininity. The Celts had large, influential settlements in what is now Turkey, Galatea, northern Italy, Switzerland, Austria, Belgium, France, Germany, Denmark, England, Ireland, Scotland, and Wales, and minor settlements in the Balkans, Spain, and Portugal. They probably figure in the ancestry of quite a few of us. Much of our information about the Celts comes from the Greeks and Romans, with whom they fought and traded. They praised the Celts for their tremendous courage and daring and for their exquisite work in gold, weaving, and other decorative arts but they disliked the Celts' great respect for women. The Roman historian Tacitus indignantly recounts how captive Celts completely ignored the Emperor Claudius and marched up to the Empress Agrippina to offer their official surrender. Roman generals frequently referred to the courage and strength of Celtic women in their military journals. One such entry said that it would take a legion to defeat a Celt when his battle fury was aroused, and an entire division to defeat him should his wife join him, as she often did. Another account tells how Roman soldiers were paralyzed with fear at the sight of the Celtic troops massed on the other side of the river. Especially frightening were the Celtic priestesses with their long, streaming hair, who rushed between the warriors, brandishing torches and shouting curses at their enemies. The general had to remind his troops they weren't supposed to be afraid of women, and only the threat of public humiliation back home in the forum induced the men to cross the river and fight.

The historian Herodotus tells us how Tomyris, queen of the Massagetae, warned Cyrus the Great of Persia not to cross her territory or start a war with her. Cyrus captured her son, who then committed suicide. When Tomyris heard this, she led her troops against Cyrus and killed him herself. Queen Boadicea of Britain was another Celtic woman renowned as a fierce warrior. She held off seventy thousand Roman soldiers, routed their army, and captured London, Colchester, and St. Albans before she was finally defeated. She chose suicide rather than the shame of being brought to Rome as a prisoner of war. Both the Roman Julius Caesar and the Carthaginian king Hannibal learned first-hand of the power and respect that Celtic women commanded, and that it was they who planned the battle strategy and made treaties.

Celtic law and Celtic leadership were premised on full sexual equality. The Celtic marriage contract guaranteed a woman that she would not lose her independence or her political, legal, and property rights by consenting to the union. Easy divorce laws also protected women. Unfortunately, early Christianity was strongly antifeminine, and the process of converting the Celts brought the gradual disenfranchisement of Celtic women. This antifeminine bias may have stemmed from the fact that Christian priests recognized the worship of the Great Goddess as the single most powerful obstacle to Celtic conversion. In Switzerland, for example, converts were required to prove their sincerity by stoning a statue of the Great Mother and reading the inscription over the poor, battered figure that said, "Once I was the Goddess and now I am nothing at all." Ironically, it was the identification of the Great Mother with Mary, Mother of God, that ultimately made Christianity acceptable to the Celts, for She was a figure immediately compatible with their view of the feminine universe.

Entire libraries of excellent scholarship have been written about the Celts, so what I've offered you here is just the simplest sketch of a highly complex people. However, I hope this helps extend the idea of what *feminine* means. Piscean femininity has little indeed to do with ruffles and bows and kittenish routines, and even less with helplessness or passivity. If we stop to think for a minute, it's easy to see that helpless, passive women would have been a terrible social liability for much of human history. Can you imagine how laughable such notions would have been to ancient Celtic women who were responsible for battle strategies, religious rituals, and whose councils were the highest decision-making bodies in their communities? We don't even have to think back thousands of years; just think what our own country's story would read like if our Indian, European, African, and Asian foremothers hadn't shouldered their enormous responsibilities.

As a Piscean, you're a water-sign person, not a wishy-washy woman. Our culture's distrust of the feminine translates feminine water into metaphors for instability, moodiness, and other negative traits. In China, however, the philosophical book, the *I Ching*, uses water as an example for right conduct in difficult or dangerous situations because water flows steadily on, attempts neither too much nor too little, and does not change its own character but moves around the obstacles in its way. From water we may learn how to maintain our personal integrity while coping with difficult people and problems. If nothing else, this instance of another culture's attitude toward water reminds us that there are at least two ways of looking at anything. The dismal view we're used to is not necessarily the best, most useful approach, so let's explore your sign with an eye to a more positive interpretation.

If you wish to read this information in terms of your Moon rather than your Sun, you'll need to shift your thinking from your identity, your will, your essential self—the way you manifest being you in the world—to focus instead on the inner you, the emotional you—your *self* at the deepest levels of your unconscious. Your Moon not only has to do with your feelings but also includes those things you take for granted in your self, those things you assume everyone else feels or is like, since they are so essential to your personality. They are ever present but elusive qualities you know intimately and yet can't quite put your finger on. The Moon also has to do with what went on in your family of origin, your home, your background. It concerns all those things that give you a sense of emotional security.

Specifically, Moon in Pisces endows you with a powerful imagination that can serve as an invaluable resource, so nurture it and allow yourself plenty of dreaming time. A Piscean Moon also emphasizes and deepens your emotions, and although you will have to exercise some discipline over your feelings so they don't run you ragged, you are virtually guaranteed a rich emotional life. Moon in Pisces creates a strong bond with your family of origin and the difficulty may be that you will feel guilty when you branch out. You'll have to come to terms with this since your need for independence and for a large circle of friends are vitally important. A Piscean Moon is expressed in the feminine side of your nature through your gentleness, kindness and courage, your quick sympathy for others, and your receptivity to feelings and ideas. It also occasionally manifests itself as a reluctance to put yourself forward, so work on strengthening your self-confidence to avoid missing out on golden opportunities. Above all, Moon in Pisces gives you a wonderful sense of humor, an ability to laugh at yourself, and a keen perception of the funny side of life.

The feminine that Pisces represents and which operates within your character is a complex of qualities and abilities related to the processes of creating, nurturing, and transforming. We resemble the ancient Goddess of Moon and Sea in that life proceeds from us: our children live first within our bodies, and after they are born we care for them until they can function independently. This miraculous biological power which most of us possess is given to us as a choice, and we make the ultimate decision as to when and if we use it. It is not the only power we possess nor is it our only mark of distinction. Doesn't it seem odd that I have to say this? But in truth many of us have come to resent any mention of our childbearing abilities because they have been used as an excuse to limit and belittle us. Think about that for a moment. Doesn't it strike you as bizarre? The fact is, though, that these are wonderful, glorious powers. Whether or not you choose to use them, you are delighted by children and wonderful as a parent, teacher, or simply as a friend.

We also tend to be suspicious of our ability to care about others and, unfortunately, our wariness is justified in a society that encourages us to care about others rather than ourselves. But I remember one bitterly cold winter evening when I saw an old woman stop by a drunk sprawled asleep on a library's steps to tuck his jacket around him; for some reason, the competence and matter-of-factness with which she performed this simple kindness brought to mind the millions upon millions of women through the long ages of time who performed similar compassionate actions and who transformed us into human beings. I felt very proud to be a woman, and very sad that we have come to distrust our heritage as the means by which we've been made history's fools. But I think we lose if we cooperate in belittling these aspects of our traditions. Compassion, concern for others, and working out humane controls to prevent destructive behavior are vital to our individual lives, and are sorely needed in our national life. However, we needn't maintain a narrow perspective on our mothering abilities, either. They are not the be-all and end-all of our existence as women, and they are not exclusively ours—which is to say that we have the right to expect compassionate behavior from men as well.

A Pisces Sun endows you with extraordinary abilities to create and to nurture. These abilities include foresight, imagination, sharp observation, thought, the perseverance to develop skills and carry projects to completion, and the patience to teach so that hard-won knowledge is not lost.

You have a very active imagination, which provides you with interesting, exciting fantasies, but you like best to direct it toward real problems. Your dreams are an especially rich source of ideas—one very good reason for you to pay serious attention to them. Like Scorpio people, you are intrigued by mysteries and unsolved problems; this extends from taking pleasure in a good puzzle or mystery story to learning every facet of whatever work you're involved in, and on to the most profound spiritual· level. Pisces not only sharpens your appreciation of life, but it also makes you aware of its mystery. You have a great desire to understand that mystery as completely as possible, and this imparts a strong religious sensibility to your temperament. You may satisfy this by joining one of the traditional religious organizations, but you're just as likely to be comfortable as a complete independent or as a member of a less conventional group.

In any case, your spiritual awareness is intensified by other Piscean gifts—namely, a very active intuition and often an unusually high degree of psychic ability. Once again, cultural attitudes may make you very uneasy with these gifts. For several centuries, these abilities have been viewed as ridiculous, contemptible, or downright dangerous. They've been used as reasons to burn people alive for witchcraft and, in easier times, they've been the butt of countless jokes. As a result, we really know very little about them, although we're finally beginning to realize that older civilizations were more sensible than we, and that these faculties are to be respected and cultivated. At the moment, however, you may be more pleased to be told that you're intuitive and psychic than to actually experience this. It may embarrass you to know without understanding *why* you know, especially when other people press you for an explanation.

Please don't belittle your insights with apologetic jokes about "women's intuition." It isn't a joke; it's a kind of thinking—one of many kinds of thinking you do—and you can do it very well. Consider one of history's more delightful ironies: Sir Francis Bacon, who developed the scientific method our century swears by, arrived at his brilliant conclusions by great, splendid leaps of intuition. Of course, you're not required to be brilliant every second in order to justify your insights, so don't harass yourself with that idea. Use your gifts, develop them as fully as you can, and learn by your own experience how they can help. They may simply give you an uncanny ability to predict who's calling on the telephone. On the other hand, they may save your life, as they did for one person who obeyed an intuition and canceled passage on the *Titanic*. They will almost certainly help you sort out the information and experience you've accumulated and to come up with new ideas, a fresh way of looking at things, or a course of action when you need it; it would be wasteful to discount that sort of assistance.

You can, however, discount the popular misconception that psychic, intuitive people are frail, other-worldly creatures who wander about with an ethereal air, trailing veils. I find this image of Pisces so exasperating that I may err on the opposite side. But it's been my observation that Piscean people have tremendous zest, dearly love a good time, and possess great physical and moral courage—qualities that are a great deal more substantial and infinitely more attractive than the shadowy, will-o'-the-wisp idea. If you do trail veils, it will be to great dramatic effect. You are concerned with appearances in that you prefer to present yourself to the best possible advantage; in this respect, you may consider yourself part of a great historical tradition. Women have been making themselves, their surroundings, and their artifacts as beautiful as possible from time immemorial. This desire to create beauty and be beautiful seems to have been even stronger in matriarchal societies, where women's survival did not depend on being attractive to men, so it seems safe to conclude that it is prompted by women's personal aesthetic sense.

Your own taste leans toward the grand, the splendid, the dramatic. In your youth you may be overly impressed by displays of wealth and by the lives of the rich and famous. Time tempers this, but while it lasts it acts as a spur to your own ambitions. You admire the comfort and freedom enjoyed by the wealthy and the personal accomplishments of the famous, because these are things you desire for yourself and you will work hard to achieve them. Fortunately, you take great pride in your own accomplishments and are not abashed when other people admire you. Keep it up! The abilities to express pleasure in a compliment and to be at ease in the spotlight are valuable assets; they make other people a great deal more comfortable than false modesty would, and they help you to take risks and to enter challenging situations. I'm not suggesting that you should expect admiration at every moment or that you should live for other people's good opinions. You may do some of that when you're young—but who of us doesn't? It takes all of us a bit of time to find our own center. You are helped in this by the fact that you form very strong, definite opinions and have the courage to express them, and therefore you learn very early that the sky will not fall when you champion your views rather than accept somebody else's ideas about how you should think, feel, and live your life.

Use this strength of mind in coming to terms with your own energy pattern. Most of us live according to some schedule or another—work, school, meetings, what-have-you—and we usually have to adapt to those schedules even when they're at odds with our particular body time. To complicate matters, we tend to expect to perform at the same level day after day, allowing perhaps for a brief lapse when we menstruate. In biological truth, no one—female or male—stays at the same level from one hour to the next, let alone from day to day. We're like the moon in that we change constantly, yet our patterns are sufficiently repetitive for us to develop some sense of continuity and stability. It would be lovely if we learned from childhood to respect the fact that we are cyclical creatures by nature. But that isn't the way we're brought up, and it's a struggle to learn as adults that we're not guilty of a major character flaw when our psychic and physical energies are temporarily unsuited to the demands we must cope with. Personally, I think it's worth the effort to shake free of the old, futile, and questionable ideal of machinelike efficiency and regain the valuable benefits our "inconsistencies" have to offer.

You, for example, experience periods of coolness—times when you feel relatively detached from other people and are able to view everything clearly and dispassionately. For a person like yourself, who is usually intensely compassionate, these intervals can be very distressing, even frightening. What's happened to you? Have you turned into a heartless icicle? Is this the real you coming to the surface? No, you're not heartless, and yes, this is the real you—or rather, a real, valid part of you that helps balance your life. Your retreats into detachment give you an emotional vacation and prevent you from carrying empathy to excess. They are times when you need more privacy and, fortunately, they provide the wherewithal for you to get it by putting your needs first. They also give you a chance to evaluate your relationships, goals, and activities to see if there are any changes you wish to make. Perhaps their most important function is to allow your psyche to restore and refresh itself. In fact, without such intervals of rest and regrouping of inner resources, so much of which is done subconsciously, it would not be possible to grow and adapt and create. There's no need to fear or to attempt to deny the cooler aspects of yourself. These do not represent an enemy within; instead, they are allies with positive contributions to make so that you can have a whole, well-integrated personality.

On a monthly basis, you tend to be most introspective when the Moon transits your sign, Pisces. External events make little impact upon you and you move through your usual routines as if through a dream. It's possible to lash yourself out of your preoccupation by feeling guilty, but frankly I see little point to that unless you have an emergency that demands your concentration. Otherwise, I recommend that you allow yourself to be absorbed in your thoughts and dreams and that, for safety's sake if nothing else, you keep your routine as simple and undemanding as possible. The Aries transit, which follows, generally finds you less preoccupied but still feeling distant. You are physically energetic but uninvolved emotionally. This is an excellent time in which to launch new projects, especially those which present initial difficulties or will arouse some opposition, either from yourself or from other people.

The Moon's transit of Taurus restores the emotional color to your life. The danger here is that, if you haven't made a friend of your cooler side, you will be so relieved to be a feeling, responsive being again that you'll overextend yourself and exhaust your energies. However, if you can be accepting of yourself during the Pisces and Aries transits, then Taurus should be a very balanced, smooth, hassle-free time in which to feel your best and accomplish a great deal. Gemini transits accentuate your sociability; whenever possible, try to schedule parties, outings, anything involving groups of people for these periods, because you will really enjoy such activities then. Reasonably enough, the urge to expand, to be with lots of people, is balanced by a need for more privacy during Cancer transits. These are not as intense as the Piscean periods, but they're definitely not the ideal time for a gala party. You are much more comfortable alone or with your immediate family or your closest friends. You get a great deal of pleasure from low-key activities such as reading, watching television, or working on a hobby. In regard to work, try to deal with routine matters that require minimum concentration. You won't find such tasks any more fascinating than usual, but their dullness will soothe rather than irritate you.

Leo transits are probably the trickiest of all for you. You feel as if you have unlimited strength and energy, but you don't quite know what to do with yourself and, consequently, you get frustrated and irritable. Also, the quality of your energy is very deceptive. You may feel as if you could move mountains, but in fact you're only able to dislodge a good-size rock or two. During these transits you're likely to experience strong urges to destroy and rebuild, and you chafe at clutter, at old ways, at any obstacle or inconvenience. Be careful. Resist the impulse to pull everything out of the closets or the files or the bookshelves or what have you, because you're liable to find that your energy deserts you and you're stuck with a worse mess than before, at the very time when disorder of any sort makes you feel absolutely frantic. Let off steam by tackling projects that are physically rather than intellectually demanding, and that can either be accomplished in a short period of time or broken down into separate stages and coped with bit by bit. An even better idea is to get out and play: walk, run, skip rope, skate, *move*. And keep your schedule as varied as possible; you don't have the patience to stick with any one thing for a long time, whereas you can make very decent progress on a variety of things.

Virgo transits are a tremendous relief. You're generally very clear about what you wish to do and your plans mesh nicely with your energy. Both Virgo and Libra transits are characterized by greater stamina, in contrast to Leo's brief rushes of intense energy, and they are far more comfortable for you. Both are excellent for activities requiring great concentration and perseverance. Virgo is exceptionally favorable for long-term planning, research, and decision making, while Libra stimulates your artistic interests.

Moon in Scorpio is another easy transit if you don't push yourself physically. It's a very easygoing period in which you feel relaxed and quite content to move at a slow tempo. It's also a reflective interval, but more on the order of quiet, peaceful musing than the intense soul-searching of a Pisces transit. You might just as well enjoy this period and be as lazy as you wish, because the intense energy that surges forth in the next transit is your guarantee that you're not sinking into the pit of sloth.

Sagittarius unleashes tremendous amounts of physical and mental power. Compared to your Scorpio self, you're a human whirlwind, eager to be with other people and do things. This is not only an excellent time to finish projects you started in Leo, but it's also perfect for travel and for new experiences. Your urge toward growth and expansion is continued during the Moon's transit of Capricorn, but at a steadier, less hectic pace. Capricorn, like Virgo, brings an intellectual emphasis, and you are more interested in exploring new ideas than in traveling to new places, unless these are somehow related to your work or private projects. Your energy starts to taper off during the Aquarian transit, which follows, and although you're at a medium level rather than a Scorpio low, it seems much less in comparison with the previous two periods. And it's erratic. You tire easily and it's difficult for you to gauge just how long you can sustain any particular activity. This may be somewhat disconcerting in terms of your usual routine, but fortunately it's no trouble to you as far as your personal needs and desires are concerned. In this transit, your focus shifts to spiritual concerns. You are still emotionally responsive, but there will be small patches of time when you'll be abstracted and not quite as attentive to the world around you. It's as if you are preparing for the intensive introspection of your Piscean transit; this, of course, returns us to the beginning of your monthly cycle, in which you are assimilating experience and getting ready for the next round of becoming.

On an annual basis, your peak period occurs in April and May. This does not necessarily mean that you are most physically active at this time, but that your imaginative and creative powers are operating at maximum. Conversely, your low period in October and November finds you quite busy, preparing for holidays, active in sports, working, and so forth, but you're not likely to come up with scads of fresh ideas or insights during these months. Your average periods generally last from June through September and then again from December through March. However, June and March are usually marked by greater creative energy and responsiveness.

Insofar as possible, try to schedule those activities that make the heaviest intellectual demands upon you for the first half of the year, when your efforts will meet with greatest success. For example, if you're in school, you'd do well to program your most difficult courses for the spring semester and go easy on yourself in the fall term.

I recommend that you go beyond the necessarily general sketch offered here and keep your own record for a couple of months to get an even better idea of your cycle. You are capable of superb self-discipline, but you achieve this by cooperating with your own rhythm and not by ignoring it or forcing yourself to run counter to it. Pisces generally makes it difficult for you to conform. You are acutely miserable in highly structured situations; obviously, you should avoid these like the plague. However, until you are guided by your energy pattern, you may waste valuable time alternately despising any discipline as so much weak-minded conformity and despairing of ever achieving the discipline you need to realize your goals. Neither of these states is especially pleasant or productive, and you can dispense with them by getting to know your cycle really well.

Pisces encourages you to be independent and ambitious, and these are powerful qualities to reckon with. I know that Pisceans are usually described as submissive, but as far as I've been able to discern there's no basis for this other than the fact that Pisces is a feminine sign and our culture considers it feminine to be submissive. If you really tried to curb your spirit to fit that idea, it would drive you to drink. Sexually, for example, you are best described as a virgin in the original sense of that word, when it meant an "independent woman." You are sensual and warm, and there's no question that you enjoy making love, but the idea of belonging to someone else is stifling. Given your compassionate, emotionally responsive nature, you might think it as natural as breathing for you to team up with someone early and live your life in partnership. The truth is that you give your deepest love and loyalty to family relationships first and to friendships second; you tend to regard your romantic attachments as entertainments. Like the Celtic women who are your spiritual foremothers, you are wary of marriage contracts and long-term commitments. No matter how much in love you may be, some portion of your soul remains on guard against encroachments on your personal freedom, and you need guarantees and reassurance that the commitment will in no way diminish you. Anyone who desires you for a wife will find it difficult to persuade you to marry, and it takes a great deal more than the exchange of vows before you fully accept your partner into the highest, kinship circle of relationships. You will be most compatible with partners who have an open, generous, affectionate nature, who are fairly easygoing, and who have a strong sense of personal identity, so that there will be no desire to try to curtail yours. Self-confidence will also enable your partners to hold their own in the spirited outbursts that you'll unleash from time to time. Such storms are bound to occur, since it is not your way to hoard up resentment and brood silently over grievances, and they also reintroduce the element of risk into your relationship, which relieves you of the sense of permanency for a time.

However, it's not too likely that you'll marry early, and there's a good portion of time in which you enjoy less serious attachments. You have a lifetime supply of sex appeal, so that whether or not you fit the current ideal of beauty, people are going to find you attractive. Paradoxically, there'll be many times when you ignore or forget this gift. One of the curious features of Pisces's influence is a tendency toward unrequited loves. You'll yearn after one person, yet accept invitations from somebody else who doesn't really matter to you. You'll see or create obstacles to union, sometimes by fixing your desire on someone who is patently unsuited for you, or by idealizing the person you love beyond mere mortal to unapproachable demigod. In my opinion, this pattern is a deliberate, although unconscious, piece of self-protection that allows you to keep the spirit of romance alive and yet permits you to concentrate on your ambitions without real interference.

The only caution I offer is that you keep clear of abusive people who would belittle you or treat your affection with contempt. Unfortunately, a lover of this type is quite socially acceptable. Few people will question why you choose to lavish time and affection on someone who continually "does you wrong." The main attraction of this sort of relationship is that it allows you to remain independent, since genuine intimacy is clearly impossible; in a way, you can have your cake and eat it, too. But I feel that you can preserve your personal autonomy with less cost to yourself, less damage to your self-esteem. Remember that your independence is your personal right, and there's no reason to punish yourself in order to have it. You commit no crime against your family or your society, either, by marrying late or by choosing not to marry at all. And you are entitled to have relationships that give you pleasure and that encourage your growth as a person.

In terms of careers, you generally excel in the sciences, particularly those related to health and medicine. Anything involving mathematics or music is also highly favored for you. However, rather than catalog all the possibilities open to you, I think it's more useful to review certain personal qualities that you might do well to keep in mind when considering any field of work. High on the list is a fact I've mentioned before: you suffer intensely in very structured situations that demand a high degree of conformity. A military career, for instance, is not ideal for you. You'd do much better in a field such as teaching or research, which allows considerable latitude for creativity and innovation. You are fortunate in being able to work well with other people and by yourself; in fact, you need to do both. It would be wise to check any job for the degree of independence it offers you and for the sort of balance between social and private contexts it provides. Whatever you choose, it's extremely important that you avoid deadend jobs and enter a field that offers at least reasonable prospects for advancement. There's no chance whatsoever that you'll eliminate ambition from your character—and no reason why you should. Instead, find ways to express that ambition so that it enhances your life rather than turns you sour in frustration and bitterness.

You might also bear in mind that you have a very retentive memory and an excellent instinct for seeing situations in their largest, most complete sense. These, combined with your humor, your warmth and charm, and your ability to create and enjoy good times, are wonderful assets in politics and public relations work. You have a gift for vivid, lively language as well, and are quite skillful at writing and speaking, talents that could serve you well in a number of fields, including such areas of communication as journalism, television, and publishing. You're quite adept at handling two things at once, and there's a very good possibility that you will either have two careers simultaneously or will use the skills and contacts from one to transform a hobby or avocation into another, full-fledged career.

By the way, I include homemaking in the category of careers because I can't think of a better word to describe it. Granted, it's different in that we have more choice about whom we'll live with than about whom we'll be with in other situations; our work is directly connected with our most intimate relationships; and as yet we're not compensated for it in outright salaries. Nevertheless, it's a whole complex of work activities and it calls forth some qualities and abilities and discourages others. You, for instance, will enjoy the variety of jobs homemaking entails but will be bored and frustrated by the repetitive tasks. It offers you a great deal of independence and enough challenges to keep you reasonably stimulated, but it doesn't provide sufficient scope for your ambition; you'll have to look elsewhere, to politics and other community affairs, to satisfy this need. If, like so many of us, you must hold an outside job in addition to running your home, be assured that you can manage this with comparative ease. However, don't let this tempt you into the Superwoman syndrome, especially since there are far better, more gratifying ways to use your energy.

Pisces has given you many splendid gifts and abilities with which to create an interesting, satisfying life for yourself. For you, these satisfactions will inevitably include the desire to meet challenges and the ability and pride to do your best by them. Your transitional periods from one nine-year cycle to the next may be difficult for you, because they'll be extensions of your cool, detached Pisces transits. Be patient with yourself, and recognize that these periods of emotional ebb are necessary for you to marshal your strength to proceed to the next stage of growth, and to decide in what direction you wish your life to proceed. Your concern for the spiritual aspects of life deepens as you grow older, and the insights you gain from your experiences can provide strength and clarity for others. Your guidance will be sought because you are sociable and caring, and your sense of humor makes you a delightful teacher. For you, old age will bring the very powerful satisfaction of sharing the wisdom and skills you've acquired. For this reason, I hope you never choose to isolate yourself in a community designed primarily for older people, but will live instead where your knowledge and companionship are available to a wide range of people. I hope also that you delight in your Piscean gifts always, and take pride in your great feminine heritage, as you add to that heritage with the qualities and achievements that are personally yours.

PISCES VISUALIZATIONS

You possess an extraordinary resource within you: your imagination. Through the power of your inward eye, you can tap into your innermost self, and into the energies of the universe. The thoughts you think, the messages you give yourself, the images you create in your imagination have tremendous power. You can literally transform your reality to fit the positive images you create mentally simply by creating those images often enough, and as specifically and clearly as you possibly can. Through such focused, purposeful "daydreaming," you can achieve an astonishing range of goals: practical goals such as weight loss, physical fitness, or money management; spiritual goals such as enhanced self-esteem, inner peace, and a deeper sense of connection with other living beings. For further information on this process, I recommend two books I've found useful, Shakti Gawain's *Creative Visualization*, and Shad Helmstetter's *The Self-Talk Solution*.

My primary concern here is empowering you to get in touch with the Goddess within you, the Eternal Feminine whose creative, nurturing, renewing energies live within us all. The Great Goddess is always ready to comfort, to heal, to strengthen, and to guide us whenever we are in need. Her images come to us from all parts of our world and from across great stretches of time. By visualizing Her in our mind's eye, by meditating on Her image, you and I not only receive help with specific problems and enhanced self-esteem but also reap the additional benefit of greater esteem for all women, past and present, and for the wonderful contributions women have made in creating and advancing civilization.

The images I sketch for you came to me through my research and through my own meditations. They may work differently for you than I've envisioned. And, of course, they're not the only images available to you. I suggest you read Merlin Stone's *Ancient Mirrors of Womanhood* and Barbara G. Walker's *The Woman's Encyclopedia of Myths and Secrets* to see what stories, prayers, and images resonate for you, and use them. I think you'll also find it illuminating simply to gaze within your own mind and see how the Goddess manifests Herself to you. I would be delighted to read your visualization experiences so if you would like to share them, please write to me, c/o the publisher.

How to go about visualization is very much a matter of personal choice: you may sit, stand, or lie down—whichever position you feel you can most comfortably maintain for ten to twenty minutes. You're probably best advised to be in a quiet, darkened room and to keep your eyes closed. Begin by relaxing your entire body. One technique is to imagine a comfortably warm, golden light surrounding you and taking away all tension in the area you're thinking of. Start with your feet and work up to the crown of your head. Once this is done, begin to construct your visualization in your mind.

What a rich array of images you have to choose from! All the mysterious feminine places like the sea, forests, and caves are yours to imagine. In profeminine traditions, these secret places are described as richly beautiful, gleaming with colors and jewels, offering heightened awareness and new perceptions, treasures, and wisdom. During those times when you are in the process of changing—of becoming—you might imagine yourself setting out on a voyage of exploration. Change evokes many emotions within us: fear, sorrow, exhilaration. We are always a little afraid to leave the familiar and we move toward the unknown with a heightened awareness of risk, even danger. As we change, we feel a sense of loss, however fleeting, at relinquishing what we once were. Yet our surrender of the past also generates tremendous excitement. And as we become familiar with the new and find out that we are not all that different, there is a distinctly pleasurable sense of our own courage, our increased competence and knowledge, and our own growth. You can use your visualizations to help you at every stage in this process.

One image that might be useful when you need comfort is that of the Goddess Ishtar of ancient Mesopotamia, who sailed the skies in her beautiful, luminous moon boat. Let Her sail into your mind and take your hand to steady you as you climb into the boat. Settle in and get comfortable. Perhaps you lean against the Goddess who is the Shining One, the Mother of All, and draw strength and solace from Her love and concern for you, for each of us. Enjoy the boat itself. It glows with a soft silver light and yet you can see through it, as if it were the clearest crystal. Despite its delicate, fragile appearance, it is solid and strong and nothing can upset or destroy it. As you sail through the sky, take in the beauties around you. You might see the sudden blaze of comets or the star-strewn Milky Way, named after the Heavenly Milk of the Goddess Hera. Beneath you is the inky blackness of the ocean, resembling in its rise and fall some great, shining sleeping beast. You notice a dove, the soft, amorous bird of the Goddess Aphrodite, symbol of Her Holy Spirit, resting, wings folded, on the waves, rocked to sleep by their peaceful rhythm. Listen to the now-gentle song of the sea and to the answering murmurs of lakes and rivers. All is serene, under the guardianship of the Great Goddess Ishtar, cloaked in Her merciful darkness, soothed by Her cool, gentle light.

There are times when the soft, gentle images of the Goddess do not answer your needs, when you need instead to call upon Her fierce courage and daring. If you feel fear and excitement mounting within you, try not to push them away or impose a quieter mood's images upon them. Ride with these feelings, match them with a vision filled with the energy of the Goddess. One that might serve you well sees you at the ocean's shore, where the waves rush in and foam coldly around your ankles. Some yards farther out you see great breakers rise like white-maned horses from the sea and come charging toward you. They are the horses of the Great Celtic Goddess, Morrigan, and the greatest of all is Morrigan Herself. Summon all your courage and leap upon the back of the wild Sea Mare. She turns and speeds away from shore, across the rolling

ocean's plains. Hold tight as She plunges into the depths of the sea's
green heart. The speed with which She moves is beyond anything
you have ever experienced. Frightened squid cloud the waters with
their ink as you streak past; other fish are merely flashes of silver or
brief glimpses of rainbow colors as they hurry out of your way. The
Morrigan gallops across the hills and valleys of the ocean's floor
toward a cave hidden deep within a coral reef. She slows to a walk
and you have the strange experience of riding upon Her back and
seeing Her face to face, simultaneously. Her eyes hold a challenge
to continue your adventure, to dismount and enter the cave and face
whatever waits for you there. I cannot presume to know what that
might be. You might meet Morrigan again in Her mermaid form,
sitting among the pearls and treasures gathered by the sea. You
might gaze into Her sea-green eyes that know all the world's
mysteries and see yourself as you have been, as you are, as you may
be. It is for you to part the seaweed curtain that masks the cave's
entrance, to enter and find out, to trust that the Goddess will not
desert you.

The times when you feel cool and detached, and not quite your
usual self, may distress you, as I mentioned earlier. An excellent way
to become more comfortable with yourself during these interludes is
to treat yourself to some playful visualizations. One I have a great
deal of fun with is imagining myself as a sea otter playing in the
ocean that is the Goddess as the Waters of Life. You might choose
to see yourself in a sunlit lagoon, the waters of the Goddess sliding
over your body as sleek as silk. The waters are so clear that you can
see every pebble, every little plant, every ridge in the golden sand of
the floor of the lagoon. It is a refuge of perfect privacy, sheltered by
beautiful trees whose leaves cast lacy shadows on the water. You
may dive and swim to your heart's content or float on the
sun-warmed surface, enjoying the cool touch of shade, the heat of
the sun on your body.

If you are feeling more adventurous or wish to get away from it
all, you may choose to ride upon a dolphin with Japan's Great
Goddess Kwannon. You may prefer to become a dolphin or great
fish, child of Tiamat of Mesopotamia, of Atargatis of Syria, of
Nuneit of Egypt, of She who was everywhere the Goddess of the

Sea, whatever Her name. Swim by Her side in perfect safety and rejoice in Her beautiful waters. Swim in the deep blue of the Pacific or travel north to the Arctic Ocean, where brilliant white islands of ice float in the water and seals and sea lions play. Explore the green mysteries of the Atlantic or the clear turquoise Caribbean or the calm sapphire of the Mediterranean. Listen to the songs of whales and dolphins, the voices of the sea that few humans are privileged to hear. Return from this visualization to the shore of your choice, your own heart singing with the wonders you have seen, the limitless bounty of the Great Goddess.

The Piscean soul reminds me of those beautiful, clear springs bubbling up unexpectedly in a forest. Priestesses used to withdraw to them to listen to the voice of the water, the voice of the Goddess unraveling the knotty problems that beset us humans, revealing the mystery of dreams. Your imaginative and intuitive powers make it virtually mandatory for you to allow yourself time for reveries, daydreams, and meditations. Withdraw within yourself to sit by a spring of your own imagining or stroll along the banks of a river that rushes singing along or slides tranquilly by, depending on your mood. The Celts used to throw in their golden jewelry as offerings to the Goddess of Waters along with their prayers. You may wish to offer your thanks for the wonderful gifts you have received, and for the ideas and insights to come. Allow the wellspring of your mind to bring you whatever it will; make no judgments on the thoughts and images that bubble up. Simply watch and listen to the voice of the Goddess within you and return from your visualization refreshed.

ARIES
March 20– April 20

ARIES: Three priestesses revivify a ram sacrificed over the sacred flame of the Great Goddess of Fire and Transformation. Based on an Attic amphora, sixth century BC, preserved in the British Museum, London, England.

Originally, your sign, Aries, whose symbol is the ram, concluded the zodiacal year, and it stayed in last place until about 2000 B.C. The ram of the earliest zodiacs is a far cry from the prancing, energetic symbol you and I are used to. The Egyptians pictured him at rest, his head facing Pisces, his tail toward Taurus. One explanation given for his posture is that he represented the time when rams were separated from ewes. However, Aries, like every other sign of the zodiac, was first and foremost a religious image commemorating the gifts we humans received from our major deity, the Great Goddess. He signified the death of winter and the rebirth of spring in its first gentle stirrings. He also symbolized the fire building within the earth—the fire of volcanoes and the fire of growth—all things that signaled a fresh start. It may seem strange to us that as a symbol of death and rebirth, of resurrection, he should be in last place. But our ancestors saw the universe as feminine, as an endless cycle created and sustained by the Goddess. In their view of life, there was no final end, and all things returned to their beginnings. It made perfect sense that there should be two spring signs: the quieter image of Aries for newly resurrected life, and the charging bull of Taurus for the rush of life forces released in spring and for the New Year.

So how did Aries get moved to first place? The explanation usually given by astronomers is a phenomenon known as the precession of the equinoxes, whereby a constellation seems to slip backwards in the sky. First Taurus gave way to Aries, then Pisces took over from Aries around the time that Christianity, whose symbol is the fish, began its ascent as a religious world power. And now Pisces gives way to Aquarius. However, nobody rushed to redraw the zodiac to keep up with these astronomical events, except for the Aries takeover from Taurus. What may seem like a minor revision to us was made at the cost of great heartbreak and struggle, and it represented a major social, political, and religious reorganization in many human communities. The ram took on a livelier aspect when it became the symbol of those who favored patriarchy, who had transformed the relatively new ritual of marriage from a contract identifying a man as a safe male, who could be trusted near a woman's children and who was entitled to the friendship and help of her brothers, into a man who owned the woman and all her children. The rewards of patriarchy, or "father-right," were private property and private leadership of one's family. Matriarchal men were really fraternal men, living within a framework of brotherhood in relationship to other males of the group. The emphasis was on group survival. Prestige and gain did not confer the right to rule others, and it was the obligation of the group to see that all members were properly provided for. A clan might grow wealthy, but that wealth was shared by all members of the clan. Property, rights, and names descended from mothers to daughters and from uncles to nephews. Patriarchy meant the chance for an individual man to become wealthy; property, rights, and names descended from father to son. Patriarchy also meant a religious shift, elevating male gods to the highest level of importance and belittling female divinities or eliminating them entirely.

Nomadic shepherd groups were the first to adopt the ram as their symbol in their bid for power, which they accomplished either by invading or grafting themselves onto agricultural settlements. It was not an easy or swift process. Patriarchy was first attempted in Egypt under the Hyksos, the shepherd kings, but their reign came to a dismal end in the eighteenth century B.C., when a matriarchal counterrevolution overthrew them. They had made an impact on Egyptian religion, however, and myths were generated in which the Great Goddess Isis was torn between Her loyalty to Her brother and Her commitment to Her husband. In Turkey and Anatolia, the archaeological evidence indicates that the struggle between the bulls and the rams went on for hundreds of years, each side destroying the others' images, and giving the final victory to the patriarchs in about 1200 B.C. Around that same time a group of Aryans under a leader named Rama invaded India from the north and set about establishing patriarchy. Their symbol was the ram and they traced the origins of Aryan life to fire. They succeeded militarily long before they triumphed in the suppression of women. The early Vedas show that women were independent, highly respected, and participated fully in all aspects of life. Eventually, however, Brahmin opposition to women succeeded; they were made totally dependent on their fathers and husbands and even forbidden to read the sacred texts they'd helped write. This was not true for the Dravidian people of southern India, who remained matriarchal for many centuries.

Let's take a quick look now at your sign in relationship to fire and see what that adds to our understanding of Aries. The gift of fire, or rather the control over fire, was one of the blessings, like agriculture, that revolutionized human life. According to the Greeks, we should be grateful to the demigod Prometheus, whose name means "forethought." Prometheus had a checkered career in relation to the Olympic gods. He alternately helped and angered Zeus, "the father of the gods." His first offense was to fashion us mortals from clay and then to teach us all the useful arts he knew. Zeus feared that we would become as powerful as the gods, and he had a fit every time Prometheus taught us something. The crowning blow came when Prometheus sneaked into Olympus and stole a fiery ember from the Sun's chariot to give to us. Enraged, Zeus chained Prometheus to a mountaintop, to be visited daily by a vulture who tore out his liver. Each night his liver would be made whole again so that he might suffer renewed agonies when the sun rose on a new day. Eventually, Prometheus was released from this horrible torment.

We know Prometheus as a hero, and the concept of Promethean man, who dares defy the gods for the sake of knowledge, is treated with great respect in our literature. But when we dig deeper, we find that our Prometheus story reverses a theme popular from a much earlier stratum of myth. In Goddess-worshipping groups, Prometheus was neither a demigod nor a benefactor. Instead, he was a young scamp who'd filched some of his grandmother's fire and caused all manner of havoc with it until she caught up with him and brought everything under control again. Scholars may not be able to pinpoint how we first mastered fire, but they are in agreement on who mastered it and the credit, they say, belongs to women.

Women's control over fire is reflected in the many fire Goddesses worshipped around the world, such as Fuji of Japan, Pele of Hawaii, the Aztecs' Cihuacoatl, and Egypt's Sekhmet, to name just a few. Judging from our rituals, we used fire first as a means of defense. Biological events such as menstruation and childbirth drew predators to us, lured by the smell of blood. So we created fire barriers to protect ourselves, placing the menstruating woman or the woman giving birth next to the fire in the center of the encampment. Holding blazing torches, we formed a ring around her and made as much noise as we could. Later on, after we'd developed agriculture, we adapted this protective rite to planting and harvest rituals, and carried torches as we circled our fields in the moonlight, protecting our Great Mother Earth.

Women turned the fear of fire to their advantage in yet another interesting way. We believed that our own blood was a form of fire, a manifestation of the moon's light, and terrible things were predicted for anyone so rash as to bother a menstruating woman. This claim may seem farfetched to us, but it carried conviction for people who were mystified by menstruation and believed it was a magical process, and who had observed the parallels between women's cycles and the moon's. The triangular equation of women, fire, and the Great Goddess as the Moon sanctified women's blood and helped safeguard us. Convinced of the Moon power of their blood, and believing it unwise to combine the two kinds of power, women excused themselves from fire-tending duties during their menses. The Vestal Virgins of Rome, like Moon priestesses elsewhere, continued this custom. With the advent of patriarchy, however, women's blood was gradually redefined from sacred to contaminating, and the dire predictions we had created as protections were turned against us to label us unclean.

History certainly does have its little ironies, doesn't it? One of the things that strikes me as ironic in our time is the striking differences in the way Aries is interpreted for men and for women. All too often Aries seems to be a sign that should have been reserved "for men only." Aries-influenced women are urged to curb their fiery, independent spirits. They are given the message that the very qualities that make for leadership in men make for awkward social relationships when they occur in women. Such ideas hark back to the Victorian era when the ideal—if you can call it that—was that men were the lords and masters and women were happily submissive to them. Women also couldn't vote, own property, or have custody of their children in the rare case of divorce. Naturally, in that kind of situation we could hardly expect that initiative, independence, assertiveness, and qualities of that sort would rank high on the list of womanly virtues—and sure enough, they didn't. Obviously also, there were a lot of women who refused to abide by that definition of femininity and who had the spirit and initiative to fight for the rights we now enjoy. Neither did your foremothers thousands of years ago sit around waiting for someone else to tell them how to survive; in fact, they took the matter of self-protection into their own capable hands. Does it make sense, then, for any of us—particularly an Aries—to take such a definition seriously? Let's loosen those Victorian stays, free ourselves from that nonsense, and explore your sign as if it came fresh from that far distant past when women were highly respected participants in every sphere of life.

If you wish to read this information in terms of your Moon rather than your Sun, you'll need to shift your thinking from your identity, your will, your essential self—the way you manifest being you in the world—to focus instead on the inner you, the emotional you—your self at the deepest levels of your unconscious. Your

Moon not only has to do with your feelings but also includes those things you take for granted in your self, those things you assume everyone else feels or is like, since they are so essential to your personality. Your Moon gifts might not be the most obvious features in your personality. They are ever present but elusive qualities you know intimately and yet can't quite put your finger on. The Moon also has to do with what went on in your family of origin, your home, your background. It concerns all those things that give you a sense of emotional security.

Specifically, Moon in Aries endows you with an active, powerful imagination that is a quick, ready source of ideas. It also provides you with a great capacity for enthusiasm and a love of action. An Arian Moon stimulates your emotions, making you quick to respond, and you will probably have to learn to control your temper and to protect your feelings from being easily hurt. If yours has been an unhappy childhood, you may choose to detach yourself in adulthood from your family of origin or live at some distance from them. Conversely, if your earliest relationships were nurturing, you will give generously of your talents and energies on behalf of your family. Moon in Aries is expressed in the feminine side of your nature in your courage, your daring, and your love of new ideas, new people and new experiences. It is also apparent in your love of children, and your open-hearted, generous approach to life. Above all, an Arian Moon strengthens your self-will, enabling you to set goals and achieve them.

Your Aries Sun influence gives you, among other things, tremendous drive, ambition, an innovative imagination, and the courage and persistence to push your plans and ideas through to completion. These are definitely not gifts you should waste. Your relationships with men can accommodate these qualities rather than suppress them. If you've been told to stop being "bossy," to let the man take the lead, have the ideas, make the decisions, you'd be well advised to ignore this advice. Let's face it; whenever we *let* someone "be the boss," we inwardly sneer at or condescend to that person. It is perfectly appropriate for a mother to let her child have something like a toy or a piece of candy, or to let her son, say, perform a responsibility and be charmed by how cute he is acting like a grown-up. But on the basis of one adult to another, nobody—female or male—has the power that *let* implies. I think it's safe to say that you and I don't go to bed with or marry little kids. So if we're sitting around our kitchens, talking with other women about how we let our men think that they make the decisions, we're either fooling ourselves or we're behaving like servants who've put one over on their masters. What exactly is so feminine and appealing about that?

You have other options to choose from. You can team up with someone without either of you being "boss" and "bossed." Decision making can shift from one to the other, depending on whose talents are best suited for the decision involved. It's also possible for you to find someone whose abilities lie in other directions than leadership, who would just as soon have you be the one who gives direction to the family and who doesn't give a rap what the neighbors think about your arrangement. You might prefer and need a partner who is very supportive of your ambitions—and that relationship is just as valid and gives each of you full value for your commitment as those in which the partner's ambitions are at the forefront. We've been taught to think of teams like these as "domineering wife and hen-pecked husband," but that is not necessarily the case.

If you're not comfortable with being the leader in your own home, find someone whose leadership you genuinely respect instead of merely pretending to. Or choose people who can speak up when they feel they are being pushed around, who will let you know directly when and if you're invading their personal sphere. It is, after all, our responsibility to notify others when we feel our rights or feelings are being abused, and to specify what constitutes an infringement on us. It is not your responsibility to read other people's minds or to second-guess them so that you can tailor yourself to some idea of what you should be in the relationship. Like the rest of us, you no doubt have weaknesses enough without having to pretend to be weak when you're not. I don't know if you were taught this, but when I was growing up we were encouraged to downplay our intelligence. What were the rewards of such behavior? To be bored to death and to miss out on all the pleasure and satisfaction of using our intelligence. We should have been urged to use our smarts to the limit, to learn, and to find boys who were as smart as we were. I urge you to be yourself and find people who are equal to you.

Aries prompts you to go out and get what you want, and that doesn't halt itself at the boundary line of sexual relationships. I see no reason why you shouldn't call up someone whom you find attractive and invite that person to go out. The worst that can happen is that your advance will be declined. Then you'll know, and you won't have spent hours waiting by the phone. You can chalk that person off, or try to figure out another way to kindle interest in your charms. And the chances are very good that you'll enjoy being the active initiator, certainly far more than if you force yourself to be passive.

When it comes to sex, you give yourself wholeheartedly to the experience. You are sensual and particularly responsive to a partner who is willing to experiment with new techniques, since the sense of novelty is important to you. It is not necessary for you to commit yourself to someone in order to have a good time, and you will probably have a great many liaisons in your lifetime. Your ardor never blinds you to your needs. You have little patience with someone who is unable to satisfy you. An unsatisfactory lover isn't likely to get too many chances to improve with you, because you'll start looking elsewhere pretty quickly. You are very candid about sex and quite comfortable discussing it with your friends. You don't hesitate to talk about your fantasies, the techniques you prefer, and what appeals to you and arouses you physically. And your conversation can be an eye-opener for other women.

It is important that your partner share your values, and this holds true for close friends, too. You usually have a highly developed sense of fairness and ethics, and an equally high regard for honesty and integrity. Despite the cost to yourself, you will speak out in defense of someone who is being treated unjustly. Even as a child, you can't stand for someone to be picked on or excluded from a group. Your pride and your sense of honor virtually guarantee that you are aboveboard in your dealings with others, and you will demand the same treatment in return. You are definitely a woman of your word and you keep your promises. Be careful, therefore, about what commitments you make.

You tend—especially in your youth—to be attracted to the rich, powerful, or famous. You're not terribly interested in the fact that they have gained wide social approval, but you're impressed that they have managed to make a personal impact upon society. I suggest that you regard your admiration as a barometer of how much you would like to do the same yourself, and direct your efforts to making your own impact. It's one thing to learn, to spend some of your early years in a sort of apprenticeship, but it would be a poor use of your own gifts to devote your life to being a fan.

Aries inclines you toward self-reliance and independence. You tend to be wary of your emotions, to experience them as a hindrance, and to be more directed toward thought and action. Naturally this doesn't mean that you don't have feelings; you can be warm and affectionate or blaze into anger or be sad or any of the rest of it. But the emotional content of a situation is not nearly as interesting to you as what you can do and what ideas or plans it generates. However, yours is a very generous nature, especially toward those you love. You are very giving of your time, money, possessions, and skills, and you will not only share all that is yours but go out of your way to be helpful. It is difficult for you to curb your generosity, but you do need to learn not to overextend yourself, not to spend every last dime on gifts, not to sacrifice your needs and plans to accommodate others on a routine basis. Save that kind of generosity for emergencies.

Your career is liable to be quite varied. You may direct yourself to one central cause and crusade for it in many different ways—for example, by writing, lecturing, making films, designing courses, campaigning and holding public office, and so forth. The issues that appeal to you are probably connected to freedom, people's rights to determine their own lives, and justice. The brashness and sarcasm that can crop up in your conversation make you an excellent choice for the spokeswoman to blast an injustice. New ideas, new ventures appeal to you strongly; you're likely to be unconventional in the way you live your life and iconoclastic in your approach to social tradition.

If you don't group your resources around a single issue, then you will probably live your life as a series of exciting adventures, moving from job to job or from field to field. This pattern satisfies your need for movement, for change of scene and change of pace. It allows you to build an immense repertoire of skills and to test yourself in a wide variety of situations. It strengthens your self-confidence to meet challenges successfully and to know that you're competent in many different areas. You possess a high degree of courage, including physical bravery, and you may enter high-risk jobs. It wouldn't trouble you at all to be a sky diver or a scuba diver or to pilot a plane or to drive a truck around hairpin curves on mountain roads. It exhilarates you to take chances and, while I can't bring myself to urge you toward daring undertakings, I wish you all the best if you do.

There is some chance that when you start out on your career you may underestimate your worth, and be so delighted to have your efforts recognized that you accept less money or less advantageous terms than you merit. Protect yourself by getting practical as swiftly as possible. It's your personal style to prefer the grand and the generous, so it may strike you as petty to quibble about a few dollars. Learn to quibble. If, for example, you're a writer, speaker, or photographer, get yourself a tough agent who will fight for your interests. In new situations in which you must handle the financial end yourself, take some time to find out just what the going rates are for someone of your experience. You tend to be honest and fair in your business dealings, and that's quite sufficient to make a good impression. Anything beyond that is unnecessary. Remember, you can't cash in those "good impressions" at the bank to buy the equipment you need or to finance the plans you have. You are excellent at swift analysis and response, and this can be applied to the financial sphere of your life as well as any other. You can easily understand contracts and other legal papers, and you sense what is or is not to your advantage even when you're reluctant to speak up. This is too important an area for you to suddenly get shy, so try to hurry yourself here. I recommend that you never delegate these matters totally to somebody else; no matter how expert your advisers are, be sure to review all documents yourself.

There is no question that you possess leadership ability. It might be described as "where you go, others will follow." You give orders, but you're not overly fond of doing so, primarily because you love your own freedom too much to want to hang around supervising others. You'd prefer that other people see for themselves what needs doing and do it promptly and skillfully. As an employee, you'll do best in jobs that give you a great deal of latitude to express your own initiative and to deal with people directly. You'll work best for someone who regards you as a protégée and is interested in teaching you as much as possible, helping you further your career. This is a role that you, too, will probably play when you are older, and you can be very generous and helpful as a guide to younger people. As an employer, you might spare yourself a lot of irritation by taking particular pains to hire highly competent people who won't need much supervision, so that you can devote yourself to the projects dear to your heart.

Your Aries influence makes it very possible for you to become a personage, a public figure with a following of your own. Your enthusiasm inspires others to see the value of new ideas. You're an excellent strategist, which can serve you well in gaining the success and respect you desire as well as for any cause you espouse. This skill may cast you in the role of consultant as you get older and your experience and expertise are more widely recognized.

All your life you demonstrate a flair for presenting yourself and your surroundings to best possible advantage. Your personal style tends to be dramatic, and you choose clothes to very great effect. Your home and your office also reflect your ability to combine comfort and drama. If you should find yourself in the spotlight, these talents will ensure that you look very good there.

You're apt to cool quickly toward people or situations who hold no challenge or do not summon your creative abilities. Harking back to your sexual relationships, again, this makes you prefer jealousy to boredom. You're apt to take people for granted once you're sure of their affections; you may hear complaints about this, but then again you may not, depending on how this casualness suits the partner you've chosen. But in general there's the likelihood that people will be more committed to you than you will to them. That also makes it easier for you to be a public figure, where you'll need to be able to deal pleasantly with a great many people while reserving your major energy for achieving your goals.

In terms of energy, you have a good deal of it—and the stamina to back it up. You might like to sleep late in the morning, but you can start early and continue well into the night if your schedule is packed with many different things to do and people to see, or if you're hot on the trail of some new scheme. You are usually fond of the night and of nightlife, when everything seems to take on an added excitement, and your energy is highest in the evening. On an annual basis, your lulls tend to occur in late December and January, and again in August, especially toward the end of the month, lasting in early September. You may not recognize these as periods of low energy, but you'd be well advised to be careful of your health and not overload your schedule if you can possibly help it. Autumn is a generally strong period, when you're building momentum. Spring starts off slowly for you; it is the period of the year when you are at your most contemplative, and most likely to be reviewing what the past has meant for you and what you plan for the future. You're one of the people who is refreshed by travel, especially in the company of close family or friends. Vacations can restore you best if they are visits to unfamiliar places, or areas in which nature is a grand, dramatic spectacle, or if they offer you an opportunity to enjoy sports for which you rarely have time during the rest of the year.

Your monthly cycle is generally characterized by a strong need for activity, particularly for new ventures, during the Moon's fire transits—Aries, Sagittarius, and Leo. The Moon's transits of Cancer and Scorpio are difficult, frustrating times when you may be bored or tired or feel as if everything is going against you. You generally enjoy the periods when the Moon is in Taurus, Virgo, or Capricorn, and you find that these days bring strong, positive energies for both work and socializing. The air transits are also excellent, especially sexually, and you feel generous and expansive in general.

Your life is very much action centered, and your transitions from one period to the next are marked by bold, highly visible, external changes such as changing a job or studying for an entirely new profession. Your most difficult period tends to be your twenties, when the grand dreams of youth seem to get bogged down and you suffer a lapse of self-confidence. It is hoped that you will be allied as a protégée to an older, powerful person in a career; this is infinitely more valuable to you than if it occurs in a sexual relationship, where it will simply delay your own start even further. Transitions give you trouble in their initial months when you're casting about for which direction to move in and you feel as if you'll go crazy from inactivity.

Another awkward time occurs in your mid-forties, when you feel as if you've exhausted all the possibilities to be had from life and the future looms as a treadmill on which you'll simply be repeating yourself. This dread is unfounded and usually signals that you're preparing to make another very large, very important change in direction. I know many Aries people who have started new businesses in their sixties, so there's no real danger that you'll stay bored or purposeless for very long.

The Arian emphasis on action surfaces in regard to your home and your children. Homemaking, per se, doesn't interest you particularly. You want your home to be interesting, to reflect you personally. It definitely will, but you're not madly interested in all the little chores involved. A rousing bout of spring or fall cleaning suits you best because it is challenging and it gets done with, and that's that. You see your home in your usual sociable light, as a gathering place for family and friends. You love to have people drop in and visit, and you have a gift for making them feel very comfortable and welcome.

The most difficult part of parenting may be those times when your children have colds and you are confined to the house together. You much prefer to be up and doing, preferably out. You will positively shine as a parent who takes her children places and arranges wonderful outings for them. You enjoy the company of children and are usually very good at teaching them skills. And in your old age, they will find you fascinating because of your stories of your experiences.

You do not seek wisdom; it will come to you. Your experiences will teach you how to curb your temper, how to present your arguments persuasively when tact rather than force is more effective.

You are realistic and become increasingly skilled at discerning the swiftest, most effective path toward achieving what you desire. The greatest mistakes you can make are to try to live vicariously or to force yourself to be meek and weak, which you're not. You have received gifts that will enable you to live a highly exciting, purposeful life. Let us hope that by the time you are a very old woman you will be passing on your stories of all the adventures you've had, the many types of people you've met, the many things you've learned and done, and the wisdom you've gained from a richness of experience.

ARIES VISUALIZATIONS

You possess an extraordinary resource within you: your imagination. Through the power of your inward eye, you can tap into your innermost self, and into the energies of the universe. The thoughts you think, the messages you give yourself, the images you create in your imagination have tremendous power. You can literally transform your reality to fit the positive images you create mentally simply by creating those images often enough, and as specifically and clearly as you possibly can. Through such focused, purposeful "daydreaming," you can achieve an astonishing range of goals: practical goals such as weight loss, physical fitness, or money management; spiritual goals such as enhanced self-esteem, inner peace, and a deeper sense of connection with other living beings. For further information on this process, I recommend two books I've found useful, Shakti Gawain's *Creative Visualization*, and Shad Helmstetter's *The Self-Talk Solution*.

My primary concern here is empowering you to get in touch with the Goddess within you, the Eternal Feminine whose creative, nurturing, renewing energies live within us all. The Great Goddess is always ready to comfort, to heal, to strengthen, and to guide us whenever we are in need. Her images come to us from all parts of our world and from across great stretches of time. By visualizing Her in our mind's eye, by meditating on Her image, you and I not only receive help with specific problems and enhanced self-esteem but also reap the additional benefit of greater esteem for all women, past and present, and for the wonderful contributions women have made in creating and advancing civilization.

The images I sketch for you came to me through my research and through my own meditations. They may work differently for you than I've envisioned. And, of course, they're not the only images available to you. I suggest you read Merlin Stone's *Ancient Mirrors of Womanhood* and Barbara G. Walker's *The Woman's Encyclopedia of Myths and Secrets* to see what stories, prayers, and images resonate for you, and use them. I think you'll also find it illuminating simply to gaze within your own mind and see how the Goddess manifests Herself to you. I would be delighted to read your visualization experiences so if you would like to share them, please write to me, c/o the publisher.

How to go about visualization is very much a matter of personal choice: you may sit, stand, or lie down—whichever position you feel you can most comfortably maintain for ten to twenty minutes. You're probably best advised to be in a quiet, darkened room and to keep your eyes closed. Begin by relaxing your entire body. One technique is to imagine a comfortably warm, golden light surrounding you and taking away all tension in the area you're thinking of. Start with your feet and work up to the crown of your head. Once this is done, begin to construct your visualization in your mind.

The Goddess of Fire is the friend of your imagination to whom you can turn in your times of need. When you are bored and life seems stale, treat yourself to a break from dull reality and visit the Goddess in Her many manifestations. You may stroll in your mind through the night and gaze upward at the small fires of the stars sparkling in the sky. The Goddess as the Moon bathes you in Her silver glow, reminding you that you will, you do, you once did carry Her Moon-fire within you. You may choose instead to see yourself at the edge of the day, standing quietly as She whom the Arunta people of Australia called Sun Woman is born anew and the sky turns pink and gold with the joy of Her arrival. You may decide instead to rise and soar, to ride the currents of the air and gaze down on Japan's beautiful Mount Fujiyama, home of the powerful Goddess Fuji, whose power pours forth from the mountain in

flaming rivers of fire. You may prefer to see in your mind's eye the
smaller fires we humans keep alive in Her ancient memory, in the
candles we light for prayers, the dishes of flame eternally burning in
memory of our esteemed and beloved dead, the torches we pass one
to the other for the high goal of excellence in our Olympic Games.

When you are low in spirit, seek comfort from the Great
Goddess, Hestia, of Greece. The Shrine of Hestia feels as familiar
and comfortable as home. The Goddess welcomes you and leads
you by the hand to the hearth and sits with you on soft rugs and
cushions before the fire. You feel wrapped in the warmth of Her
love, perfectly content to watch the flames, green and blue, red and
fiery gold, dancing on the logs. You listen to the fire's song and
smell the perfume of the wood as it burns. As you dream before the
fire, the Goddess strokes your hair. All tension dissolves at Her touch
and you feel completely at peace. You can feel your spirit heal
within you, grow strong again, glow with the awareness that you are
loved as a child of the Goddess.

At points of change, when you are bewildered and seek to know
the direction you should take, visit the Temple of Vesta in Ancient
Rome. Set on the Palatine Hills, it shines white and splendid in the
sun. A priestess quietly welcomes you and, realizing your need, she
leads you to the tripod at the center of the temple, where the eternal
flame of the Goddess burns. You follow her, the marble floor cool
beneath your bare feet. You stand before the flames that sanctify the
city, in this temple dedicated to truth and justice and mercy. The
priestess leaves you before the altar. If you wish, she will stay a while
and listen as you sort out your thoughts. But she will neither judge
nor tell you what to do. You are at a point where you must seek your
own truth, your own path, and she withdraws in recognition of this.
Concentrate your mind on the flame of the Goddess. Its energy
purifies and transforms. Let your thoughts come as they will,
unchecked. Your steady gaze on the flame itself will purify your
mind, cleansing it of clutter and distraction, creating a clear, open
beautiful space in which to bring forth a vision of the way you must
go. Do not be discouraged if the way is not revealed immediately or
in its entirety. This is the type of vision that may need to be repeated
several days in succession or returned to at intervals.

If you're anything like the rest of us, there will be times when you feel guilty about something you've said or done or left undone. Feeling guilty, feeling "bad," makes us helpless and prolongs our difficulties. You have an excellent recourse at your disposal. Withdraw into your mind and march yourself up to the temple dedicated to Sekhmet, Egypt's Great Goddess of Fire. Holy Sekhmet, Lady of the Tongues of Flame, is tall and beautiful. She Who Burns All Evil has the head of a lion and She looks at you steadily with a lion's golden eyes. It is not easy to meet the gaze of Sekhmet, but you can do it. Stand quietly before Her and tell Her what you have done or failed to do. If you find yourself making excuses and shifting the blame onto other people or circumstances, try again. This time declare yourself: state what you have done and declare that you are responsible for it and whatever consequences may proceed from it. Be as specific as possible. If you need to, repeat this declaration until you become aware that you do accept responsibility for them. Sekhmet will not tell you that you are bad, or that everything's all right. She stands before you in Her strength so that you may regain your own, so that you may discard the role of victim and reempower yourself. When you return from this visualization, you will notice that you feel lighter and calmer, and that you now have the strength to face whatever lies ahead.

When the people around you are cynical or are less than honorable in their dealings, take your anger and discouragement to the Goddess. Stand before Her altar in your mind and rededicate yourself to Her precepts of truth, of generosity, of kindness to others. Declare your allegiance to these ideals by which She has guided us. Your declaration will serve to fortify you. Your own commitment may create commitment in others, may have effects far beyond what you can now imagine. You can also use this visualization to express your commitment to achieve any goal you aim for, and again you may be surprised at the profound results it brings about.

The following exercise is also one that may serve several purposes. You can use it when you feel threatened and in need of protection, or when you feel lonely and seek companionship, or when you feel discouraged and want a boost for your resolve. Imagine that you are in a beautiful forest at night. You are seated

next to a fire, in front of a cave, all your favorite possessions and your
gear in a sturdy bag beside you. Sit there by yourself for a moment
or two, noticing the details of the scene: the shape and color of the
rocks that hem in the fire, the great boulders near the mouth of the
cave, the trees as they bend slightly to catch the moon's light. Now,
one by one, invite the members of your family, even those who have
died or who live far away from you, to join you in a circle around
the fire. Next invite your friends to sit with you, and then your
casual acquaintances. As you sit together, you might tell each other
your favorite stories, jokes, and memories of each other and sing
your favorite songs. Become aware that other people have joined
you—people from the past, even from thousands of years ago. They
stand holding torches, forming a protective ring around you. They,
too, laugh and sing and tell stories. They tell you how Grandmother
braved the darkness and in her trust of the Goddess, snatched a
burning branch from a lightning-struck tree and brought it home to
them to guard forever. They tell you of their council fires where they
sorted out the problems of their people, and of their wonderful
dances and songs. You hear of the teachers and healers and all those
who in the name of the Great Mother helped light our way. As you
listen, your spirit expands and connects with those women of the
past. You realize that they and all those you love are always with
you, and that you are adding your stories and your efforts to theirs,
and continuing the Great Round of Life.

CHARTS OF THE
MOON'S TRANSITS

The moon is a relatively fast-moving heavenly body. It travels through each sign of the zodiac in the course of each month. The charts that follow will help you keep track of the moon's travels from now until 2000. That's a good eleven years in which you can anticipate and make the most of your own fluctuations in energy and mood as these are influenced by the moon. The charts are fairly simple to use: the listing for each month tells you first the day of the month the moon enters a sign; then the zodiac symbol for the sign it enters; and then the hour and minute of its entry. For example, on January 1, 1990 the moon enters Pisces at 6:11 A.M. If you need to know where the moon is on January 2 and there is no entry on that date, then you know that the moon is still in Pisces; you will see that it doesn't enter Aries until January 3 at 10:57 A.M.

For graciously preparing these charts, I thank Neil Michelsen, Astro Computing Services, Inc., P.O. Box 16430, San Diego, California, 92116-0430.

Key to the Zodiac Symbols

♈ Aries	♉ Taurus	♊ Gemini
♋ Cancer	♌ Leo	♍ Virgo
♎ Libra	♏ Scorpio	♐ Sagittarius
♑ Capricorn	♒ Aquarius	♓ Pisces

1989

January

1	♏	4pm34
4	♐	2am12
6	♑	8am14
8	♒	11am31
10	♓	1pm31
12	♈	3pm36
14	♉	6pm36
16	♊	10pm57
19	♋	4am57
21	♌	1pm02
23	♍	11pm32
26	♎	12pm01
29	♏	0am49
31	♐	11am30

February

2	♑	6pm30
4	♒	9pm51
6	♓	10pm52
8	♈	11pm18
11	♉	0am45
13	♊	4am22
15	♋	10am40
17	♌	7pm33
20	♍	6am34
22	♎	7pm05
25	♏	7am57
27	♐	7pm29

March

2	♑	3am58
4	♒	8am36
6	♓	9am59
8	♈	9am36
10	♉	9am25
12	♊	11am16
14	♋	4pm27
17	♌	1am13
19	♍	12pm39
22	♎	1am24
24	♏	2pm10
27	♐	1am54
29	♑	11am25
31	♒	5pm45

April

2	♓	8pm37
4	♈	8pm51
6	♉	8pm07
8	♊	8pm31
10	♋	11pm58
13	♌	7am31
15	♍	6pm39
18	♎	7am31
20	♏	8pm13
23	♐	7am38
25	♑	5pm15
28	♒	0am33
30	♓	5am03

May

2	♈	6am50
4	♉	6am55
6	♊	7am03
8	♋	9am19
10	♌	3pm23
13	♍	1am30
15	♎	2pm07
18	♏	2am48
20	♐	1pm52
22	♑	10pm54
25	♒	6am01
27	♓	11am13
29	♈	2pm25
31	♉	3pm59

June

2	♊	5pm02
4	♋	7pm17
7	♌	0am28
9	♍	9am29
11	♎	9pm31
14	♏	10am11
16	♐	9pm12
19	♑	5am41
21	♒	11am57
23	♓	4pm36
25	♈	8pm06
27	♉	10pm45
30	♊	1am08

July

2	♋	4am19
4	♌	9am37
6	♍	6pm04
9	♎	5am30
11	♏	6pm09
14	♐	5am31
16	♑	2pm01
18	♒	7pm35
20	♓	11pm07
23	♈	1am41
25	♉	4am10
27	♊	7am15
29	♋	11am32
31	♌	5pm41

August

3	♍	2am19
5	♎	1pm28
8	♏	2am05
10	♐	2pm02
12	♑	11pm16
15	♒	4am59
17	♓	7am46
19	♈	8am59
21	♉	10am10
23	♊	12pm39
25	♋	5pm13
28	♌	0am12
30	♍	9am29

September

1	♎	8pm47
4	♏	9am23
6	♐	9pm51
9	♑	8am13
11	♒	3pm02
13	♓	6pm07
15	♈	6pm38
17	♉	6pm22
19	♊	7pm16
21	♋	10pm50
24	♌	5am44
26	♍	3pm32
29	♎	3am15

October

1	♏	3pm53
4	♐	4am29
6	♑	3pm45
9	♒	0am07
11	♓	4am37
13	♈	5am41
15	♉	4am52
17	♊	4am19
19	♋	6am09
21	♌	11am47
23	♍	9pm15
26	♎	9am11
28	♏	9pm56
31	♐	10am23

November

2	♑	9pm46
5	♒	7am09
7	♓	1pm25
9	♈	4pm08
11	♉	4pm09
13	♊	3pm19
15	♋	3pm51
17	♌	7pm46
20	♍	3am54
22	♎	3pm25
25	♏	4am13
27	♐	4pm30
30	♑	3am26

December

2	♒	12pm42
4	♓	7pm48
7	♈	0am11
9	♉	1am59
11	♊	2am15
13	♋	2am49
15	♌	5am41
17	♍	12pm19
19	♎	10pm45
22	♏	11am18
24	♐	11pm37
27	♑	10am10
29	♒	6pm38

Key to the Zodiac Symbols

♈ Aries	♉ Taurus	♊ Gemini
♋ Cancer	♌ Leo	♍ Virgo
♎ Libra	♏ Scorpio	♐ Sagittarius
♑ Capricorn	♒ Aquarius	♓ Pisces

1990

January

1	♓	1am10
3	♈	5am56
5	♉	9am04
7	♊	11am02
9	♋	12pm52
11	♌	4pm02
13	♍	9pm57
16	♎	7am18
18	♏	7pm16
21	♐	7am44
23	♑	6pm27
26	♒	2am25
28	♓	7am51
30	♈	11am34

February

1	♉	2pm27
3	♊	5pm12
5	♋	8pm27
8	♌	0am51
10	♍	7am13
12	♎	4pm09
15	♏	3am34
17	♐	4pm07
20	♑	3am30
22	♒	11am52
24	♓	4pm49
26	♈	7pm16
28	♉	8pm43

March

2	♊	10pm37
5	♋	2am02
7	♌	7am24
9	♍	2pm47
12	♎	0am09
14	♏	11am25
16	♐	11pm56
19	♑	12pm01
21	♒	9pm31
24	♓	3am08
26	♈	5am15
28	♉	5am26
30	♊	5am42

April

1	♋	7am50
3	♌	12pm50
5	♍	8pm42
8	♎	6am44
10	♏	6pm18
13	♐	6am48
15	♑	7pm15
18	♒	5am53
20	♓	12pm57
22	♈	3pm58
24	♉	4pm03
26	♊	3pm12
28	♋	3pm39
30	♌	7pm08

May

3	♍	2am18
5	♎	12pm28
8	♏	0am22
10	♐	12pm56
13	♑	1am21
15	♒	12pm30
17	♓	8pm54
20	♈	1am31
22	♉	2am42
24	♊	2am00
26	♋	1am34
28	♌	3am29
30	♍	9am08

June

1	♎	6pm31
4	♏	6am21
6	♐	6pm59
9	♑	7am12
11	♒	6pm09
14	♓	3am00
16	♈	8am55
18	♉	11am43
20	♊	12pm14
22	♋	12pm10
24	♌	1pm25
26	♍	5pm42
29	♎	1am47

July

1	♏	1pm01
4	♐	1am35
6	♑	1pm39
9	♒	0am07
11	♓	8am29
13	♈	2pm36
15	♉	6pm29
17	♊	8pm32
19	♋	9pm44
21	♌	11pm29
24	♍	3am17
26	♎	10am19
28	♏	8pm39
31	♐	9am00

August

2	♑	9pm09
5	♒	7am19
7	♓	2pm54
9	♈	8pm13
11	♉	11pm55
14	♊	2am41
16	♋	5am12
18	♌	3am11
20	♍	12pm33
22	♎	7pm17
25	♏	4am56
27	♐	4pm57
30	♑	5am23

September

1	♒	3pm51
3	♓	11pm06
6	♈	3am23
8	♉	5am55
10	♊	8am05
12	♋	10am53
14	♌	2pm52
16	♍	8pm19
19	♎	3am34
21	♏	1pm06
24	♐	0am52
26	♑	1pm36
29	♒	0am54

October

1	♓	8am42
3	♈	12pm42
5	♉	2pm06
7	♊	2pm47
9	♋	4pm29
11	♌	8pm16
14	♍	2am21
16	♎	10am26
18	♏	8pm24
21	♐	8am09
23	♑	9pm03
26	♒	9am14
28	♓	6pm22
30	♈	11pm14

November

2	♉	0am31
4	♊	0am06
6	♋	0am07
8	♌	2am24
10	♍	7am48
12	♎	4pm08
15	♏	2am39
17	♐	2pm39
20	♑	3am31
22	♒	4pm07
25	♓	2am32
27	♈	9am06
29	♉	11am37

December

1	♊	11am23
3	♋	10am27
5	♌	11am00
7	♍	2pm39
9	♎	10pm00
12	♏	8am28
14	♐	8pm44
17	♑	9am35
19	♒	9pm59
22	♓	8am48
24	♈	4pm45
26	♉	9pm09
28	♊	10pm26
30	♋	10pm02

Key to the Zodiac Symbols

♈ Aries	♉ Taurus	♊ Gemini
♋ Cancer	♌ Leo	♍ Virgo
♎ Libra	♏ Scorpio	♐ Sagittarius
♑ Capricorn	♒ Aquarius	♓ Pisces

1991

January

1	♌	9pm54
3	♍	11pm57
6	♎	5am33
8	♏	2pm59
11	♐	3am06
13	♑	4pm00
16	♒	4am04
18	♓	2pm23
20	♈	10pm28
23	♉	4am01
25	♊	7am06
27	♋	8am23
29	♌	9am03
31	♍	10am44

February

2	♎	3pm02
4	♏	11pm01
7	♐	10am23
9	♑	11pm16
12	♒	11am16
14	♓	8pm59
17	♈	4am11
19	♉	9am24
21	♊	1pm10
23	♋	3pm56
25	♌	6pm13
27	♍	8pm50

March

2	♎	1am03
4	♏	8am08
6	♐	6pm35
9	♑	7am14
11	♒	7pm31
14	♓	5am11
16	♈	11am37
18	♉	3pm40
20	♊	6pm37
22	♋	9pm27
25	♌	0am43
27	♍	4am41
29	♎	9am49
31	♏	5pm01

April

3	♐	2am59
5	♑	3pm20
8	♒	4am00
10	♓	2pm17
12	♈	8pm49
15	♉	0am06
17	♊	1am41
19	♋	3am17
21	♌	6am04
23	♍	10am29
25	♎	4pm36
28	♏	0am34
30	♐	10am42

May

2	♑	10pm55
5	♒	11am51
7	♓	11pm04
10	♈	6am34
12	♉	10am07
14	♊	11am02
16	♋	11am14
18	♌	12pm30
20	♍	4pm00
22	♎	10pm08
25	♏	6am41
27	♐	5pm21
30	♑	5am40

June

1	♒	6pm42
4	♓	6am36
6	♈	3pm25
8	♉	8pm13
10	♊	9pm36
12	♋	9pm16
14	♌	9pm10
16	♍	11pm03
19	♎	4am01
21	♏	12pm18
23	♐	11pm16
26	♑	11am49
29	♒	0am47

July

1	♓	12pm51
3	♈	10pm33
6	♉	4am52
8	♊	7am42
10	♋	8am03
12	♌	7am35
14	♍	8am12
16	♎	11am34
18	♏	6pm41
21	♐	5am16
23	♑	5pm55
26	♒	6am49
28	♓	6pm35
31	♈	4am20

August

2	♉	11am32
4	♊	3pm54
6	♋	5pm47
8	♌	6pm09
10	♍	6pm35
12	♎	8pm52
15	♏	2am34
17	♐	12pm11
20	♑	0am34
22	♒	1pm27
25	♓	0am51
27	♈	10am01
29	♉	5pm00
31	♊	10pm02

September

3	♋	1am19
5	♌	3am13
7	♍	4am35
9	♎	6am52
11	♏	11am42
13	♐	8pm14
16	♑	8am04
18	♒	8pm58
21	♓	8am20
23	♈	4pm56
25	♉	10pm59
28	♊	3am25
30	♋	6am58

October

2	♌	9am58
4	♍	12pm45
6	♎	4pm00
8	♏	9pm00
11	♐	4am58
13	♑	4pm10
16	♒	5am04
18	♓	4pm53
21	♈	1am33
23	♉	6am55
25	♊	10am09
27	♋	12pm37
29	♌	3pm20
31	♍	6pm47

November

2	♎	11pm13
5	♏	5am09
7	♐	1pm21
10	♑	0am16
12	♒	1pm06
15	♓	1am33
17	♈	11am08
19	♉	4pm49
21	♊	7pm22
23	♋	8pm25
25	♌	9pm37
28	♍	0am12
30	♎	4am47

December

2	♏	11am33
4	♐	8pm32
7	♑	7am41
9	♒	8pm27
12	♓	9am19
14	♈	8pm06
17	♉	3am10
19	♊	6am21
21	♋	6am55
23	♌	6am38
25	♍	7am24
27	♎	10am37
29	♏	5pm03

Key to the Zodiac Symbols

♈ Aries	♉ Taurus	♊ Gemini
♋ Cancer	♌ Leo	♍ Virgo
♎ Libra	♏ Scorpio	♐ Sagittarius
♑ Capricorn	♒ Aquarius	♓ Pisces

1992

January

1	♐	2am30
3	♑	2pm09
6	♒	2am59
8	♓	3pm52
11	♈	3am22
13	♉	12pm00
15	♊	4pm55
17	♋	6pm26
19	♌	5pm57
21	♍	5pm22
23	♎	6pm42
25	♏	11pm32
28	♐	8am20
30	♑	8pm07

February

2	♒	9am09
4	♓	9pm51
7	♈	9am15
9	♉	6pm36
12	♊	1am08
14	♋	4am31
16	♌	5am15
18	♍	4am47
20	♎	5am05
22	♏	8am11
24	♐	3pm26
27	♑	2am33
29	♒	3pm34

March

3	♓	4am11
5	♈	3pm07
8	♉	0am05
10	♊	7am03
12	♋	11am50
14	♌	2pm20
16	♍	3pm13
18	♎	3pm55
20	♏	6pm20
23	♐	0am13
25	♑	10am08
27	♒	10pm44
30	♓	11am23

April

1	♈	10pm04
4	♉	6am18
6	♊	12pm33
8	♋	5pm18
10	♌	8pm46
12	♍	11pm09
15	♎	1am10
17	♏	4am10
19	♐	9am40
21	♑	6pm41
24	♒	6am38
26	♓	7pm20
29	♈	6am13

May

1	♉	2pm09
3	♊	7pm28
5	♋	11pm09
8	♌	2am07
10	♍	4am56
12	♎	8am05
14	♏	12pm15
16	♐	6pm22
19	♑	3am13
21	♒	2pm43
24	♓	3am25
26	♈	2pm52
28	♉	11pm16
31	♊	4am19

June

2	♋	6am58
4	♌	8am35
6	♍	10am28
8	♎	1pm33
10	♏	6pm27
13	♐	1am29
15	♑	10am50
17	♒	10pm19
20	♓	11am00
22	♈	11pm03
25	♉	8am28
27	♊	2pm14
29	♋	4pm42

July

1	♌	5pm15
3	♍	5pm37
5	♎	7pm27
7	♏	11pm53
10	♐	7am17
12	♑	5pm16
15	♒	5am03
17	♓	5pm44
20	♈	6am07
22	♉	4pm36
24	♊	11pm44
27	♋	3am08
29	♌	3am39
31	♍	3am01

August

2	♎	3am17
4	♏	6am16
6	♐	12pm57
8	♑	11pm00
11	♒	11am06
13	♓	11pm51
16	♈	12pm11
18	♉	11pm10
21	♊	7am36
23	♋	12pm36
25	♌	2pm15
27	♍	1pm46
29	♎	1pm11
31	♏	2pm38

September

2	♐	7pm50
5	♑	5am06
7	♒	5pm08
10	♓	5am56
12	♈	6pm02
15	♉	4am47
17	♊	1pm40
19	♋	7pm59
21	♌	11pm19
24	♍	0am08
25	♎	11pm55
28	♏	0am44
30	♐	4am33

October

2	♑	12pm29
4	♒	11pm53
7	♓	12pm38
10	♈	0am36
12	♉	10am48
14	♊	7pm08
17	♋	1am36
19	♌	6am01
21	♍	8am27
23	♎	9am39
25	♏	11am04
27	♐	2pm29
29	♑	9pm18

November

1	♒	7am43
3	♓	8pm13
6	♈	8am19
8	♉	6pm19
11	♊	1am49
13	♋	7am19
15	♌	11am23
17	♍	2pm28
19	♎	5pm03
21	♏	7pm52
24	♐	0am01
26	♑	6am38
28	♒	4pm19

December

1	♓	4am23
3	♈	4pm49
6	♉	3am16
8	♊	10am37
10	♋	3pm05
12	♌	5pm47
14	♍	7pm56
16	♎	10pm33
19	♏	2am20
21	♐	7am42
23	♑	3pm04
26	♒	0am43
28	♓	12pm28
31	♈	1am07

Key to the Zodiac Symbols

♈ Aries   ♉ Taurus   ♊ Gemini
♋ Cancer   ♌ Leo   ♍ Virgo
♎ Libra   ♏ Scorpio   ♐ Sagittarius
♑ Capricorn   ♒ Aquarius   ♓ Pisces

1993

January

2	♉	12pm30
4	♊	8pm42
7	♋	1am10
9	♌	2am49
11	♍	3am20
13	♎	4am30
15	♏	7am42
17	♐	1pm30
19	♑	9pm46
22	♒	8am00
24	♓	7pm47
27	♈	8am28
29	♉	8pm37

February

1	♊	6am15
3	♋	11am56
5	♌	1pm51
7	♍	1pm29
9	♎	12pm58
11	♏	2pm24
13	♐	7pm08
16	♑	3am20
18	♒	2pm05
21	♓	2am12
23	♈	2pm50
26	♉	3am11
28	♊	1pm52

March

2	♋	9pm16
5	♌	0am40
7	♍	0am52
8	♎	11pm46
10	♏	11pm40
13	♐	2am33
15	♑	9am28
17	♒	7pm52
20	♓	8am11
22	♈	8pm51
25	♉	8am59
27	♊	7pm48
30	♋	4am14

April

1	♌	9am21
3	♍	11am10
5	♎	10am54
7	♏	10am32
9	♐	12pm10
11	♑	5pm24
14	♒	2am36
16	♓	2pm32
19	♈	3am14
21	♉	3pm08
24	♊	1am27
26	♋	9am45
28	♌	3pm39
30	♍	7pm00

May

2	♎	8pm20
4	♏	8pm57
6	♐	10pm34
9	♑	2am51
11	♒	10am44
13	♓	9pm51
16	♈	10am24
18	♉	10pm16
21	♊	8am07
23	♋	3pm38
25	♌	9pm03
28	♍	0am46
30	♎	3am18

June

1	♏	5am22
3	♐	8am01
5	♑	12pm26
7	♒	7pm39
10	♓	5am57
12	♈	6pm14
15	♉	6am19
17	♊	4pm12
19	♋	11pm05
22	♌	3am26
24	♍	6am18
26	♎	8am45
28	♏	11am37
30	♐	3pm28

July

2	♑	8pm49
5	♒	4am14
7	♓	2pm10
10	♈	2am11
12	♉	2pm37
15	♊	1am07
17	♋	8am08
19	♌	11am47
21	♍	1pm24
23	♎	2pm40
25	♏	5pm00
27	♐	9pm13
30	♑	3am27

August

1	♒	11am36
3	♓	9pm44
6	♈	9am39
8	♉	10pm22
11	♊	9am47
13	♋	5pm46
15	♌	9pm43
17	♍	10pm41
19	♎	10pm35
21	♏	11pm27
24	♐	2am45
26	♑	8am58
28	♒	5pm42
31	♓	4am19

September

2	♈	4pm21
5	♉	5am09
7	♊	5pm16
10	♋	2am37
12	♌	7am51
14	♍	9am20
16	♎	8am44
18	♏	8am15
20	♐	9am53
22	♑	2pm54
24	♒	11pm19
27	♓	10am13
29	♈	10pm29

October

2	♉	11am13
4	♊	11pm27
7	♋	9am42
9	♌	4pm34
11	♍	7pm36
13	♎	7pm47
15	♏	7pm01
17	♐	7pm23
19	♑	10pm42
22	♒	5am49
24	♓	4pm17
27	♈	4am39
29	♉	5pm20

November

1	♊	5am13
3	♋	3pm25
5	♌	11pm06
8	♍	3am47
10	♎	5am42
12	♏	6am00
14	♐	6am20
16	♑	8am34
18	♒	2pm08
20	♓	11pm27
23	♈	11am30
26	♉	0am14
28	♊	11am48
30	♋	9pm17

December

3	♌	4am33
5	♍	9am43
7	♎	1pm03
9	♏	3pm04
11	♐	4pm39
13	♑	7pm06
15	♒	11pm51
18	♓	7am59
20	♈	7pm19
23	♉	8am05
25	♊	7pm46
28	♋	4am46
30	♌	10am59

Key to the Zodiac Symbols

♈ Aries	♉ Taurus	♊ Gemini
♋ Cancer	♌ Leo	♍ Virgo
♎ Libra	♏ Scorpio	♐ Sagittarius
♑ Capricorn	♒ Aquarius	♓ Pisces

1994

January

1	♍	3pm15
3	♎	6pm31
5	♏	9pm29
8	♐	0am34
10	♑	4am16
12	♒	9am25
14	♓	5pm04
17	♈	3am42
19	♉	4pm22
22	♊	4am35
24	♋	1pm55
26	♌	7pm38
28	♍	10pm39
31	♎	0am34

February

2	♏	2am49
4	♐	6am14
6	♑	11am02
8	♒	5pm16
11	♓	1am23
13	♈	11am49
16	♉	0am20
18	♊	1pm05
20	♋	11pm27
23	♌	5am48
25	♍	8am27
27	♎	9am06

March

1	♏	9am43
3	♐	11am54
5	♑	4pm24
7	♒	11pm15
10	♓	8am09
12	♈	6pm59
15	♉	7am27
17	♊	8pm29
20	♋	7am54
22	♌	3pm39
24	♍	7pm14
26	♎	7pm46
28	♏	7pm15
30	♐	7pm41

April

1	♑	10pm38
4	♒	4am45
6	♓	1pm51
9	♈	1am09
11	♉	1pm48
14	♊	2am48
16	♋	2pm41
18	♌	11pm45
21	♍	4am58
23	♎	6am40
25	♏	6am18
27	♐	5am48
29	♑	7am05

May

1	♒	11am34
3	♓	7pm47
6	♈	7am01
8	♉	7pm50
11	♊	8am43
13	♋	8pm27
16	♌	5am58
18	♍	12pm31
20	♎	3pm54
22	♏	4pm51
24	♐	4pm43
26	♑	5pm17
28	♒	8pm19
31	♓	3am03

June

2	♈	1pm31
5	♉	2am14
7	♊	3pm03
10	♋	2am22
12	♌	11am29
14	♍	6pm16
16	♎	10pm48
19	♏	1am20
21	♐	2am32
23	♑	3am37
25	♒	6am10
27	♓	11am44
29	♈	9pm07

July

2	♉	9am23
4	♊	10pm12
7	♋	9am17
9	♌	5pm43
11	♍	11pm48
14	♎	4am15
16	♏	7am35
18	♐	10am09
20	♑	12pm30
22	♒	3pm38
24	♓	8pm56
27	♈	5am31
29	♉	5pm13

August

1	♊	6am05
3	♋	5pm22
6	♌	1am31
8	♍	6am42
10	♎	10am07
12	♏	12pm56
14	♐	3pm53
16	♑	7pm18
18	♒	11pm34
21	♓	5am27
23	♈	1pm55
26	♉	1am13
28	♊	2pm07
31	♋	2am00

September

2	♌	10am37
4	♍	3pm33
6	♎	5pm57
8	♏	7pm26
10	♐	9pm25
13	♑	0am44
15	♒	5am42
17	♓	12pm31
19	♈	9pm30
22	♉	8am47
24	♊	9pm41
27	♋	10am12
29	♌	7pm55

October

2	♍	1am39
4	♎	3am56
6	♏	4am22
8	♐	4am47
10	♑	6am44
12	♒	11am09
14	♓	6pm18
17	♈	3am56
19	♉	3pm34
22	♊	4am28
24	♋	5pm15
27	♌	4am05
29	♍	11am21
31	♎	2pm46

November

2	♏	3pm19
4	♐	2pm46
6	♑	3pm02
8	♒	5pm48
11	♓	0am04
13	♈	9am44
15	♉	9pm44
18	♊	10am41
20	♋	11pm21
23	♌	10am33
25	♍	7pm09
28	♎	0am22
30	♏	2am21

December

2	♐	2am13
4	♑	1am42
6	♒	2am52
8	♓	7am24
10	♈	4pm03
13	♉	3am56
15	♊	5pm00
18	♋	5am25
20	♌	4pm13
23	♍	1am01
25	♎	7am27
27	♏	11am17
29	♐	12pm45
31	♑	12pm57

Key to the Zodiac Symbols

♈ Aries	♉ Taurus	♊ Gemini
♋ Cancer	♌ Leo	♍ Virgo
♎ Libra	♏ Scorpio	♐ Sagittarius
♑ Capricorn	♒ Aquarius	♓ Pisces

1995

January

2	♒	1pm39
4	♓	4pm49
6	♈	11pm56
9	♉	10am58
11	♊	11pm57
14	♋	12pm20
16	♌	10pm36
19	♍	6am39
21	♎	12pm54
23	♏	5pm32
25	♐	8pm37
27	♑	10pm26
30	♒	0am03

February

1	♓	3am05
3	♈	9am12
5	♉	7pm09
8	♊	7am44
10	♋	8pm17
13	♌	6am31
15	♍	1pm52
17	♎	7pm00
19	♏	10pm55
22	♐	2am13
24	♑	5am11
26	♒	8am14
28	♓	12pm16

March

2	♈	6pm30
5	♉	3am50
7	♊	3pm55
10	♋	4am40
12	♌	3pm28
14	♍	10pm54
17	♎	3am18
19	♏	5am52
21	♐	7am57
23	♑	10am31
25	♒	2pm10
27	♓	7pm18
30	♈	2am26

April

1	♉	11am59
3	♊	11pm49
6	♋	12pm40
9	♌	0am16
11	♍	8am39
13	♎	1pm20
15	♏	3pm13
17	♐	3pm52
19	♑	4pm54
21	♒	7pm38
24	♓	0am51
26	♈	8am41
28	♉	6pm53

May

1	♊	6am53
3	♋	7pm45
6	♌	7am55
8	♍	5pm33
10	♎	11pm30
13	♏	1am53
15	♐	1am58
17	♑	1am36
19	♒	2am39
21	♓	6am40
23	♈	2pm13
26	♉	0am47
28	♊	1pm07
31	♋	1am59

June

2	♌	2pm17
5	♍	0am46
7	♎	8am13
9	♏	12pm03
11	♐	12pm50
13	♑	12pm05
15	♒	11am52
17	♓	2pm13
19	♈	8pm29
22	♉	6am35
24	♊	7pm02
27	♋	7am56
29	♌	8pm02

July

2	♍	6am35
4	♎	2pm55
6	♏	8pm19
8	♐	10pm38
10	♑	10pm43
12	♒	10pm21
14	♓	11pm37
17	♈	4am23
19	♉	1pm20
22	♊	1am23
24	♋	2pm16
27	♌	2am07
29	♍	12pm12
31	♎	8pm23

August

3	♏	2am29
5	♐	6am14
7	♑	7am52
9	♒	8am28
11	♓	9am46
13	♈	1pm41
15	♉	9pm25
18	♊	8am40
20	♋	9pm24
23	♌	9am13
25	♍	6pm50
28	♎	2am15
30	♏	7am51

September

1	♐	11am57
3	♑	2pm45
5	♒	4pm47
7	♓	7pm08
9	♈	11pm14
12	♉	6am21
14	♊	4pm48
17	♋	5am16
19	♌	5pm19
22	♍	3am01
24	♎	9am50
26	♏	2pm20
28	♐	5pm30
30	♑	8pm10

October

2	♒	10pm59
5	♓	2am35
7	♈	7am42
9	♉	3pm05
12	♊	1am10
14	♋	1pm20
17	♌	1am46
19	♍	12pm11
21	♎	7pm15
23	♏	11pm07
26	♐	0am56
28	♑	2am15
30	♒	4am23

November

1	♓	8am17
3	♈	2pm21
5	♉	10pm35
8	♊	8am55
10	♋	8pm57
13	♌	9am37
15	♍	9pm02
18	♎	5am18
20	♏	9am40
22	♐	10am56
24	♑	10am48
26	♒	11am15
28	♓	1pm59
30	♈	7pm51

December

3	♉	4am40
5	♊	3pm35
8	♋	3am44
10	♌	4pm24
13	♍	4am26
15	♎	2pm09
17	♏	8pm07
19	♐	10pm13
21	♑	9pm46
23	♒	8pm52
25	♓	9pm45
28	♈	2am06
30	♉	10am21

Key to the Zodiac Symbols

♈ Aries	♉ Taurus	♊ Gemini
♋ Cancer	♌ Leo	♍ Virgo
♎ Libra	♏ Scorpio	♐ Sagittarius
♑ Capricorn	♒ Aquarius	♓ Pisces

1996

January

1	♊	9pm29
4	♋	9am56
6	♌	10pm30
9	♍	10am29
11	♎	8pm55
14	♏	4am30
16	♐	8am25
18	♑	9am07
20	♒	8am15
22	♓	8am02
24	♈	10am37
26	♉	5pm16
29	♊	3am42
31	♋	4pm11

February

3	♌	4am46
5	♍	4pm22
8	♎	2am30
10	♏	10am35
12	♐	3pm58
14	♑	6pm29
16	♒	7pm00
18	♓	7pm09
20	♈	8pm58
23	♉	2am08
25	♊	11am14
27	♋	11pm10

March

1	♌	11am47
3	♍	11pm13
6	♎	8am40
8	♏	4pm05
10	♐	9pm32
13	♑	1am08
15	♒	3am15
17	♓	4am50
19	♈	7am15
21	♉	11am59
23	♊	8pm00
26	♋	7am06
28	♌	7pm37
31	♍	7am15

April

2	♎	4pm26
4	♏	10pm57
7	♐	3am21
9	♑	6am30
11	♒	9am09
13	♓	12pm00
15	♈	3pm43
17	♉	9pm05
20	♊	4am54
22	♋	3pm25
25	♌	3am44
27	♍	3pm49
30	♎	1am27

May

2	♏	7am42
4	♐	11am05
6	♑	12pm54
8	♒	2pm39
10	♓	5pm29
12	♈	10pm00
15	♉	4am25
17	♊	12pm48
19	♋	11pm16
22	♌	11am28
24	♍	11pm58
27	♎	10am33
29	♏	5pm30
31	♐	8pm43

June

2	♑	9pm29
4	♒	9pm45
6	♓	11pm19
9	♈	3am23
11	♉	10am11
13	♊	7pm16
16	♋	6am08
18	♌	6pm22
21	♍	7am07
23	♎	6pm37
26	♏	2am53
28	♐	7am01
30	♑	7am47

July

2	♒	7am05
4	♓	7am07
6	♈	9am42
8	♉	3pm43
11	♊	0am52
13	♋	12pm08
16	♌	0am31
18	♍	1pm16
21	♎	1am14
23	♏	10am43
25	♐	4pm24
27	♑	6pm17
29	♒	5pm47
31	♓	5pm01

August

2	♈	6pm05
4	♉	10pm33
7	♊	6am49
9	♋	5pm57
12	♌	6am29
14	♍	7pm07
17	♎	6am55
19	♏	4pm50
21	♐	11pm48
24	♑	3am22
26	♒	4am10
28	♓	3am49
30	♈	4am15

September

1	♉	7am20
3	♊	2pm08
6	♋	0am29
8	♌	12pm54
11	♍	1am28
13	♎	12pm51
15	♏	10pm20
18	♐	5am31
20	♑	10am12
22	♒	12pm39
24	♓	1pm43
26	♈	2pm46
28	♉	5pm24
30	♊	11pm01

October

3	♋	8am14
5	♌	8pm12
8	♍	8am49
10	♎	8pm00
13	♏	4am46
15	♐	11am07
17	♑	3pm37
19	♒	6pm51
21	♓	9pm22
23	♈	11pm50
26	♉	3am11
28	♊	8am35
30	♋	4pm56

November

2	♌	4am16
4	♍	4pm57
7	♎	4am29
9	♏	1pm02
11	♐	6pm26
13	♑	9pm44
16	♒	0am14
18	♓	3am00
20	♈	6am34
22	♉	11am12
24	♊	5pm20
27	♋	1am37
29	♌	12pm30

December

2	♍	1am11
4	♎	1pm23
6	♏	10pm39
9	♐	3am58
11	♑	6am15
13	♒	7am14
15	♓	8am44
17	♈	11am55
19	♉	5pm10
22	♊	0am17
24	♋	9am14
26	♌	8pm09
29	♍	8am45
31	♎	9pm32

Key to the Zodiac Symbols

♈ Aries	♉ Taurus	♊ Gemini
♋ Cancer	♌ Leo	♍ Virgo
♎ Libra	♏ Scorpio	♐ Sagittarius
♑ Capricorn	♒ Aquarius	♓ Pisces

1997

January

3	♏	8am02
5	♐	2pm27
7	♑	4pm55
9	♒	5pm00
11	♓	4pm51
13	♈	6pm22
15	♉	10pm40
18	♊	5am53
20	♋	3pm29
23	♌	2am50
25	♍	3pm26
28	♎	4am21
30	♏	3pm48

February

1	♐	11pm51
4	♑	3am44
6	♒	4am21
8	♓	3am34
10	♈	3am29
12	♉	5am56
14	♊	11am53
16	♋	9pm13
19	♌	8am52
21	♍	9pm38
24	♎	10am23
26	♏	9pm57

March

1	♐	7am01
3	♑	12pm38
5	♒	2pm54
7	♓	2pm57
9	♈	2pm33
11	♉	3pm37
13	♊	7pm48
16	♋	3am51
18	♌	3pm08
21	♍	3am59
23	♎	4pm35
26	♏	3am42
28	♐	12pm40
30	♑	7pm07

April

1	♒	10pm59
4	♓	0am42
6	♈	1am19
8	♉	2am20
10	♊	5am28
12	♋	12pm03
14	♌	10pm22
17	♍	11am00
19	♎	11pm36
22	♏	10am19
24	♐	6pm32
27	♑	0am32
29	♒	4am50

May

1	♓	7am50
3	♈	9am59
5	♉	12pm04
7	♊	3pm21
9	♋	9pm13
12	♌	6am33
14	♍	6pm43
17	♎	7am27
19	♏	6pm11
22	♐	1am51
24	♑	6am51
26	♒	10am20
28	♓	1pm18
30	♈	4pm18

June

1	♉	7pm39
3	♊	11pm55
6	♋	6am02
8	♌	2pm58
11	♍	2am43
13	♎	3pm35
16	♏	2am51
18	♐	10am39
20	♑	3pm02
22	♒	5pm20
24	♓	7pm09
26	♈	9pm39
29	♉	1am23

July

1	♊	6am35
3	♋	1pm33
5	♌	10pm45
8	♍	10am22
10	♎	11pm21
13	♏	11am20
15	♐	8pm02
18	♑	0am45
20	♒	2am29
22	♓	3am00
24	♈	4am03
26	♉	6am53
28	♊	12pm04
30	♋	7pm38

August

2	♌	5am27
4	♍	5pm15
7	♎	6am17
9	♏	6pm50
12	♐	4am45
14	♑	10am42
16	♒	12pm58
18	♓	1pm01
20	♈	12pm45
22	♉	1pm57
24	♊	5pm56
27	♋	1am11
29	♌	11am19
31	♍	11pm27

September

3	♎	12pm30
6	♏	1am10
8	♐	11am54
10	♑	7pm23
12	♒	11pm10
14	♓	11pm59
16	♈	11pm25
18	♉	11pm21
21	♊	1am39
23	♋	7am33
25	♌	5pm12
28	♍	5am27
30	♎	6pm32

October

3	♏	6am57
5	♐	5pm43
8	♑	2am04
10	♒	7am29
12	♓	9am59
14	♈	10am25
16	♉	10am16
18	♊	11am26
20	♋	3pm45
23	♌	0am10
25	♍	11am59
28	♎	1am05
30	♏	1pm15

November

1	♐	11pm27
4	♑	7am31
6	♒	1pm33
8	♓	5pm35
10	♈	7pm44
12	♉	8pm45
14	♊	10pm05
17	♋	1am32
19	♌	8am38
21	♍	7pm33
24	♎	8am29
26	♏	8pm43
29	♐	6am28

December

1	♑	1pm38
3	♒	6pm58
5	♓	11pm07
8	♈	2am24
10	♉	5am00
12	♊	7am35
14	♋	11am25
16	♌	5pm58
19	♍	4am00
21	♎	4pm35
24	♏	5am07
26	♐	3pm07
28	♑	9pm48
31	♒	1am58

Key to the Zodiac Symbols

♈ Aries	♉ Taurus	♊ Gemini
♋ Cancer	♌ Leo	♍ Virgo
♎ Libra	♏ Scorpio	♐ Sagittarius
♑ Capricorn	♒ Aquarius	♓ Pisces

1998

January
- 2 ♓ 4am56
- 4 ♈ 7am43
- 6 ♉ 10am52
- 8 ♊ 2pm42
- 10 ♋ 7pm43
- 13 ♌ 2am45
- 15 ♍ 12pm31
- 18 ♎ 0am44
- 20 ♏ 1pm34
- 23 ♐ 0am25
- 25 ♑ 7am39
- 27 ♒ 11am27
- 29 ♓ 1pm08
- 31 ♈ 2pm21

February
- 2 ♉ 4pm25
- 4 ♊ 8pm09
- 7 ♋ 1am57
- 9 ♌ 9am57
- 11 ♍ 8pm10
- 14 ♎ 8am17
- 16 ♏ 9pm13
- 19 ♐ 8am56
- 21 ♑ 5pm30
- 23 ♒ 10pm10
- 25 ♓ 11pm42
- 27 ♈ 11pm42

March
- 2 ♉ 0am00
- 4 ♊ 2am15
- 6 ♋ 7am27
- 8 ♌ 3pm46
- 11 ♍ 2am35
- 13 ♎ 2pm58
- 16 ♏ 3am51
- 18 ♐ 3pm56
- 21 ♑ 1am43
- 23 ♒ 8am01
- 25 ♓ 10am43
- 27 ♈ 10am49
- 29 ♉ 10am06
- 31 ♊ 10am38

April
- 2 ♋ 2pm10
- 4 ♌ 9pm36
- 7 ♍ 8am25
- 9 ♎ 9pm04
- 12 ♏ 9am56
- 14 ♐ 9pm52
- 17 ♑ 8am05
- 19 ♒ 3pm41
- 21 ♓ 8pm06
- 23 ♈ 9pm30
- 25 ♉ 9pm09
- 27 ♊ 8pm55
- 29 ♋ 10pm57

May
- 2 ♌ 4am49
- 4 ♍ 2pm47
- 7 ♎ 3am19
- 9 ♏ 4pm10
- 12 ♐ 3am48
- 14 ♑ 1pm39
- 16 ♒ 9pm30
- 19 ♓ 3am03
- 21 ♈ 6am06
- 23 ♉ 7am06
- 25 ♊ 7am25
- 27 ♋ 8am58
- 29 ♌ 1pm38
- 31 ♍ 10pm21

June
- 3 ♎ 10am17
- 5 ♏ 11pm06
- 8 ♐ 10am34
- 10 ♑ 7pm50
- 13 ♒ 3am03
- 15 ♓ 8am31
- 17 ♈ 12pm23
- 19 ♉ 2pm47
- 21 ♊ 4pm26
- 23 ♋ 6pm39
- 25 ♌ 11pm04
- 28 ♍ 6am54
- 30 ♎ 6pm05

July
- 3 ♏ 6am45
- 5 ♐ 6pm24
- 8 ♑ 3am27
- 10 ♒ 9am52
- 12 ♓ 2pm22
- 14 ♈ 5pm45
- 16 ♉ 8pm33
- 18 ♊ 11pm18
- 21 ♋ 2am43
- 23 ♌ 7am49
- 25 ♍ 3pm34
- 28 ♎ 2am14
- 30 ♏ 2pm44

August
- 2 ♐ 2am48
- 4 ♑ 12pm18
- 6 ♒ 6pm31
- 8 ♓ 10pm04
- 11 ♈ 0am10
- 13 ♉ 2am04
- 15 ♊ 4am46
- 17 ♋ 8am55
- 19 ♌ 3pm01
- 21 ♍ 11pm21
- 24 ♎ 10am02
- 26 ♏ 10pm25
- 29 ♐ 10am55
- 31 ♑ 9pm23

September
- 3 ♒ 4am21
- 5 ♓ 7am48
- 7 ♈ 8am52
- 9 ♉ 9am16
- 11 ♊ 10am40
- 13 ♋ 2pm20
- 15 ♌ 8pm48
- 18 ♍ 5am52
- 20 ♎ 4pm57
- 23 ♏ 5am22
- 25 ♐ 6pm05
- 28 ♑ 5am30
- 30 ♒ 1pm53

October
- 2 ♓ 6pm23
- 4 ♈ 7pm32
- 6 ♉ 6pm57
- 8 ♊ 6pm44
- 10 ♋ 8pm48
- 13 ♌ 2am25
- 15 ♍ 11am32
- 17 ♎ 11pm02
- 20 ♏ 11am36
- 23 ♐ 0am16
- 25 ♑ 12pm05
- 27 ♒ 9pm44
- 30 ♓ 3am58

November
- 1 ♈ 6am27
- 3 ♉ 6am12
- 5 ♊ 5am11
- 7 ♋ 5am39
- 9 ♌ 9am33
- 11 ♍ 5pm37
- 14 ♎ 4am58
- 16 ♏ 5pm41
- 19 ♐ 6am13
- 21 ♑ 5pm45
- 24 ♒ 3am43
- 26 ♓ 11am14
- 28 ♈ 3pm34
- 30 ♉ 4pm52

December
- 2 ♊ 4pm30
- 4 ♋ 4pm28
- 6 ♌ 6pm55
- 9 ♍ 1am21
- 11 ♎ 11am43
- 14 ♏ 0am16
- 16 ♐ 12pm47
- 18 ♑ 11pm55
- 21 ♒ 9am17
- 23 ♓ 4pm45
- 25 ♈ 10pm04
- 28 ♉ 1am05
- 30 ♊ 2am22

Key to the Zodiac Symbols

♈	Aries	♉	Taurus	♊	Gemini
♋	Cancer	♌	Leo	♍	Virgo
♎	Libra	♏	Scorpio	♐	Sagittarius
♑	Capricorn	♒	Aquarius	♓	Pisces

1999

January

1	♋	3am15
3	♌	5am31
5	♍	10am49
7	♎	7pm53
10	♏	7am49
12	♐	8pm23
15	♑	7am29
17	♒	4pm11
19	♓	10pm40
22	♈	3am25
24	♉	6am52
26	♊	9am29
28	♋	11am57
30	♌	3pm16

February

1	♍	8pm37
4	♎	4am56
6	♏	4pm06
9	♐	4am38
11	♑	4pm10
14	♒	0am57
16	♓	6am40
18	♈	10am06
20	♉	12pm29
22	♊	2pm54
24	♋	6pm09
26	♌	10pm44

March

1	♍	5am05
3	♎	1pm34
6	♏	0am22
8	♐	12pm46
11	♑	0am54
13	♒	10am32
15	♓	4pm30
17	♈	7pm13
19	♉	8pm09
21	♊	9pm05
23	♋	11pm33
26	♌	4am22
28	♍	11am34
30	♎	8pm49

April

2	♏	7am49
4	♐	8pm07
7	♑	8am39
9	♒	7pm24
12	♓	2am35
14	♈	5am46
16	♉	6am07
18	♊	5am39
20	♋	6am27
22	♌	10am06
24	♍	5pm04
27	♎	2am46
29	♏	2pm12

May

2	♐	2am36
4	♑	3pm12
7	♒	2am40
9	♓	11am16
11	♈	3pm53
13	♉	4pm56
15	♊	4pm07
17	♋	3pm39
19	♌	5pm37
21	♍	11pm15
24	♎	8am29
26	♏	8pm05
29	♐	8am37
31	♑	9pm06

June

3	♒	8am37
5	♓	6pm00
8	♈	0am08
10	♉	2am44
12	♊	2am48
14	♋	2am14
16	♌	3am07
18	♍	7am12
20	♎	3pm10
23	♏	2am18
25	♐	2pm51
28	♑	3am12
30	♒	2pm19

July

2	♓	11pm34
5	♈	6am21
7	♉	10am22
9	♊	12pm00
11	♋	12pm27
13	♌	1pm26
15	♍	4pm39
17	♎	11pm19
20	♏	9am30
22	♐	9pm48
25	♑	10am08
27	♒	8pm54
30	♓	5am27

August

1	♈	11am47
3	♉	4pm09
5	♊	6pm57
7	♋	8pm53
9	♌	10pm55
12	♍	2am22
14	♎	8am24
16	♏	5pm40
19	♐	5am32
21	♑	5pm59
24	♒	4am49
26	♓	12pm50
28	♈	6pm09
30	♉	9pm41

September

2	♊	0am25
4	♋	3am10
6	♌	6am29
8	♍	10am57
10	♎	5pm16
13	♏	2am08
15	♐	1pm35
18	♑	2am13
20	♒	1pm38
22	♓	9pm51
25	♈	2am34
27	♉	4am51
29	♊	6am21

October

1	♋	8am31
3	♌	12pm13
5	♍	5pm40
8	♎	0am52
10	♏	10am01
12	♐	9pm18
15	♑	10am04
17	♒	10pm17
20	♓	7am33
22	♈	12pm41
24	♉	2pm25
26	♊	2pm33
28	♋	3pm09
30	♌	5pm47

November

1	♍	11pm07
4	♎	6am57
6	♏	4pm46
9	♐	4am15
11	♑	5pm00
14	♒	5am46
16	♓	4pm21
18	♈	10pm57
21	♉	1am26
23	♊	1am14
25	♋	0am29
27	♌	1am19
29	♍	5am11

December

1	♎	12pm29
3	♏	10pm35
6	♐	10am27
8	♑	11pm14
11	♒	11am59
13	♓	11pm18
16	♈	7am30
18	♉	11am45
20	♊	12pm39
22	♋	11am52
24	♌	11am32
26	♍	1pm34
28	♎	7pm14
31	♏	4am36

Key to the Zodiac Symbols

♈ Aries	♉ Taurus	♊ Gemini
♋ Cancer	♌ Leo	♍ Virgo
♎ Libra	♏ Scorpio	♐ Sagittarius
♑ Capricorn	♒ Aquarius	♓ Pisces

2000

January

2	♐	4pm32
5	♑	5am24
7	♒	5pm53
10	♓	4am59
12	♈	1pm48
14	♉	7pm38
16	♊	10pm25
18	♋	11pm01
20	♌	10pm58
23	♍	0am07
25	♎	4am09
27	♏	12pm01
29	♐	11pm18

February

1	♑	12pm10
4	♒	0am31
6	♓	11am02
8	♈	7pm17
11	♉	1am21
13	♊	5am23
15	♋	7am45
17	♌	9am11
19	♍	10am53
21	♎	2pm21
23	♏	8pm58
26	♐	7am10
28	♑	7pm45

March

2	♒	8am14
4	♓	6pm30
7	♈	1am54
9	♉	7am01
11	♊	10am46
13	♋	1pm51
15	♌	4pm43
17	♍	7pm48
19	♎	11pm57
22	♏	6am18
24	♐	3pm43
27	♑	3am51
29	♒	4pm34

April

1	♓	3am12
3	♈	10am22
5	♉	2pm29
7	♊	4pm58
9	♋	7pm16
11	♌	10pm16
14	♍	2am19
16	♎	7am36
18	♏	2pm35
20	♐	11pm58
23	♑	11am47
26	♒	0am42
28	♓	12pm06
30	♈	7pm55

May

2	♉	11pm54
5	♊	1am23
7	♋	2am14
9	♌	4am01
11	♍	7am41
13	♎	1pm27
15	♏	9pm16
18	♐	7am09
20	♑	7pm01
23	♒	8am00
25	♓	8pm07
28	♈	5am08
30	♉	10am02

June

1	♊	11am34
3	♋	11am30
5	♌	11am46
7	♍	1pm57
9	♎	6pm59
12	♏	2am55
14	♐	1pm18
17	♑	1am27
19	♒	2pm26
22	♓	2am52
24	♈	12pm55
26	♉	7pm19
28	♊	9pm59
30	♋	10pm09

July

2	♌	9pm38
4	♍	10pm19
7	♎	1am47
9	♏	8am48
11	♐	7pm06
14	♑	7am28
16	♒	8pm27
19	♓	8am44
21	♈	7pm09
24	♉	2am44
26	♊	7am01
28	♋	8am30
30	♌	8am24

August

1	♍	8am27
3	♎	10am31
5	♏	4pm04
8	♐	1am30
10	♑	1pm44
13	♒	2am43
15	♓	2pm41
18	♈	0am44
20	♉	8am31
22	♊	1pm55
24	♋	5pm00
26	♌	6pm17
28	♍	6pm55
30	♎	8pm33

September

2	♏	0am55
4	♐	9am08
6	♑	8pm47
9	♒	9am44
11	♓	9pm34
14	♈	7am00
16	♉	2pm05
18	♊	7pm22
20	♋	11pm16
23	♌	2am00
25	♍	4am02
27	♎	6am22
29	♏	10am30

October

1	♐	5pm50
4	♑	4am42
6	♒	5pm33
9	♓	5am36
11	♈	2pm51
13	♉	9pm06
16	♊	1am19
18	♋	4am37
20	♌	7am42
22	♍	10am52
24	♎	2pm30
26	♏	7pm23
29	♐	2am40
31	♑	1pm02

November

3	♒	1am41
5	♓	2pm13
8	♈	0am02
10	♉	6am12
12	♊	9am27
14	♋	11am21
16	♌	1pm19
18	♍	4pm15
20	♎	8pm35
23	♏	2am33
25	♐	10am33
27	♑	8pm57
30	♒	9am27

December

2	♓	10pm23
5	♈	9am17
7	♉	4pm27
9	♊	7pm50
11	♋	8pm48
13	♌	9pm09
15	♍	10pm30
18	♎	2am01
20	♏	8am12
22	♐	4pm57
25	♑	3am54
27	♒	4pm25
30	♓	5am27

BIBLIOGRAPHY

ALEXANDER, HARTLEY BURR. *The World's Rim: Great Mysteries of the North American Indians.* Lincoln, Nebr.: University of Nebraska Press, 1953.

ANDRESKI, IRIS. *Old Wives' Tales: Life Stories of African Women.* New York: Schocken Books, 1971.

ASTROV, MARGOT, ed. *American Indian Prose and Poetry,* "The Winged Serpent." New York: Capricorn Books, 1962.

BACHOFEN, JACOB J. *Myth, Religion, and Mother Right.* Translated by Ralph Manheim. Bollingen Series 84. Princeton, N.J.: Princeton University Press, 1967.

BETTELHEIM, BRUNO. *Symbolic Wounds: Puberty Rites and the Envious Male.* Glencoe, Ill.: Free Press, 1954.

BLACK, ELK. *Black Elk Speaks: Being the Life Story of a Holy Man of the Oglala Sioux.* Told through John G. Neihardt. Lincoln, Nebr.: University of Nebraska Press, 1961.

BLY, ROBERT. *Sleepers Joining Hands.* New York: Harper & Row, 1973.

BRIFFAULT, ROBERT. *The Mothers: The Matriarchal Theory of Social Origins.* Abridged and with an introduction by Gordon Rattray Taylor. London: Ruskin House/George Allen & Unwin, 1959.

CAMPBELL, JOSEPH. *The Masks of God: Primitive Mythology.* New York: Viking Press, 1959.

CARUS, PAUL. *Chinese Astrology*. La Salle, Ill.: Open Court, 1974.

CAVANDAR, KENNETH. "The Astarte Phenomenon." *Horizon* 13, no. 2 (Spring 1971): 15ff.

CHADWICK, JOHN. "Life in Mycenaean Greece." *Scientific American* 227, no. 4 (Oct. 1972): 36–49.

CHAUVIN, REMY. *Animal Societies*. London: Sphere Books, 1968.

CHIÑAS, BEVERLY L. *The Isthmus Zapotecs: Women's Roles in Cultural Context*. New York: Holt, Rinehart & Winston, 1973.

CHRISTIE, ANTHONY. *Chinese Mythology*. London: Paul Hamlyn, 1968.

COTTRELL, LEONARD. *The Horizon Book of Lost Worlds*. New York: Laurel/Dell, 1964.

CURTIS, EDWARD SHERIFF. *The North American Indians: A Selection of Photographs*. Text compiled and Introduction by Joseph Epes Brown. New York: Aperture, 1972.

CURTIS, NATALIE, ed. *The Indians' Book*. Unabridged, unaltered republication of 2d ed. by Harper & Brothers, 1923. New York: Dover Publications, 1968.

DAVIS, ELIZABETH GOULD. *The First Sex*. New York: Putnam, 1971.

DELORIA, VINE, JR. *God is Red*. New York: Delta/Dell, 1973.

DISSELHOFF, HANS-DIETRICH AND SIGVALD LINNÉ. *The Art of Ancient America*. Translated by Ann Keep. New York: Greystone Press, 1966.

EARTHY, E. DORA. *Valenge Women*. London: Frank Cass & Co., 1968.

EHRENREICH, BARBARA, AND DEIRDRE ENGLISH. *Witches, Midwives and Nurses: A History of Women Healers*. Old Westbury, N.Y.: Feminist Press, 1973.

ELIADE, MIRCEA. *Zalmoxis, the Vanishing God*. Translated by Willard R. Trask. Chicago: University of Chicago Press, 1970.

EVANS, SIR ARTHUR. "Minoan Civilization and Its Discovery"; "Scenes From Minoan Life"; "Restorations at Knossos," reprinted in *The World of the Past, Vol. II*, ed. by Jacquetta Hawkes. New York: Touchstone Books/ Simon and Schuster, 1963.

FAGAN, CYRIL. *Astrological Origins*. St. Paul, Minn.: Llewellyn Publications, 1971.

FALK, NANCY. "An Image of Women in Old Buddhist Literature: The Daughters of Mara." In *Women and Religion*, ed. by Judith Plaskow and Joan Arnold Romero. Working Group on Women and Religion, American Academy of Religion. Missoula, Mont.: Scholar's Press, 1974.

FELDMANN, SUSAN, ed. *The Story Telling Stone*. New York: Laurel/Dell, 1965.

FINLEY, M. I. "The Rediscovery of Crete." *Horizon* 7, no. 3 (Summer 1965).

FRAZER, SIR JAMES GEORGE. *The Golden Bough: A Study in Magic and Religion.* One-volume abridged edition. New York: Macmillan, 1963.

GARBINI, GIOVANNI. *The Ancient World.* New York: McGraw-Hill, 1966.

GAUQUELIN, MICHEL. *The Cosmic Clocks: From Astrology to a Modern Science.* London: Paladin Press, 1973.

GAWAIN, SHAKTI. *Creative Visualization.* California: Whatever Publishing, 1978.

GIBSON, ARRELL M. *The Chickasaws.* Norman, Okla.: University of Oklahoma Press, 1971.

GIUGANINO, ALBERTO, AND ADOLFO TAMBURELLO. *National Museum, Tokyo.* Great Museums of the World, ed. by Carlo Ludovico Ragghianti. New York: Newsweek, Inc. and Arnoldo Mondadori Editore, 1968.

GLOTZ, GUSTAVE. *The Aegean Civilization.* Translated by M. R. Dobie and E. M. Riley. New York: Barnes & Noble, 1968.

GOETZ, HERMANN. *The Art of India: Five Thousand Years of Indian Art.* New York: Greystone Press, 1964.

GRAVES, ROBERT. *The Greek Myths.* 2 vols. New York: George Braziller, 1959.

——. *The White Goddess: A Historical Grammar of Poetic Myth.* Amended and enlarged edition. New York: Farrar, Strauss & Giroux, 1966.

HALL, MANLEY. *The Story of Astrology: The Belief in the Stars As a Factor in Human Progress.* Los Angeles: Phoenix Press, 1933.

HARDING, M. ESTHER. *Woman's Mysteries.* New York: Bantam Books, 1973.

HELMSTETTER, SHAD. *The Self-Talk Solution.* New York: Pocket Books, 1987.

HUNT, R. C., ed. *Personalities and Cultures: Readings in Psychological Anthropology.* Garden City, N.Y.: Natural History Press/Doubleday & Company, 1967.

JACKSON, J. WILFRID. "The Aztec Moon-Cult and Its Relation to the Chank Cult of India." *Manchester Literary and Philosophical Society Memoirs and Proceedings.* 60, no. 5 (May 17, 1916).

KIM, YONG IK. *The Moons of Korea.* Seoul: Korea Information Service, 1959.

KINSELLA, THOMAS, trans. *The Tain.* From the Irish epic *Tain Bo Cuailnge.* London: Oxford University Press, 1969.

KLAUSER, HENRIETTE ANNE. *Writing on Both Sides of the Brain.* San Francisco: Harper & Row, 1987.

KLEIN, RICHARD M. "A Naturalist at Large: Maypoles and Earth Mothers." *Natural History* 85, no. 5 (May 1976): 4–8.

LaRousse Encyclopedia of Ancient and Medieval History. Foreword by Arnold Toynbee. London: Paul Hamlyn, 1967.

LOMMEL, ANDREAS, *Prehistoric and Primitive Man.* New York: McGraw-Hill, 1966.

LUCE, GAY GAER. *Body Time.* New York: Bantam Books, 1973.

MACKENZIE, JEAN. "How Bio Rhythms Affect Your Life." *Science Digest* 74 (August 1973).

MALINOWSKI, BRONISLAW. *Magic, Science and Religion.* Garden City, N.Y.: Doubleday & Company, 1954.

MARKALE, JEAN. *Women of the Celts.* Translated by A. Mygind, C. Hauch, and P. Henry. London: Gordon Cremonesi, 1975.

MEAD, MARGARET. *Sex and Temperament in Three Primitive Societies.* New York: William Morrow, 1963.

MELLAART, JAMES. *Earliest Civilizations of the Near East.* London: Thames and Hudson, 1965.

MERTZ, BARBARA. *Temples, Tombs and Hieroglyphics: The Story of Egyptology.* New York: Dell Publishing Co., 1964.

MIDDLETON, JOHN, ed. *From Child to Adult: Studies in the Anthropology of Education.* Garden City, N.Y.: Natural History Press/Doubleday & Company, 1970.

MODI, DR. JIVANJI JAMSHEDJI. "The Ancient Iranian Belief and Folklore About the Moon." *Journal of the Anthropological Society of Bombay* 11 (1921).

"MOON MADNESS." *Science Digest* 72, no. 3 (Sept. 1972): 28–32.

MORAN, HUGH. *The Alphabet and the Ancient Calendar Signs.* UNESCO. Palo Alto, Calif.: Pacific Books, 1953.

MORGAN, ELAINE. *The Descent of Woman.* New York: Bantam Books, 1973.

MURPHY, YOLANDA, AND ROBERT F. MURPHY. *Women of the Forest.* New York: Columbia University Press, 1974.

NEUMANN, ERICH. *The Great Mother.* Translated by Ralph Manheim. Bollingen Series 47. Princeton, N.J.: Princeton University Press, 1963.

——. *The Origins and History of Consciousness.* Bollingen Series 42. Princeton, N.J.: Princeton University Press, 1970.

New LaRousse Encyclopedia of Mythology. Introduction by Robert Graves. London: Paul Hamlyn, 1968.

NICHOLSON, IRENE. *Mexican and Central American Mythology*. London: Paul Hamlyn, 1967.

NILSSON, MARTIN P. *The Mycenaean Origin of Greek Mythology*. Berkeley: University of California Press, 1932, 1972.

OLIVER, DOUGLAS L. *The Pacific Islands*. New York: American Museum of Natural History and Anchor Books/Doubleday, 1961.

PARTRIDGE, ERIC. *Origins: The Encyclopedia of Words*. New York: Macmillan, 1958.

PAULME, DENISE, ed. *Women of Tropical Africa*. Translated by H. M. Wright. Berkeley: University of California Press, 1971.

Personalities and Cultures: Readings in Psychological Anthropology. Garden City, N.Y.: Natural History Press/Doubleday, 1967.

PLATON, NICHOLAS. "Kato Zakro: A Rediscovered Palace." *Horizon* 7, no. 3 (Summer 1965): 65–75.

POMEROY, SARAH B. *Goddesses, Whores, Wives and Slaves: Women in Classical Antiquity*. New York: Schocken Books, 1976.

POWILLS, DOROTHY. "Mythology and Playing Cards." *Hobbies* 77, no. 1 (March 1972): 140–141.

RAMIREZ, VAZQUEZ, P. *National Museum of Anthropology, Mexico City*. Great Museums of the World, ed. by Carlo Ludovico Ragghianti. New York: Newsweek, Inc. and Arnoldo Mondadori Editore, 1970.

RAPPORT, SAMUEL, AND HELEN WRIGHT. *Archaeology*. New York: Washington Square Press, 1964.

RAUM, O. T. "Female Initiation Among the Chaga." *American Anthropologist* 41, no. 4: (Oct.–Dec. 1939) 554–65.

REED, EVELYN. *Woman's Evolution: From Matriarchal Clan to Patriarchal Family*. New York: Pathfinder Press, 1975.

REIK, THEODOR. *The Creation of Woman*. New York: George Braziller, 1960.

ROSS, ANNE. *Everyday Life of the Pagan Celts*. New York: G. P. Putnam, 1970.

RUDHYAR, DANE. *The Lunation Cycle*. Berkeley: Shambala, 1971.

RUSSELL, FRANKLIN. "Road to Ur." *Horizon* 14, no. 3 (Summer 1972): 90.

STEN, MARIA. *The Mexican Codices*. Translated by Carolyn B. Czitron. Mexico: Ediciones Lara, S.A., 1974.

STONE, MERLIN. *Ancient Mirrors of Womanhood*. Boston: Beacon Press, 1979.

———. *The Paradise Papers*. London: Virago, 1976.

————. *When God Was a Woman*. New York: Dial Press, 1976.

STUBBINGS, FRANK H. *Prehistoric Greece*. New York: John Day Company, 1973.

TACITUS, P. CORNELIUS. *The Annals*. Chicago: Encyclopedia Brittania, 1952.

THOMSON, J. OLIVER. *Everyman's Classical Atlas*. 3d ed. New York: E. P. Dutton, 1961.

TUCKER, W. J. *Foundations of Astrology*. Kent, England: Pythagorean Publications, 1960.

VAN HOESEN, H. B. "Greek Horoscopes." *The American Philosophical Society* 48: (1959).

VOLGUINE, ALEXANDRE. *Lunar Astrology*. New York: ASI Publishers, 1974.

VON CLES-REDEN, SIBYLLE. *The Realms of the Great Goddess*. Englewood Cliffs, N.J.: Prentice-Hall, 1962.

VON HAGEN, VICTOR W. *World of the Maya*. New York: New American Library, 1960.

WALKER, BARBARA G. *The Woman's Dictionary of Symbols and Sacred Objects*. San Francisco: Harper & Row, 1988.

————. *The Woman's Encyclopedia of Myths and Secrets*. San Francisco: Harper & Row, 1983.

WILLETTS, R. F. *Ancient Crete: A Social History from Early Times Until the Roman Occupation*. Toronto: University of Toronto Press, 1965.

WITHERSPOON, GARY. *Navajo Kinship and Marriage*. Chicago. University of Chicago Press, 1975.